Training to work in the early years

Training to work in the early years

Developing the climbing frame

Edited by
Lesley Abbott *and* **Gillian Pugh**

Open University Press
Buckingham · Philadelphia

Open University Press
Celtic Court
22 Ballmoor
Buckingham
MK18 1XW

email: enquiries@openup.co.uk
world wide web: http://www.openup.co.uk

and
325 Chestnut Street
Philadelphia, PA 19106, USA

First Published 1998

A catalogue record of this book is available from the British Library

ISBN   0 335 20031 1 (hb)   0 335 20030 3 (pb)

Library of Congress Cataloging-in-Publication Data
Training to work in the early years / edited by Lesley Abbott and
  Gillian Pugh.
      p.   cm.
  Includes bibliographical references and index.
  ISBN 0-335-20031-1 (hb). – ISBN 0-335-20030-3 (pb)
  1. Early childhood teachers – Training of – Great Britain.
  I. Abbott, Lesley. 1945–   . II. Pugh, Gillian.
    LB1732.3 T73   1998
    370′ 71–dc21   98–3316
                                                                    CIP

Typeset by Type Study, Scarborough
Printed in Great Britain by St Edmundsbury Press Ltd, Bury St Edmunds, Suffolk

Contents

Contributors

Lesley Abbott is Professor of Early Childhood Education at the Manchester Metropolitan University where she heads the Early Years/Multi-professional Centre. She has served on the Council for the Accreditation of Teacher Education (CATE), the Rumbold Committee and the RSA Early Learning Inquiry. She is firmly committed to multi-professional training and is responsible for the development of one of the first interdisciplinary degrees, the BA(Hons) Early Childhood Studies. Research interests include Educare for the Under-Threes and Play and Training, areas in which she has published a number of books and articles. Recent publications include: *Working with the Under-3s: Training and Professional Development* and *Working with the Under-3s: Responding to Children's Needs*, with Helen Moylett (Open University Press 1997).

Pamela Calder is a Senior Lecturer in Psychology at South Bank University in the School of Education, Politics and Social Science, where she teaches social and developmental psychology and early childhood education. She graduated in Psychology at Nottingham University in 1963. For many years she has been involved in both campaigning for more nursery provision and for provision that better meets the needs of both children, women and families. To this end she has been concerned with developing education and training for early childhood workers. She has developed in-service diplomas at South Bank and is currently part of a European Erasmus/Socrates postgraduate programme in early childhood education. She has two children, a son now at university and a daughter who has just graduated. She worked full-time from the time they were born and thus has first-hand experience of the UK's early childhood provision.

Tricia David is a Professor of Early Childhood Education at Canterbury Christ Church College. She is probably best known for her publications about young children, such as *Under Five – Under-educated?* (Open University Press 1990) and on children and society, for example, *Child Protection and Early Years*

Teachers (Open University Press 1993). Tricia feels she has been fortunate to have her thinking on early childhood challenged by her many contacts in and visits to other countries. She is currently enjoying learning so much more from her first grandchild.

Pat Dench has worked in the early years education and adult education fields for a number of years as a practitioner and an adult education teacher. She has been a member of staff at the Pre-school Learning Alliance, a national educational charity, for nine years. She has been a regional Training and Development Officer, the Services Liaison Officer (responsible for developing training and support to armed forces preschools and their families) and is currently responsible for training and quality assurance programmes for the charity. Pat represents the charity on the Early Childhood Education Forum and as a board member on CACHE.

Mary Fawcett is a lecturer at the University of Bristol in the School for Policy Studies and she has also been involved with the School of Education running INSET courses. Drawing on experiences with the multi-professional Advanced Diploma in work with children and families in the then Department of Social Work, she established the new degree in Early Childhood Studies along with Sonia Jackson. In her role as course convenor she has seen the course become a popular and established feature of an initially sceptical university. She is a founder member of STAR (Support and Training Against Racism for Under-Fives Workers and Parents). She has been a member of the Early Years Training Group at the National Children's Bureau since it began and contributed to their publication, *Education and Training for Work in the Early Years*. In 1996, her handbook, *Learning Through Child Observation*, was published by Jessica Kingsley.

Sue Griffin is Training Officer of the National Childminding Association. Previously she was employed by NCMA as Development Officer for South West England. She has made contributions to the development of National Vocational Qualifications in Child Care and Education, as a member of the Under Sevens Project which developed standards for these NVQs, and in the subsequent implementation and current review. She is currently undertaking consultancy work for the Local Government Management Board on the establishment of an Early Years Forum for the Care Sector Consortium, and exploring the possibility of an Early Years National Training Organisation. She has published widely in the training field, contributing to BBC and local government publications. Her major contribution is *The Key to Quality: Guide and Resource Materials for Training Childminders* (1993).

Ian Kane is the Head of the Didsbury School of Education at the Manchester Metropolitan University. He is currently the Chair of the University Council for the Education of Teachers (UCET). He has been, variously, Chief Examiner for nine initial training courses in England and Scotland. He was co-director of the Esmée Fairbairn project on 'Mentoring in Schools', 1993–6.

Janet Moyles was a nursery/first school teacher and head teacher for several years before becoming a Senior Lecturer in Education at the University of Leicester. Her research interests are in aspects of children's learning including play and in the professional development and training of early years practitioners, including mentoring roles. She has published widely, both books and articles.

Pamela Oberhuemer has a background in teaching (in London, Hamburg and Munich) and has worked in research and development projects at the State Institute of Early Childhood Education and Research (IFP) in Munich since 1976. Research interests include: comparative perspectives on early childhood provision, professionalization and professionalism; teaching and learning in a multicultural society. Pamela is an editorial board member of the International journal of *Early Years Education*.

Maureen O'Hagan is Director of Quality Assurance to the Council for Awards in Children's Care and Education (CACHE) a post to which she was appointed following the merger of NNEB and CEYA, an awarding body formed specifically to award NVQs in Child Care and Education and related areas, of which she was Director. Her qualifications include SRN, BEd and MEd for which her dissertation involved extensive work with ethnic minority communities. She has worked in Romania, devising and writing training programmes for staff in Romanian orphanages. She has published widely in the field of National Vocational Qualifications and improving the quality of training for workers in early childhood care and education.

Sue Owen has worked in the field of childcare and education since 1968 when she first volunteered in a preschool playgroup. She is currently Principal Officer in the Early Childhood Unit at the National Children's Bureau. Previously, she was Early Years Development Officer for Humberside County Council with a brief to coordinate and develop services across the statutory, voluntary and private sectors. This involved the creation of a number of partnership bodies, including groups setting up childminding networks, training and support strategies and economic development initiatives. Before moving to Humberside, Sue worked as Information Officer for the National Childminding Association. She has also worked as playgroup adviser for Manchester City Council, Childminding Adviser for the Save the Children Fund and as a freelance researcher.

Helen Penn is Senior Research Fellow at the Social Science Research Unit, Institute of Education, London University. She has been researching aspects of nursery practice for a number of years. Her current research is on 'centres of early excellence'. She also acts as a consultant to Save the Children UK in Southern Africa and the Far East, and has conducted a review for the Department for International Development on initiatives in early childhood in the Majority World.

John Powell is Senior Lecturer in the Department of Educational Studies at the Manchester Metropolitan University. He is course leader of the BA(Hons) Early

Childhood Studies degree and manager of the Multi-professional Centre. His background is in social work. He has worked in inner-city Manchester as an education social worker and senior team leader with a major specialism in child protection. He has taught in further education as a lecturer in social studies where he worked with students taking the ADCE, and later as an assessor for NVQs and GNVQs in Child Care. He is currently a verifier for the ADCE for CACHE. He has an MA in teaching and is currently studying for a PhD.

Gillian Pugh has been Chief Executive of the Thomas Coram Foundation for Children since early 1997, having previously been Director of the Early Childhood Unit at the National Children's Bureau. She has published books and training materials on policy development, on coordination of services, on curriculum, on parental involvement and on parent education. Recent publications include *The Contribution of Mainstream Services to Preventive Work with Families* with Ruth Sinclair and Barbara Hearn (1997), *Contemporary Issues in the Early Years* (2nd edition 1996) and *Confident Parents, Confident Children: Policy and Practice in Parent Education* with Erica De'Ath and Celia Smith (1994). Gillian was a member of the Rumbold Committee on the education of children of 3- to 5-year-olds, of the RSA Start Right enquiry and of the Audit Commission study of early education. She set up and chaired the Early Childhood Education Forum and the Early Years Training Group, and was a founder member of the Parenting Education and Support Forum.

Wendy Suschitzky was a nursery/infant teacher before becoming a part-time tutor at the University of Leicester. She is also a part-time research assistant contributing both to the research reported in the chapter and to research on mentoring and the particular needs of ethnic-minority personnel.

Barbara Thompson is the Courses Development Officer for the Pre-school Learning Alliance where she is working on the review and development of courses for parents, preschool staff, volunteers, tutors and development workers within the Pre-school Learning Alliance. Previously she was Training and Development Officer for the PLA where she was involved with the charity's quality assurance system and with the professional development of tutors. In her previous life she was a research chemist and holds a BSc in Industrial Chemistry and a MEd in Continuing Education.

Gill Thorpe is a freelance trainer and consultant in early years and community development work. She has gained her professional career experience with Save the Children Fund, managing and working on projects linked to supporting young families and children; the last was setting up an assessment centre for childcare and education NVQs.

Foreword

Lesley Abbott and Gillian Pugh

In 1992 a group of early years trainers and advisers started to meet at the National Children's Bureau to discuss the future of training to work with young children. The group was principally concerned with the mismatch between the training needs of those working in schools, nurseries and other settings with young children and the training opportunities that were available to them. As a direct result of the group's discussions, some of the members based in university departments of education and social work took forward plans that evolved into new early childhood studies degrees. The group was also concerned about some of the changes in teacher training as these impacted on early years teachers, and on the lack of progress in developing National Vocational Qualifications in childcare and education. All three of these areas were covered in *The Future of Training in the Early Years: A Discussion Paper* (National Children's Bureau 1993).

In 1993, the Early Childhood Education Forum (ECEF) was established, bringing together the forty major national organizations working with and for young children across the statutory, voluntary and independent sectors. This provided a focus for wide-ranging discussions across a number of areas – policy, curriculum, training, inspection and funding of services. With the growing interest in the education of young children during 1995, and the announcement of the Conservative Government's nursery voucher scheme for 4-year-olds, members of the original training group reconvened and merged with the training subgroup of ECEF – thus creating a strong and representative group of early years practitioners and trainers who were able to argue their case with both government and opposition. The joint group, which met during 1996 and 1997, included, among others, almost all of those who have contributed to this book. Members were among those who advised the current government while in opposition on its early years policy and on the need for a coherent policy on training including a 'climbing frame' of qualifications. This concept was included in the Labour Party's pre-election manifesto *Early Excellence* (1996) which also supported the development of integrated Early Childhood Studies degrees. Other developments since the new Government came into power also reflect the ECEF's recommendations, notably the requirement on every local authority to produce an early years development plan, and the establishment nationwide of early years partnerships. While both of these initiatives should improve access to training, there is still no national policy on training to work in the early years.

The post-election circular (May 1997) confirmed many of the commitments made earlier. With regard to staffing, the paper indicates that 'a qualified teacher should be involved in all settings providing early years education within an early years development plan'. Precisely what 'involvement' means is not spelt out and while the recommendation is made that 'there should be improvement in the training of early years workers, including a review of the qualifications available' (Labour Party 1997: 7) no indication is given as to who should undertake this task and how it might be funded. While such developments are laudable, without clear guidance and financial support little progress will be made. The requirement for the establishment of an early years partnership in each authority should promote cooperative or collaborative activity, but will do little to increase the number of appropriately trained staff available to work in early years establishments unless training providers are involved, and access and support made available to staff.

During 1996, the early years training group published a further report on *Education and Training for Work in the Early Years* (Pugh 1996b), a snapshot of developments in the three main areas of training and accreditation in this field – teacher training, early childhood studies degrees and vocational training in childcare and education and NVQs – and an agenda for further action. That report was based on a number of underpinning assumptions, and these are repeated here as the value base from which this book has evolved.

- Young children are valued and their full development is possible only if they live in an environment which reflects and respects their individual identity, culture and heritage.
- Central and local government have a duty, working in partnership with parents, to ensure that a range of services and support is available to families as and when they need them and at a price they can afford.
- These services should encourage children's cognitive, social, emotional and physical development; and meet parents' need for support for themselves and day care for their children.
- The skills and experience necessary to support the growth and development of young children are seriously underestimated and undervalued. Initial and ongoing training are essential if the quality of services for young children and their families are to be ensured.
- The provision of adequate early childhood services is an essential requirement of an effective equal opportunities policy, enabling women to have equal access to employment and training.
- Services should enable parents to reconcile work and family responsibilities.

The report also took account of the underpinning principles of the Early Childhood Education Forum in relation to children's learning. These are also repeated here as the basis for the arguments in this book.

- Learning begins at birth.
- Care and education are inseparable – quality care is educational, and quality education is caring.
- Every child develops at his/her own pace, but adults can stimulate and encourage learning.
- All children benefit from developmentally appropriate care and education.
- Skilled and careful observation is the key to helping children learn.
- Cultural and physical diversity should be respected and valued: a proactive anti-bias approach should be adopted and stereotypes challenged.
- Learning is holistic and is not compartmentalized in the early years: trust, motivation, interest, enjoyment and social skills are as important as purely cognitive gains.
- Young children learn best through first hand experience, through play and talk.
- Carers and educators should work in partnership with parents, who are their child's first educators.

In summary, the training group believed that the early years from birth to 6 years should be seen as a distinct phase, in which care and education are combined, and for which specialist training is required.

Training to Work in the Early Years is the logical development from the above-mentioned two reports. Members of the training group have been joined by others in raising key issues about the training and professional development of those who work with young children, issues that urgently need to be addressed. Although the profile of early education is now much higher than it was in the early 1990s, and the amount of provision has increased, there is still no coherent national training strategy and many questions that await an answer. It is these questions that this book addresses.

Acknowledgements

To Jean Davidson for her skill and patience in the preparation of this book and to the staff of the Didsbury Research Centre at the Manchester Metropolitan University for their continuing support.

Glossary of terms

ADCE	Advanced Diploma for Child Care and Education
APEL	Accreditation of Prior Experience and Learning
APL	Accreditation of Prior Learning
ARTEN	Anti-Racist Teacher Education Network
BAECE	British Association of Early Childhood Education
CACHE	Council for Awards in Child Care and Education
CATS	Credit Accumulation and Transfer
CCETSW	Central Council for Education and Training of Social Workers
CEYA	Council for Early Years Awards
ECEF	Early Childhood Education Forum
EECERA	European Early Childhood Research Association
ESF	European Social Fund
FEFC	Further Education Funding Council
GEST	Grants for Education Support and Training
GNVQ	General National Vocational Qualification
GTC	General Teaching Council
HMI	Her Majesty's Inspector (of Schools)
KS1	Key Stage 1
LEA	Local Education Authority
NAEYC	National Association for the Education of Young Children
NCMA	National Childminding Association
NNEB	Nursery Nurse Examination Board
NNTARN	Nursery Nurse Trainers Anti-Racist Network
NTO	National Training Organization
NVQ	National Vocational Qualifications
OFSTED	Office for Standards in Education
PGCE	Post-Graduate Certificate of Education
PLA	Pre-school Learning Alliance
QCA	Qualifications and Curriculum Authority

SCAA	School Curriculum and Assessment Authority
SENCOs	Special Educational Needs Coordinators
SOC	Sector Occupational Codes
SSD	Social Services Department
STA	Specialist Teacher Assistants
STAR	Support and Training Against Racism for Under Fives Workers and Parents
SVQs	Scottish Vocational Qualifications
TEC	Training and Enterprise Council
TTA	Teacher Training Agency
UCET	University Council for the Education of Teachers

1 Early years training in context

Gillian Pugh

One is forced to conclude that this lack of concern over training and qualifications for what are in reality highly responsible roles . . . reflects confused and outmoded public attitudes which commonly regard the care of young children as an extension of the mothering role, and assume it all comes naturally to women. Such attitudes in turn reinforce the low status of early years work, helping to keep pay low and turnover high.

(Hevey and Curtis 1996: 212)

Research studies show the importance of appropriate training as being significant in influencing the quality of provision.

(Rodger *et al.* 1994)

The increasing level of debate in the last decade about the importance of the early years of children's lives and the need to increase access to early education has, until very recently, not been accompanied by a debate about the skills required to work effectively with young children nor – more importantly – about how as a country we view young children and childhood.

This is primarily a book about the education, training and professional development of those who work with young children – a book that tries to make sense of the confusing tangle of courses and qualifications that have grown, somewhat chaotically, over the past years, and to suggest a path that could take us out of this muddle. But the confusion over training, the piecemeal way in which courses have developed, the low status that many carry, the lack of funding for students enrolling on them and the generally low level of qualification that besets the field, are but a symptom of a wider malaise within the early years field. Until as a nation we recognize the importance of the early years of education and create an integrated service that reflects the rights and needs of children and their families, and until we have a common view about what kind of service we should be creating and why, then we will not be in a position to recruit, train and continue to support a workforce with the skills that we need.

The wider environment in which children are growing up in the UK at the end of the twentieth century presents policymakers and providers of services with a number of challenges. Changes in family patterns and in the economic circumstances of many families' lives suggest an increasingly divided society. Whereas continuing unemployment has contributed to some one in three children living on or below the poverty line, those families where one or both parents have found employment must often struggle to balance the demands of the workplace with their family responsibilities. Among the countries of the European Union, the UK now has the second highest number of women with children under five who are economically active (49 per cent), and the highest percentage of fathers working long hours (European Commission Network on Childcare 1996b). And yet the amount of day care available, as we shall see shortly, is still negligible. An increasing number of parents are also struggling to bring children up on their own, with one in five children now experiencing life in a single parent family at any one time.

The circumstances of children's lives must provide one of the starting points in our consideration of early years services and the training of those who work in them. But central to this book is the concept of childhood, of young children's development and of the limitations of some of our assumptions about how young children's needs should be met. A number of themes are apparent in the chapters which follow:

- What do we know about the nature of children's development during their first five years, and what is the most effective response?
- Do young children only need warm, loving and consistent carers?
- What role should parents play, when we know that parental attitudes to their children's learning is vital?
- What is the role of trained professionals and what kind of training do they need, when research points to the significance of the training received by educators in determining the quality of early years provision (Rodger *et al.* 1994)?
- How much structure do children need? Research shows that only high-quality preschool education leads to lasting gains, through encouraging high aspirations, motivation to learn and a sense of mastery, fostering the belief in children that attainment is not innate but is achieved in part by effort (see Sylva 1994). What are the implications of these findings for the training of early years workers?
- Do we listen to children's voices in our planning of services and our training programmes?

These are some key dilemmas for a group of workers that is struggling to create a profession but is at the centre of wider unresolved issues about the nature of childhood and the kind of early childhood services that society should provide.

The current scene

The complexity of the range of early years services in the UK and the overall lack of coordination has been well described elsewhere (Pugh 1988, 1996a; David 1990; DES 1990; Ball 1994; Moss and Penn 1996). For the purposes of this book, the main forms of provision and the staff employed within them are briefly described here and summarized in Table 1.1.

State nursery schools and classes

These are mainly for 3- and 4-year-olds and are provided by local education authorities. Provision is non-statutory and there are thus considerable regional differences. Nursery schools are separate institutions with their own head teacher, while nursery classes are attached to primary schools. Both are open for the normal school day and school terms, but the majority of children attend either morning or afternoon. Nursery provision is staffed by qualified teachers assisted by trained nursery nurses, in a ratio of two members of staff to 26 children.

Reception classes

Reception classes of primary schools are taking an increasing number of 4-year olds, although children are not required to start school until the term after their fifth birthday. There are no restrictions on numbers and while some schools may employ nursery nurses, many children are in classes of between 30 and 40 children with one teacher.

Combined nursery centres

These are usually jointly funded and managed by the education authority and social services department. Since their inception in the 1970s, they have developed in different ways across the country, but most provide integrated nursery education and day care for the whole working day throughout the year. There are currently about a hundred, but the new Labour Government's 'early excellence centre' initiative suggests that their numbers may increase. Ratios and staff qualifications are similar to those of local authority nursery schools and day nurseries.

Local authority day nurseries/family centres

These are run by social service departments mainly for children who are thought to be 'at risk'. At least half of the staff must have a relevant qualification for working with young children, and this is usually the old Nursery Nurse Examination Board (NNEB) diploma, National Vocational Qualifications (NVQ) level 2 or 3, the CACHE Diploma in Nursery Nursing (NNEB) or Edexcel (formerly BTEC) Diploma in Nursery Nursing. The number of local

Table 1.1 Services for under-fives in England

Type of provision	Age of children	Percentage of children*	Opening hours	Administration	Qualifications required
Nursery school nursery class	3–4 years	27	9.00–3.00 term time (often either morning or afternoon)	LEA	*Teacher:* BEd or degree and PGCE *Nursery Nurse:* NNEB or equivalent
Reception class in primary school	3–4 years	26	9.00–3.00 term time	LEA	*Teacher:* see above
Combined nursery centre/community centre	0–4 years	no information	8.00–5.00 all year	LEA/SSD	As for nursery schools and day nurseries
Independent schools	2–4 years	4	9.00–3.00 term time	Private	Unknown
Day nursery/family centre	0–4 years	0.6	8.00–5.00 full and part-time places	SSD	At least half staff must have some qualifications (unspecified, usually NNEB/NVQ)
Playgroup/pre-school	2–4 years	56	Vary. Average 8 hours per child per week	Private and voluntary sector, SSD regulates	At least half staff must have some qualifications (unspecified, usually PLA/NVQ)
Private nurseries	0–4 years	4.3	Usually 8.00–5.00	Private and voluntary sector, SSD regulates	At least half staff must have some qualification (unspecified, usually NNEB/NVQ)
Childminders	0–8 years	11.6 (of 0–5-year-olds)	8.00–5.00	Self-employed, SSD regulates	None required. Some following NVQ-related courses

* Percentage of children using services in England in 1995.
Source: Statistics: Under Fives and Pre-school Services 1995, Early Childhood Unit, National Children's Bureau, 1997.

authority nurseries is diminishing and many are now more closely linked with education-based provision.

Playgroups or preschools

These are usually parent-managed groups within the voluntary sector. Although many have extended their hours over the last few years, the majority are open for three or four days during the week in term time and the average time attended by any one child is two and a half sessions – between seven and eight hours. Playgroups or preschools are usually run by parents, at least half of whom must have had some training. This is usually provided by the Preschool Learning Alliance. They must be registered by social service departments within the requirements of the Children Act (1989).

Private nurseries

Private nurseries include a wide range of groups, including some playgroups, nursery schools and day nurseries. Those with more than five children over the age of five are registered by the Department for Education, but the majority fall within the remit of the Children Act and are registered and inspected by social services departments. There are no specific qualifications required, although at least half of the staff are required to have some relevant qualification.

Childminders

These normally provide for children up to the age of eight, on a self-employed basis. They too fall within the remit of the Children Act and are registered and inspected by social services departments. A childminder may care for up to three children under five. No qualifications are required, and training is provided at the discretion of the local authority.

In summary, the different services outlined here:

- are provided by different agencies (education, social services, leisure departments, health authorities, and the voluntary and private sectors);
- have different aims and objectives and underpinning philosophies, some focusing on children's learning and cognitive development, some more overtly concerned with children's care and welfare;
- operate to different standards set down by different legislation, some within the welfare tradition (Children Act 1989 – the requirements are laid down in Department of Health 1991) and some as part of the education legislation;
- fall within different inspection regimes, schools being inspected by Ofsted, and voluntary and private sector nurseries by social services under the Children Act and by the new Ofsted nursery inspections;
- require different levels of staffing, and different levels of training and qualifications;

- have different hours of opening, with the majority of provision still only available for two or three hours a day;
- have different fee structures, with statutory provision free and private and voluntary sector provision charging parents (although funding is now available for 4-year-olds in services which comply to government standards).

It is hardly surprising, given this lack of coordination or overall policy direction, that the education and training of those who work with young children has been so sadly neglected.

What kind of services?

The Early Childhood Education Forum, representing all the types of provision summarized above, drew on Holtermann's report *Investing in Young Children: A Reassessment of the Cost of an Education and Day Care Service* (1995) to argue that every child should have access to a free 'nugget' of early childhood education. Working within the system as it currently exists, this might be provided in nursery schools, or classes, reception classes, playgroups, pre-schools or day nurseries – provided they are of a comparable standard in terms of appropriate curriculum and trained staff. These centres could be linked to childminding networks. In this report, it was suggested that day care could be paid for by parents according to their means, with a third of parents paying nothing.

Looking towards the way in which services should develop, the Forum described a vision for early childhood care and education in a paper outlining an approach which combined centres with networks or other services (Duffy and Griffin 1994). Others have described their own vision (Pugh and McQuail 1996; Moss and Penn 1996) and, drawing on all of these, the Labour Party subsequently published its own vision (*Early Excellence* 1996). This has subsequently become government policy, and a current initiative is seeking to establish 25 early excellence centres across the country, linked into local early years development plans. As yet, this initiative puts little emphasis on training.

There are, of course, already many such centres, and although no two are the same they do have a number of common features:

- flexible and multifunctional services, providing education and care for children and support for parents and access to training where it is required;
- continuous provision from birth to five or beyond;
- open access rather than segregated or stigmatized services;
- provision of a developmentally appropriate anti-bias curriculum;
- well-qualified and well-paid staff, with continuing access to further training;
- partnership between parents and early years workers;
- a common and coherent system of funding;
- high-quality premises and equipment;
- adherence to a range of models of delivery of services, provided they are coherently organized.

For further discussion of such centres see *Not Just A Nursery* (Makins 1997).

Implications for training

Although centres such as those described above are not as yet widely available, they have been slowly developing over the last 25 years, and their further development is part of current government policy. This gives the provision of appropriate training even greater urgency. Little existing training equips staff to work in multi-agency settings. Teacher training does not include working with, and understanding, the needs of children under the age of three. Many of the lower-level courses do not include a very strong emphasis on children's cognitive development. Not all courses equip students to work in inner-city areas and with families from a range of cultural and religious backgrounds; nor is there always a very strong emphasis on working with parents or with professionals from other agencies. These concerns and the specific requirements of a more coordinated approach to service provision led to the establishment of the first integrated early childhood studies degrees, whose development is outlined in Chapter 8. But there are other demands as well, which have a relevance to all provision – for example, the expanded responsibilities in relation to child protection procedures, the implementation of the Code of Practice for children with special educational needs, and the requirements of the new inspection regime linked into the 'desirable learning outcomes' for children of four. All of these issues require early childhood educators to be well trained and to have access to continuing training and professional development during their working lives.

Why is high-quality training for early years important?

After decades of neglect, a series of influential reports over the last few years have built up a more coherent case for the importance of investment in early childhood education for educational, social and economic reasons. One of the most influential of these was the Rumbold report *Starting with Quality* (DES 1990) which based its recommendations on an understanding of how young children learn (with a particularly strong emphasis on playing and talking) and of the critical role of adults – well-trained adults – in taking that learning forward. The report argued that there should be comparable quality in all settings in which young children find themselves and placed a heavy emphasis on the skills, knowledge and attitudes required by teachers and other early childhood educators. It was also the first public recognition of the importance of multi-agency training:

> We see as essential needs: a closer linkage between the three strands of health, care and education in initial and in-service training. A pattern of vocational training and qualifications for childcare workers which will bridge the gap between the vocational and academic qualifications, safeguarding both the rigour and relevance of initial training for teachers of the under fives, and affording improved opportunities of in-service training for childcare workers in educational settings.
>
> (DES 1990: 27)

It further remarked that 'sound standards of teaching will not be developed or sustained without extensive and varied provision for in-service training' (paragraph 188).

Further reports followed, including the National Commission on Education (1993) which placed the expansion of nursery education as its highest priority in its reflections on the future of education and training in the UK, and commented:

> We place particular emphasis on appropriate training. Whether in day care facilities, playgroups, nursery schools and classes or primary school infant classes, the education of children under compulsory school age should be the responsibility of staff with an appropriate early years qualification. Teaching very young children is a complex task, demanding a high level of skill and understanding. The Commission supports graduate level training. We welcome the efforts now being made to establish a variety or routes to qualification, including high level NVQs and modular degrees specialising in early childhood study, which might be combined with teacher training. Consideration should also be given to incorporating a multi-professional dimension in training so that both childcare and education are covered.
>
> (ibid.: 132)

Both the Royal Society of Arts *Start Right* report (Ball 1994) and the Audit Commission (1996) study of the education of under-fives point to the calibre and training of those who work with young children as the key determinants of high-quality provision. The RSA report argues that early years teachers require a breadth of knowledge, understanding and experience which is not needed by those training to teach older children:

> They must have mastery of the curriculum content as well as having a sound knowledge of child development, including language acquisition, cognitive, social, emotional and physical development. They are required to lead and plan for a team of other professionals including parents, nursery nurses, students and other including speech therapists, language support teachers, psychologists and social workers. They are responsible for the assessment of children and for monitoring progress and ensuring continuity and progression between stages and establishments.
>
> (Ball 1994: 59)

These reports reflect an emerging recognition that during the first five years of their life children are not only at their most vulnerable, but are at a stage of development when learning is most rapid and most intense. As children begin to work out who they are and how they feel about themselves, how they relate to other people, how to communicate their excitements and their fears, how their bodies work and what the world is like, it is critical that those around them – their close family and their early childhood workers – can understand and support their development. Recent research into brain formation and development in very young children and into the impact of social and environmental factors on changes in brain structure and functioning, reaffirms the importance of an enriched early environment (Carnegie Corporation 1994). Young children are naturally curious and eager to learn – and as the Rumbold report argues, it is important that early years educators are able to 'turn children on' to learning:

Early years educators play a critical role in young children's learning. It is within their power to encourage feelings of fun and discovery in learning on the one hand or of dull drudgery on the other. Attitudes and behaviour patterns established during the first years of life are thus central to future educational and social development. Particular attention has thus to be given in these early years to the process by which a child acquires the disposition to learn and the necessary competencies for learning.

(DES 1990: 36)

Given the strength of the research evidence, it is extraordinary that the gradual increase in the amount of provision over recent years, and recent legislation (both the Children Act and education legislation) have both ignored the need to provide a qualified and well-trained workforce. Later chapters in this book outline developments in NVQs, teacher training and the development of new courses, such as the integrated early childhood studies degrees described in Chapter 8. But none of these developments has taken place against an overall strategy that has planned a coherent expansion of services. No additional training places have been established, there has been no national training initiative, no additional funding for either initial or in-service training, and the regulations have not required any specific qualifications for staff working in the private and voluntary sectors. The Children Act requires half of all staff to be trained, but fails to specify what type of training is required or to what level, and the short-lived voucher initiative failed to require staff in voucher-redeeming institutions to be qualified. Research from Goldsmith's College (Blenkin *et al.* 1996) shows that over half of the heads of all types of early childhood institutions believe that 'staff not trained for early years specialism' is the most constraining factor in developing an appropriate curriculum for young children.

Most recently, the Labour Government's White Paper (DfEE 1997) does require 'the *involvement* [italics added] of a qualified teacher in all settings providing early years education within the early years development plan', although it is not clear how involvement is defined. While stronger than previous legislation, this illustrates a continuing struggle between the wish to value the contribution of existing providers, many of whom are not well qualified, and the recognition of the importance of a highly skilled workforce. This may be a pragmatic short-term solution, but does not create a longer-term strategy. This continues to be a contentious issue and one on which the contributors to this book continue to have different views.

Perhaps more encouragingly, the White Paper draws on discussions with many of the contributors to this book to refer to 'a climbing frame of vocational qualifications which will allow people to come in at different points, to develop their skills and knowledge on a modular basis . . . We will encourage the emergence of new courses which offer integrated training, like those at Manchester Metropolitan University and Suffolk College' (Labour Party 1996: 14).

Who are the workers and how are they trained?

As we have seen, the early years workforce is a disparate one, ranging from teachers with graduate and postgraduate qualifications through to workers with no formal qualifications but often considerable practical experience. For most childcare staff, training and qualifications are not legally required, and the most common training is a two-year course for 16-year-old school-leavers. Table 1.2, giving the qualifications held by a sample of 530 early years practitioners across all types of group settings shows that less than one in five are graduates, and that one in ten have no qualifications at all. One of the central discussions of the training working party whose work gave rise to this book was whether or not this should be a graduate profession, and how much early

Table 1.2 Qualifications held by practitioners working with children under eight (*n* = 530)

Qualification	Percentage
BA(Ed)/BEd/BAdd	13.8
PGCE	3.3
Cert Ed (2 years)	2.2
Cert Ed (3 years)	15.8
NNEB, City & Guilds	20.9
NVQs	0.5
BTEC	0.8
Montessori certificate	2.4
PPA Diploma in playgroup practice	7.9
PPA tutor and fieldwork course	0.5
PPA short course	6.6
PPA further course	1.5
BA	4.0
BSc	1.5
SRN	0.9
MA/MEd/MAdd	0.8
MPhil/PhD	0.1
Others	6.1
None	10.4
More than one qualification	7.0

Source: Blenkin *et al.* (1996).

years establishments should continue to rely on those who bring commitment and experience but no qualifications and little training or continuing professional development.

The UK is still one of the few countries in the world where all nursery teachers are fully qualified teachers, qualified to teach at any stage in the education system. A recent review of training across Europe (Oberhuemer and Ulich 1997) points out that other countries are gradually moving towards a graduate level qualification, often for all early years workers and not just teachers. This review highlights a dilemma that is facing a number of European countries but is particularly acute in the UK at the present time: should the early years be a separate phase or be an integral part of primary education? In this country, as in France, Ireland and The Netherlands, early years teacher training is integral to primary teacher training. But in a country where the majority of children are starting school at four, there is a very real fear that the downward pressure of the National Curriculum will have an unhelpful downwards thrust on the education of the younger children, and that a more child-centred approach will be abandoned. This issue is further discussed in Chapter 5.

Does the answer then lie in a separate phase, perhaps integrating all training to work with children before they start school across the statutory, voluntary and private sectors? The author's view is that this would further reduce the status of early years education. A more productive solution would be to establish an integrated 'climbing frame' of qualifications, linked to changes in the structure of primary education, in which the years from birth to six or seven are seen as the first stage of a system of care and education. This concept is discussed further in Chapter 12.

If most children in the UK start school at four, it follows that most 4-year-olds are in reception classes, where studies have consistently shown that the majority of teachers are not trained to work with young children. A recent national survey of qualifications found that only a quarter of qualified teachers were initially trained to work with the three to eight age group and of this group only one-third were trained to work specifically with 3- to 5-year-olds. Further, only 20 per cent of teachers of children under eight were graduates (Blenkin *et al.* 1996). Also of concern was the fact that many practitioners received little or no in-service training – only 15 per cent were engaged in any form of in-service award bearing training, there were few incentives to encourage practitioners to undertake further training, and once they had qualified they were unlikely to pursue any further training. While initial training is important, so too is a culture of continuous training, reflection and staff development. At present only nursery schools and classes within the statutory education system have five days closure per year for in-service training. Until this becomes common practice across all settings, then initiatives such as the Effective Early Learning Project (Pascal *et al.* 1994b) and the Goldsmith's Principles into Practice project (Blenkin *et al.* 1996), which provide practitioners with a framework for reflecting on and improving their own practice, will have little long-term value.

In a recent review of training for early years workers, Hevey and Curtis

(1996) point out that it sometimes comes as a surprise to find that the majority of day care and preschool education services in the UK are not staffed by teachers but by a

largely unqualified army of more that 200,000 child care and education workers. In England and Wales alone there are roughly 100,000 self-employed childminders and at least 50,000 playgroup leaders and assistants in some 20,000 playgroups. Workers with young children and their families are also found in day nurseries, nursery and primary schools, crèches, parent and toddler groups, family centres, parent support and home visiting schemes, toy libraries, playbuses and many other types of provision.

(Hevey and Curtis 1996: 212)

Hevey and Curtis point out that the majority (97 per cent) of these people who work with young children are women, most with family responsibilities of their own. Many work part-time and some work as unpaid volunteers. Wages are low and turnover rates high. The European Commission Network on Childcare (1996b) reports that nannies earn just over half the average pay of women workers and childminders less than half.

A more recent study by Penn and McQuail (1997) found that only 1 per cent of students in training were male and argue that childcare is deeply gendered in the nature of the work and in the limitations and lack of career opportunities. Colleges were attracting working-class women who were low achievers, most of whom were drawn to childcare as a 'natural' occupation for women. Helen Penn discusses some of the issues that this raises in Chapter 3. There are, of course, strategies which can be adopted to promote the recruitment and employment of more men in work with young children and some initiatives elsewhere in Europe are described by the European Commission Network on Childcare (1996a).

The only education and training opportunities open to the majority of non-teaching staff are part-time, low cost and are not formally assessed or accredited. A recent survey of 419 day care providers in England and Wales revealed that the commonest qualification for heads of nurseries and nursery staff was the NNEB while playgroup workers had most frequently attended courses by the Preschool Learning Alliance or other agencies. 'The great majority of childminders had no relevant qualifications' and neither did a third of playgroup workers or a fifth of private day nursery staff (Moss *et al.* 1995).

While the gradual introduction of NVQs as described in Chapters 6 and 7 should provide opportunities for accreditation, unless there is funding for training to provide the 'underpinning knowledge and understanding' and a change in attitude about the need for such training, then this situation is likely to continue. New initiatives such as the Kirklees course, described in Chapter 9, go some way towards combining the vocational and academic aspects, but funding is still an issue if this approach is to be more widely adopted.

The Early Childhood Education Forum has been pressing for acceptance of a requirement that all managers of centres, nurseries and playgroups should be graduates or hold NVQ level 4 or equivalent; and that all who work in centres or as childminders should be at level 3. Even if this argument were to be accepted in principle, however, there is as yet still no level 4 available.

Developments in education and training

The chapters in this book reflect the main developments in early years training across England and Wales. There are no national figures available on the numbers of staff holding different qualifications, nor on the extent to which on-going training and staff development is available throughout the sector. The variety of routes is complex but some of the key points can be drawn out. The main route to teaching is via either a 3 or 4 year BEd degree or a 1 year Post Graduate Certificate in Education (PGCE) following a three-year degree course (see Chapter 5). An increasingly popular option for early years teachers is the integrated early childhood studies degree, which is a valuable degree in its own right but can lead on to a teaching qualification (see Chapter 8). This degree can also provide the basis for a career in social work or healthcare. Discussions with regard to future career routes for graduates of multidisciplinary degrees must continue in order to provide the choice originally envisaged by the early years training group. It is also important that the currency of early childhood studies degrees is more widely advertised.

Routes to vocational qualifications are somewhat more varied and complex. The most common are: the CACHE (Council for Awards in Children's Care and Education) Diploma and Advanced Diploma; the BTEC National Diploma; and the Diploma in Pre-school Practice. All these provide underpinning knowledge and understanding for NVQs at levels 2 and 3 (see Chapter 6). The NVQ system and a growing number of training courses are becoming more flexible in response to the considerable number of mature students, often women, who have brought up their own children and are now returning to work, bringing practical experience on which they can draw in their training. Chapter 9 on the developments in Kirklees illustrates one such course. The HERA project in Suffolk, funded through the European Social Fund New Opportunities for Women scheme, which has trained over 2000 women in 18 months, is another. Developments in the UK such as the introduction of less rigid entry requirements into higher education, modular and part-time courses, and the new integrated early childhood studies degrees are all commended in a recent review of training in Europe (Oberhuemer and Ulich 1997).

Another development which could bring some greater coherence to the training of early years workers is the emergence of a National Training Organisation (NTO) specifically for the early years sector. This could play a central role in promoting the training needs of the sector, and create a two-way access route between vocational and academic qualifications, but it will only succeed in doing this if it can develop close working links with the Teacher Training Agency (TTA) and with the personal social services NTO being established by the Central Council for the Education and Training of Social Workers (CCETSW). A major difficulty in its longer-term establishment, however, is the absence of any obvious sources of funding in a sector with few employers of any size, and with a low-paid workforce.

With regard to recent developments in government policy, the overall thrust of *Early Excellence* (Labour Party 1996) was incorporated into the government's White Paper *Excellence in Schools* (DfEE July 1997a). Key issues with regard to quality assurance include staff training and qualifications, including early years training for qualified teachers and common standards of regulation and inspection, but no indication is given as to how developments will take place in these areas. There is clearly a need for Ofsted and social services inspection to be brought together and while there is evidence that inspection is bringing more rigour into early years work, it is also highlighting the need for more appropriately trained staff. Support for staff both pre- and post-inspection is needed but availability of, and access to, continuing professional development for early years staff continues to cause concern. Inspectors should be highly trained, knowledgeable, experienced and well qualified if they are to bring the required rigour to this important role, yet there is evidence that in some instances inspectors themselves have little knowledge and experience of the early years. The proposed new course requirements for initial teacher training make heavy demands on early years students to cover all that general primary students will address in addition to those highlighted within the document as early years specific (DfEE 1997b). These include management of a team, leadership, working with other professionals, parents and carers, recording, monitoring and conducting baseline assessment. There is still no recognition of the centrality of child development and play in early years training nor is there acknowledgement of the need for early years students to experience a range of contexts other than schools in which they may be employed in the future. At least one BEd course is now offering Early Childhood Studies as a special subject. This would seem to be an appropriate way forward in dealing with the demand for appropriately trained early years teachers. While the new proposals make no specific requirements for early years students to address the curriculum with regard to the *Desirable Outcomes for Children's Learning* (SCAA 1996), *The Career Entry Profile for Qualified Teachers* (Teacher Training Agency 1997) requires additional standards to this effect for early years teachers on 3–8 and 3–11 courses.

In conclusion, there are a number of issues of concern which will be discussed in the pages that follow. For example: the inappropriateness of the content of teacher training for those working in infant and nursery classes; the number of teachers working in these classes who are not trained to work with young children; the very slow growth in the availability of NVQs and the lack of availability of NVQs at level 4; the problems of funding for students on vocational courses; the continuing range of training courses and accrediting bodies; and the lack of opportunities for ongoing professional development. We return to these in our final chapter, but end this introduction with the conclusions of the National Child Care Staffing Study carried out in the USA in 1988, a substantial study of which we have no equivalent in the UK:

As a nation we are reluctant to acknowledge child care settings as a work environment for adults, and to commit resources to improving them. Even though many Americans recognise that child care teachers are underpaid, outdated attitudes about women's work and the family obscure our view of teachers' economic needs and the demands of their work. If a job in childcare is seen as an extension of women's familial role of rearing children, professional preparation and adequate resource compensation seem unnecessary.

(Whitebook *et al.* 1990)

As the RSA *Start Right* report concluded:

The calibre and training of the professionals who work with children are the key determinants of high quality provision.

(Ball 1994, para 6.13)

(2) Changing minds: young children and society

Tricia David

Here in the UK there seems to be little respect for young children as people and this is reflected in the view that they do not learn much until they begin to attend primary school. An editorial in *The Times* 1995 exemplified this assumption by suggesting that nursery education could prepare children so that 'the reception class can begin the proper process of education' (*The Times* 1995: 17). Such a statement makes one aware that, according to mainstream society:

- babies and young children are not capable of doing or learning very much;
- if they do learn anything in the first five years it is not very important;
- the older one becomes the more serious and important the learning (and therefore more worthy of investment by society).

The dominant view of young children in this country tends to be based on limited and outdated theories and beliefs. Ideas about maternal deprivation and children's emotional needs (Bowlby 1953) have been used as arguments against the provision of nurseries in the past and interpretations of Piagetian theory (Piaget 1954) have limited some of the experiences thought relevant by teachers in nursery and infant classes. The idea that young children are active learners capable of co-constructing their own view of the world with caring, familiar others participating in the creation of knowledge from the moment of birth, has not been used to inform a coherent policy for our youngest children.

Recent research (e.g. Bruner and Haste 1987; Trevarthen 1992) indicates that babies and children live 'up' or 'down' to societal expectations, that they will try to please those around them, both adults and older children, in order to become part of their social group, to be valued, loved and accepted. Far from being a biological bundle, babies come into the world programmed to make sense of the context in which they are growing (Trevarthen 1992). So why do we continue with an outdated 'model' of early childhood and where does it come from?

Biology, culture and theories of child development

'That children have certain characteristics, that adults have others, and that it is natural to grow from one to the other, are messages that we receive from all forms of mass communication' (Morss 1996: 29). In each of his challenging studies, John Morss (1990, 1996) questions the taken-for-granted nature of developmentalism in Western/Northern thinking about children. He cites Rom Harre's (1983, 1986) argument that:

> stage-based accounts of childhood make the pretence that a sequence of stages unfolds through some natural process . . . The world or worlds of the child, Harre argued, have to be described not as if biologically determined but more as forms of culture.
>
> (Morss 1996: 33–4)

Just over a decade ago Harre and others (for example, Harre 1983, 1986; Ingleby 1986) were challenging the roots of developmental psychology and its biological basis. Before this, the social construction movement, which was especially strong in the UK, with its foundations in sociology, had been ushered in by the publication of Berger and Luckman's *The Social Construction of Reality* (1967). Yet even this book propounded a view of babies as part of their mothers and as largely biological beings, who *become* human through socialization in the culture.

However, it was probably the ground-breaking paper 'The American child and other cultural inventions' by William Kessen (1979) which really put the cat among the pigeons. Kessen could see that childhood is defined by a particular society at a particular time in a particular way. In fact, according to studies such as that by Aries (1962), childhood did not exist at certain times in the history of Western Europe. And according to Postman (1985), childhood was invented with the printing press, since children then required a period of time in which to become literate. What Kessen, who in the mid-1970s led a delegation visiting educational settings for children in communist China (Kessen 1975), was really highlighting was the question of why different societies construct childhood in particular ways and why certain childhoods are assigned to particular children. By claiming that one version of childhood is a correct or true version and by demanding conformity, developmental psychologists and early years practitioners appear to have operated in a culture- or context-blind fashion. As Morss (1996) remarks, developmentalism may be hegemonic. We must ask if in defining stages in development and in seeking to protect young children, we also limit their achievements. Concluding that we end up with 'the children we deserve', Ros Miles (1994) argues for greater attention to children's rights and personhood.

What has been especially powerful about many Western academic studies of child development has been the assumption that findings can be generalized and applied to other societies. The impact of cultural context and the beliefs about young children permeating the shared meanings in any social group or nursery have been largely ignored. Psychologists such as the Newsons (1963, 1967) were attempting, as early as the 1960s, to show how parents and small children together create their own meanings and family culture. And in the USA, Bronfenbrenner (1975, 1979), another member of Kessen's delegation to China, attempted to bring together context and biology in his ecological theory of child development. He proposed that each child's 'ecological niche' is unique because each will experience the relationships and processes of interaction between home, nursery, wider world and the ideology in which all these are embedded. He also argued that children themselves, like the others around them, actively influence their 'ecological niche'. Since that time, the idea that members of a group or society co-construct particular childhoods and that children are active participants in that construction, has provided a powerful challenge to decontextualized theories of child development.

Yet despite these challenges, most research about young children and their learning has continued to be dominated by assumptions and approaches derived from the natural sciences. The problem is that this has led to under-estimates of their potential and capabilities (Deloache and Brown 1987). Morss (1990) shows how even Piaget ignored his own evidence when it did not fit contemporary preconceptions about young children's thinking. Watching two-and-half-year-old Arthur helping my 18-month-old grand-daughter onto a garden bench, where he had never been before nor seen an adult model this behaviour, I was spurred to reflect on the reported egocentricity of Piaget's children. Similarly, we see numerous examples of babies and young children hypothesizing in extremely sophisticated ways. An exhibit from the Reggio Emilia nurseries at the Bethnal Green Museum of childhood in summer 1997 consisted of a series of photographs of eight-month-old Laura. In the first she is looking at a catalogue with an educator. The page displays a range of watches. Laura then looks at the worker's watch, which by chance is the type which ticks. The worker puts her watch to Laura's ear. In the final photo Laura has laid her ear on the page of watches.

It may be that alliances between early years professionals from a range of fields and disciplines will move us on even further in our ability to comprehend and respond reflectively to young children. For example, stimulating new ideas concerning the complementary nature of genetic and epigenetic factors in children's brain development are being researched by psycho-physiologists such as Lambert (1996) in Paris. He suggests that contrary to the notion that babies and young children have to wait for their nervous connections to grow and for interaction with the environment to stimulate that growth, there are in fact many connections already in existence and it is through the complementarity of biology and experience that just one nervous connection (for a particular muscle action let's say) survives – the others die off. We can see how such a theory makes sense in the way human babies display all the sounds necessary to speak any language – but by around 12 months of age, a child will begin to lose all the sounds not used in the home language or languages.

We can no longer claim, as scientists did during this century, that newborn babies do not feel pain, that children cannot understand the world from another's viewpoint, that they cannot communicate or interact with others. Recent research suggests that children come into this world 'programmed' to make sense of the situation in which they find themselves and to communicate with other human beings (Trevarthen 1992) and that they learn more in their first five years than in all the other years of their lives. We need to throw out limiting old assumptions and respect what Howard Gardner (1993) has called 'the most remarkable features of the young mind – its adventurousness, its generativity, its resourcefulness, and its flashes of flexibility and creativity' (Gardner 1993: 111).

It would appear that young children have dispositions to learn different things, that they are not simply bundles of biological urges slowly being transformed, as they pass through universal pre-set stages of development, until they become fully formed humans as adults. On the contrary, once we have decided what kind of society we want, it is in everyone's interests to pay attention to the impact of policies on young children and those who share their lives, even those policies which appear irrelevant to early childhood.

Constructions of childhood and societal values

Once we become aware of the ways in which childhood itself is constructed in different societies or at different times, we also begin to ask ourselves why children are treated in certain ways, what is considered an appropriate education for children at different stages in their lives and what does all this tell us about that society.

While new research demonstrates children's amazing capacity for learning in their earliest years (e.g. Bruner and Haste 1987; Trevarthen 1992), the effects of what Eileen Byrne calls *The Snark Syndrome* (Byrne 1993) mean that policy and practice often lag behind, failing to adjust to the new knowledge. Byrne argues that old understandings are embedded in practices to such an extent they are difficult to overcome. She uses Lewis Carroll's poem, *The Hunting of the Snark*, with the lines

'Just the place for a Snark! I have said it thrice:
What I tell you three times is true'.

Byrne's 'Snark syndrome', about the constraints which can arise out of cultural assumptions and 'norms', is similar to the idea of 'regimes of truth' theorized by Foucault (1977). Being told repeatedly that babies and young children cannot understand or do very much becomes a self-fulfilling prophecy. Opportunity sampling in airport lounges and supermarkets has led me to conclude that we, as a nation, discourage young parents from interacting with or talking to their babies in public. I have been told they do not want to be thought strange. Yet viewed from a different perspective, it is this reserve which seems strange. An ex-Warwick colleague, Caroline Currer, writes of how English culture is perceived by people from the Indian subcontinent. She writes:

> one old man recounted to me in horror that, on a visit to Britain, he had seen a woman carrying a dog and pushing a baby [in a pram]. He had remembered this because it seems to epitomize the strange ordering of values here.
>
> (Currer 1991: 44)

Our value system is also implicit in the view of children as 'adults in waiting'. This represents a particularly Western/Northern approach to both childhood and learning (Hazareesingh *et al.* 1989) and, in its rationalist stance, an education system which separates the intellect from the emotions denies the holistic nature of human being. As Cathy Nutbrown writes:

> Perspectives on childhood that include the concept of children as 'adults in waiting' do not value children as learners and therefore create systems of educating, and design curricula, that can be narrow-minded rather than open-minded and which transmit to children, rather than challenge children to use their powers as thinkers and nurture their humanity.
>
> (Nutbrown 1996: xiv)

Childhood in contemporary Britain

Using both international comparisons with other Western/Northern nations and comparisons with our own national records, we find the following:

- The reported infant mortality rate is higher in the UK than in Sweden, Norway, Switzerland, and The Netherlands and higher proportions of the UK population live in relative poverty than in those countries – and the divide between rich and poor has increased during the last fifteen years.
- The UK and Denmark have the highest percentages of lone parents in the European Union (EU) and there are links between lone parenthood and poverty (Utting 1995).
- Studies have shown that there is evidence of a decline in average reading standards unaffected by teaching methods but related to the rapid increase in relative deprivation (Wilkinson 1994) and achievements (or lack of them) in the later years of school are also related to socio-economic factors.
- More than half the children in London's poorest boroughs are entitled to 'free' school meals (Brindle 1994) and the growing differentials in access to a healthy environment and diet carry risks such as increased risk of early death (Kumar 1993).
- The UK has the fastest increase of maternal employment outside the home yet more than one-third of fathers of children aged between birth and nine years work more than 50 hours a week – the highest levels in the EU (Cohen 1990). The result can be little time to spend together as a family, yet we have known for many years that isolation can lead to parental depression.

- Meanwhile, parental anxiety about the potential for child physical abuse as a result of the stress caused by unemployment has been documented by the NSPCC. The UK has the second highest proportion of unemployed fathers of children under nine in the EU (Moss 1996).
- The risk of homicide for babies under one year old is four times that of any other age group. The UK has the fifth highest rate of infant homicide in the EU (Butler 1996).

This litany serves to show how the childhoods experienced by all our children are not the same. Just as diet casts a long shadow forward, so too does the family and community's ability to provide emotional, social and intellectual stimulation. If, as a parent or carer, you do not have sufficient information or resources, how can you help your child? If our society fails to provide the necessary support, is it a sign that the construction of different and unequal childhoods are useful to those in power?

The purposes of early childhood services

It seems likely that we, as a nation, underestimate the learning capacity of children in these first years of life because of our assumptions and accepted notions about young children. Received wisdom about very young children in UK society, or established 'regimes of truth' (Foucault 1977), have resulted in our having one of the worst records of nursery provision in the EU and even 'lifelong education' plans propose the start at three years of age. The new Labour Government's White Paper *Excellence in Schools* ((DfEE 1997a) ostensibly devotes a whole chapter to 'A sound beginning' yet it fails to grasp the importance, in learning terms, of the years before three. The idea of babies and young children as people with the capacity to learn and the need to relate to others in meaningful ways, not as objects or possessions who should be mainly restricted to their own homes with only their own mothers for company, remains largely unrecognised. Parents need support and information to help them in their role as the primary educators of their very young children. Can we remedy or reduce the impact of all the negative factors in young children's lives and can early childhood education make a difference?

First, as a society, we need to decide what we want preschool provision to do – what it is 'for'. Politicians have all too often confused the issue by arguing that government has no responsibility to provide services so that women can go out to work, a message reiterated very recently in this connection by a former Minister at the DfEE (Gillan 1996). Does this former British government view reflect the ideology of society? In Sweden, for example, it is generally accepted that everyone has a responsibility towards children and as a result childcare, in which education is embedded, is high on the Swedish agenda.

To improve educational standards, we must ensure relevant and appropriate early learning opportunities. In terms of European comparisons of state-funded or state-subsidized provision for children under five, the UK does not fare particularly well. Despite the fact that almost all our 4- and 5-year-olds are in school (not always the best solution for either children or parents), we come out badly because of our relative lack of provision for children aged three and under (Moss 1996). In the majority of our European partner countries, there is much more widespread support for parents in the form of childcare services, parental leave and recognition for public responsibility towards the children of working parents, so alleviating and sharing the challenges of bringing up small children in today's rapidly changing world.

Further, there is greater coherence, a more holistic view of what the services should be for as far as the children themselves are concerned (Penn 1997a). In many of our partner countries, what happens to the children, the kind of curriculum offered while in the services provided is subject to evaluation and communal debate (Dahlberg and Åsén 1994) and a recent EU Recommendation called for all Member States to take measures to ensure the provision of childcare facilities for working parents and that those services should combine 'reliable care with a pedagogical approach' (Moss 1996: 48).

No British government to date has actually made a real commitment to ensuring an entitlement to the provision of full-time, publicly subsidized educare facilities for all children under five, which would support parents in their roles as both primary educators and as earners. We are the only EU country to provide nursery education on a 'part-time, shift system as a matter of policy' (Moss 1996: 37). Most 3- to 6-year-olds in other parts of the European Union can expect three years of continuous nursery education, while those in the UK experience what is probably the greatest period of discontinuity in their lives. Parents are sometimes forced to use more than one form of provision within a single day and children frequently move from playgroup, to private nursery, to reception class year on year. If children aged 11 to 14 experienced the same number of discontinuities in their learning, it would be perceived as a national scandal. Why do we not become incensed that this is what is actually happening to children during their most vulnerable, yet their most productive learning period?

In the light of US and other evidence (Barnett and Escobar 1990; Andersson 1992; Sylva 1994), such as that from the HighScope longitudinal study (Schweinhart *et al.* 1993a), when will the UK wake up to the fact that spending on the early years is an investment? It is significant that the HighScope curriculum demanded not only good home–school liaison but also highly educated, qualified early years teachers. The importance of investment in the training of those who work with young children is also emerging as a key factor in a number of other studies (see David 1996a).

Research has shown that, if we want children's early experiences to have beneficial effects in terms of their emotional stability, present contentment and later achievements, we need to pay attention to certain key factors (Field 1991). Those key ingredients include:

- the development of self-esteem in young children;
- investment in young children;

- stable childcare arrangements ensuring children interact with a limited number of familiar carers each day;
- low staff turnover;
- good training;
- and low adult : child ratios.

Yet one has the impression that numeracy and literacy have been accorded superordinate importance by successive governments, all of whom seem to believe that the earlier children focus on these areas of learning the more successful they will be later. Making the assumption that all we need to do is to teach children the mechanics of reading earlier and earlier, as seems to be the thrust of the government-inspired *Desirable Outcomes for Children's Learning on Entering Compulsory Schooling* from the School Curriculum and Assessment Authority (SCAA 1996) and other initiatives, may actually be wasting children's time and preventing them from acquiring other important knowledge and skills. Drawing on wide-ranging comparative evidence, Terenzina Nunes has commented:

> In Britain a six-year-old can be labelled a 'backward reader' and be assigned to remedial classes, whereas in Brazil or Sweden there is no room for such labelling at six.
>
> (Nunes 1994: 17)

Indeed, there is something sadly awry when a minister or an official fulminates (as Kenneth Clarke did when Secretary of State for Education in 1991) over the 'reading failure' of a quarter of our 7-year-olds, when in most of our partner countries children of this age are only just embarking on lessons in reading.

A high performance (on academic tasks) on school entry is not the magic key to educational success (Sylva 1992). A number of studies, as Bridie Raban concluded, demonstrate that

> the most important learning in the preschool years concerns task persistence, social skills, feelings of confidence and aspirations for the future.
>
> (Raban 1995: 15)

Perhaps belatedly, 'emotional intelligence' (Goleman 1996) has become a high priority. The foundations of robust emotional health and the ability to relate well to others seem to be laid during these very early years. Children can only develop the qualities listed by Bridie Raban (see above) and the emotional intelligence advocated by Goleman if the adults to whom we entrust them can engender those feelings of confidence and self-worth. The adults, whether parents or educators, can only undertake such a task if they have the necessary resources and feel valued in their turn.

Collective responsibility for young children

As a nation, the UK has signed up to the UN Convention on the Rights of the Child (United Nations 1989). Furthermore, we have the Children Act 1989, which requires we act in the best interests of the child, heed the child's views, support parents in their role as responsible carers and, as professionals involved with children and their families, work together effectively to these ends.

For the first time in British legal history, parents are portrayed as having *responsibilities for*, rather than *rights over*, their children. For child liberationists, the Children Act 1989 was only a beginning, a small move towards some sort of representation for children. As Louise Sylwander, Children's Ombudsman for Sweden, has pointed out, 'the Convention is something which has to be lived' (Sylwander 1996: 49). The way we think of and, as a result, treat children, especially those in their earliest years, has consequences. In the end, we get the children we deserve. *The Child as Citizen* (Council of Europe 1996) reminds readers that children form one of the largest groups in society but they do not form a lobby and are rarely represented in decision-making processes. Valuing children, the inheritance of a 'civic covenant' which includes a moral responsibility for the generations which follow us, is John O'Neill's (1994) argument in *The Missing Child in Liberal Theory*. He suggests that the power of the global market must be restrained, that capitalism has always been dependent upon moral and political restraints to keep it from destroying itself. In other words, if we do not have government which pays attention to the needs of its least powerful members and we allow individualism free rein, ignoring social responsibility, we risk a total collapse of society. We cannot disembed the economy from the polity.

When one traces the history of 'child politics' in its global, as opposed to nation-state, nature, many of the advances in awareness of children and their position in different societies have been due to the work of international NGOs (non-governmental organizations). In particular the breakthroughs of child politics and child policy of the 1960s and 1970s were, in part, due to the impact of the rise of feminism in making children more visible in society worldwide (Therborn 1996), through women's recognition that children's position in society paralleled their own.

Historically, the majority of early childhood educators have been women and there is an urgent need to review that history. Childminders have tended to be given a bad press, just as dame schools had earlier this century. There is evidence that proposals to create highly trained professionals to work with this age group have, and still do, run into opposition and sometimes derision, presumably because those who oppose are holding onto outdated ideas about young children, so they fail to grasp the complexity of learning in the first years of life. An example of that thinking occurred in the early 1990s, when the then Conservative Government proposed a 'Mum's Army' of preschool workers. Other important episodes in that history include the King of Prussia banning Froebelian training in the mid-eighteenth century and Franco ordering the closure of nurseries in Spain during the 1930s – what were they afraid of? So as well as asking ourselves, 'Why that model of early childhood in that place at that time?' we should also ask, 'Why this model of educator (or educators) in this place at this time?' As Caroline Steedman (1988) pointed out, the 'mother made conscious', probably the model of an early years teacher held by those who believe young children do not learn very much during this stage of life, is typically middle class and not very clever.

The early years teachers society wants

As early childhood educators we need to be able to explore our own thinking. Are we able to disembed our understandings from the cultural context in which we have grown, developed, and indeed, been trained for our professional roles? Can we problematize the constructions of childhood extant in our cultures and communities? To be capable of such reflective and reflexive practice requires high levels of understanding, education and empathy. Early educators seem to require the ability to stand in a child's shoes, or to stand in a parent's shoes, and to examine the ecological niche within which the family is living; to try to make sense of and expose the challenges and constraints – and the benefits – which impact on that child and that family in ways which may assist or prevent the child in the achievement of his or her human potential.

So what are the implications for training?

Probably the most important implications for training, apart from high levels of knowledge in a range of relevant disciplines, involve the need for early childhood educators to be able to de-centre (to view the world from another's viewpoint); to 'problematize' their favoured theories and to engage in reflexivity (examining how their own thinking, views and actions influence their ecological niche). Thus training should not be about acquiring facts and knowledge but about exploring bodies of knowledge and submitting them to critical analysis in the light of real-life experience. There should be opportunities for experiencing and reflecting on teamwork with other adults, leading to open, depersonalized self-evaluation of strengths and weaknesses. In particular, in relation to the main thrust of this chapter, there should be discussion of the ways in which societies construct different versions of early childhood and the services deemed appropriate as a result.

Conclusion

The constant reminders that our education system is failing our children always seem to omit the fact that we do not, as a society, pay enough attention to the very earliest years. Perhaps our current malaise is in part due to our lack of attention to the 'needs' and rhythms of young children (David 1996a). Changing children's minds to help them achieve their potential means changing the minds around them, so that they are no longer seen as 'adults in waiting' but as people, social beings who are trying to participate in and make sense of their world – whatever their age.

(3) | Facing some difficulties

Helen Penn

What does it take to educate and care for a group of young children? What special aptitudes are necessary? What kind of skills must be acquired? What sort of knowledge needs to inform practice? How should this blend of aptitude, skills and knowledge be rewarded? What is it worth in the market-place? These are simplistic questions but they bedevil discussions about early years training. It would be accurate to say there is no consensus about the answers, since they are not questions of evidence but of opinion. To put it another way, we are asking about what kinds of services do we think are appropriate for young children and who should be working in them?

In trying to come up with answers, we uncover all kinds of assumptions: about childhood and the needs of children and how they should be met; about the lives of women and particularly mothers who are childcarers without any training; about the role of the state and the borders of its intervention in family life; and about the nature and organization of places where young children come and spend their time and what they are like as working environments, not only for the children, but for those who look after the children. This chapter tries to explore, or to use a more fashionable word, 'deconstruct', some ideas about training.

What do young children need?

As many writers have pointed out (Woodhead 1990; Burman 1994) ideas and beliefs about what young children need in order to grow, develop and thrive rest more on an expression of the moral and ideological concerns of adults than on a description of children. Indeed, it is now theoretically questionable whether there are any 'natural' scientifically established attributes of child-hood, that is universal aspects of development which aspiring practitioners need to know about in order to inform their practice (Morss 1996). The idea of 'developmentally appropriate practice' (Bredekamp 1987), that is, a body of knowledge about child development which every practitioner should know – and which certainly is presumed as underpinning the NVQ and NNEB qualifications – is increasingly seen to be problematic by psychologists themselves.

Developmental psychology, like so many other empirical sciences, is fragmenting, and offers competing views of itself as a discipline. In a famous essay entitled 'The child and other cultural inventions' (1983) William Kessen, professor of psychology at Harvard, analyses some of the assumptions of child development and makes a number of radical claims, among them that different human cultures have invented different children and what typifies the Anglo-American view above all is a view of a child as

> a free standing isolable being who moves through development as a self-contained and complete individual . . . The ubiquity of such radical individualism in our lives makes the consideration of alternative images of childhood extraordinarily difficult.
>
> (Kessen 1983: 268)

He suggests that, as a starting point, we need to accept the variety of children's lived experiences, what he calls 'the awesome variety of mankind'. Other developmental psychologists have taken up these ideas, and most recently Michael Cole (1996) has argued that the only kind of psychology which makes sense is 'Cultural Psychology.' He defines this as an attempt to derive principles from activities located at the level of everyday practices and to return to those practices as a grounding for its theoretical claims. Another way of describing it is that child development is domain-specific – what you are doing depends where you are and why you are doing it. Having the tools and skills to analyse and theorize practice is what makes for good practice, rather than referring to a supposedly universal set of prescriptions which one calls 'child development'.

If Cole's suggestions seem too abstract, let me give a very practical example. Nelson Mandela, in his autobiography, recalls that up to the age of 7 he never remembers being alone. There were always other children present, of different ages and from different families (even the use of the word 'family' will not do to describe the variety of kinship and household arrangements which exist outside the Minority World[1]). For most of the world's children, separation, privacy and individual ownership of possessions, things which we in the Minority World take absolutely for granted, simply do not exist. It does not make sense in this context to talk of children 'learning to share'; in fact, 'learning to share' might be more appropriately be called 'learning to handle and police private possessions'.

To follow through Kessen's concept of 'individualism' it is possible to claim that such individualism permeates practice in nursery education, day nurseries and most other forms of childcare in the UK. For instance in a recent book, *Comparing Nurseries* (Penn, 1997a), I compare the daily experiences of staff and children in day nurseries in Spain, Italy and the UK. What was so striking to me as an observer in the nurseries over a period of time, was not only the individualism in the UK nurseries, as compared with the other non-UK nurseries, but the way in which the staff had no means of understanding or analysing their practice because this individualism was so embedded and yet so unarticulated in what they did.

> . . . individualism dominates practice. There is no other rationale, no basis for action when children and adults come together, no sense that the nursery as an organization can or should add anything different or new to the children's daily lives, no sense that the lived experiences are anything more than an aggregate of separate and individual reactions. When I prompted, the most articulate explanation that was offered of what the nursery was doing is that staff are trying to make the nursery as much like home as possible – but the presence of a token strip of carpet or an armchair cannot begin to turn an institution for 40 or 50 children into a home; it does not remotely resemble one. In fact it is cut off in its practices from anything ordinary or daily that is going on around it – shopping, cashing benefits, going on a bus, collecting a brother or sister from school, rocking the baby to stop it crying, chasing a cat or exercising a dog, even making a cup of tea. The staff implicitly deny that the nursery is not a home, and try to convince themselves that it is; that they can substitute for the (idealized) mother–child experiences which the child is deemed to be lacking. This accounts for the overstaffing in some of the nurseries, and the belief that the child is incapable of learning anything valuable unless in a one to one situation. In one of the nurseries . . . they had even invented a verb to describe the process 'one to oneing'.
>
> (Penn 1997a: 125)

I use this example as an illustration of the shortcomings of the child development theory which many of the staff had been taught as students, that is, a view of children as isolated individuals, highly dependent for their emotional support and learning on the presence of adults. This had resulted in particular and sometimes unhelpful practices in the nurseries.

There is, then, considerable and accumulating debate about the viability of child development as a source of ideas about practice. This comes from a variety of angles, from within child development itself, which is what I have very briefly recounted here, but also from other disciplines. The growing body of research on the sociology of childhood (for example, the findings of social anthropology and the methodologies of history) suggest that we must treat with caution any claims to present childhood as constant, or to understand development as invariable, or to represent the needs of children as universal.

Women, mothers and other childcarers

Caring work has traditionally been done by women in informal situations, and much of it still is undertaken in this way. As Rose (1994) has remarked:

Yet women's work is of a particular kind. Whether menial or requiring the sophisticated skills involved in childcare it almost always involves personal service . . . emotionally demanding labour requires that the carer gives something of themselves to the person being cared for, so that even while childcare is capable of immense variation within societies, across societies and across time, it remains the case that nurturance – a matter of feeding, touching, comforting and cleaning bodies – is cross-culturally the preserve of women.

(Rose 1994: 22, 31)

Once childcare becomes professionalized and institutionalized, what happens to these conceptions of caring as both bodily and emotionally intimate? The evidence suggests that these ideas about caring as a woman's 'natural' occupation are widespread. Ninety-nine per cent of those working in early childhood services are women, which makes it one of the most heavily gendered of all occupations. In a recent study of nursery workers in training, carried out for the Department for Education and Employment, we asked why students had chosen to undertake childcare training, and whether the training was what they expected (Penn and McQuail 1997). The women we interviewed felt that they all brought intrinsic 'natural' talent to the job of childcare, and this talent was at least as important, if not more important than any training.

'The caring bit attracted me. I feel comfortable around children and they feel comfortable around me. But now I understand more about children.'

'It's intrinsic to being a woman.'

'I felt I was a natural.'

'You can use your own experience as a mum, you feel comfortable.'

'All the courses in the world will never give you that feeling of knowing and working with children. That feeling comes from within, its a good good feeling.'

'At home it's the women's role, that's why women do it, they are used to it.'

'Mothering is natural, its an instinct, it comes naturally to most mothers.'

'You need to be a little bit mumsy to work with babies, it comes from within.'

'Whether trained or not, if you are not a natural, you can't hack it, you've got to get down to their level.'

Almost all of the respondents considered that aptitude was more important or as least as important as training. The most frequently mentioned qualities that were seen as important in caring for children – patience, kindness, understanding, tolerance, flexibility, consistency, reliability – were seen as qualities which students brought with them rather than qualities they had acquired through training. Tied in with this view of themselves as already caring and competent women, was a view of young children as a more vulnerable group, uniquely susceptible to their influence.

> 'They are vulnerable, I want to protect them, they depend on you. When they are older they don't.'

> 'I enjoy helping them, the first 5 or 7 years are important to their life, its important to help them on their way, by 9 or 10 they have learnt it all, the older children answer you back, they are harder to control.'

> 'They are more open to learning, older children are more stubborn.'

> 'We can control them more. You say don't do it and they understand. You say it to an older child and they get back at you.'

Many women therefore turn to childcare because it is perceived as easy and unthreatening; it builds on what they know and think they can do; it does not carry too many risks; and it is a useful and fulfilling, and sometimes very pleasant job to be doing. As one student summed it up:

> 'You get more self-esteem, it confirms what you already know. I am able to do it.'

These heavily gendered attitudes, which I would argue are fairly widespread amongst those taking childcare training in the UK, are problematic for a number of reasons. First of all, they amount to a devaluing of theory and professionalism. If childcare is 'natural' then the theory and the knowledge of practice, and the ethics and standards associated with professionalism, are to an extent superfluous. The tutors of the students were uncomfortably aware of this contradiction, and tried to insist on the professionalism of the job of childcare, and although the students accepted some of the rhetoric of professionalism they also felt their instincts and accumulated experience as mothers and carers was the most important thing they had to offer.

But, second, if childcare is a 'natural' occupation for women, then it follows that it is 'unnatural for men'. Most of the men and women in our student sample thought that men working with children was 'unnatural' and would be perceived as such by the outside world. This could only be resolved by arguing that men brought something different and special to childcare. Men were said to offer a 'male role model'. Men were perceived as being more physical, more able to engage in rough-and-tumble play, better at organizing children, but less able to deal with babies or work with very young children. Underlying this description of men was a basic and divisive conception of sexuality and gender – men are men and what they are and do and want is fundamentally different from what women are and do and want.

> 'For a man, he's a wally, he doesn't fit in.'

> 'The man is seen as a woman when he changes a nappy.'

'It's good to have male role models, it's essential but the skills of men are different . . . it's an attitude to physical activity, an ability to team lead children.'

'They play with children differently, they get the rough play.'

'A man is different.'

Stereotypes of gender, then, are likely to permeate basic childcare training, based as they are on lived daily experiences. Addressing such stereotypes is not merely a matter of confronting them on training courses, but is an indication of a wider societal unease about gender equity.

What should the state provide?

One difficulty about training is the nature of the material, particularly child development material, traditionally provided on training courses. Another difficulty is the very strong preconceptions about gender which permeate training and work in childcare. A third major difficulty is how to answer the question, what are we training people to do? As many reports and books have pointed out, early childhood services in the UK are fragmented and confusing. Different services have different aims and objectives, operate in different ways for different hours, have different expectations of the staff who work in them and remunerate them in different ways. Parents may pay nothing, or an entire weekly wage, towards the costs of these services. Nursery schools and classes, playgroups, day nurseries, family centres, private day nurseries and workplace nurseries, crèches, childminders and nannies all offer some kind of service for children, although there is rarely a straight and unambiguous choice for parents between them. Is it possible to have a coherent training without coherent services? Is the same childcare training appropriate for work with disturbed children and families in a family centre in a run-down inner-city area, working as a nanny to a rich family in New York, being a crèche attendant in a health and fitness club, and acting as an assistant to a teacher in an infant class?

Apart from a very small percentage of children, around 1 per cent, who are defined as children in need, and for whom family centres and day nurseries are deemed appropriate, unlike many other European countries, the state accepts no responsibility to provide comprehensive early childhood services. Local authorities now have to show that all 4-year-olds can have access to part-time nursery education in the area, although it is left open as to how it is defined, how it will be provided, and what kind of compatibility there will be between the different providers in terms of staffing or premises. But children of working parents remain 'a private responsibility' despite the fact that under the Welfare to Work programme, families on benefits, particularly single mothers, are being urged to seek work and find whatever childcare they can. Until education departments, nationally and locally, accept responsibility for the children of working parents, the present confusion is likely to continue and provision is likely to be as fragmented as ever, with those who can afford paying for private in-home services or private day nurseries, leaving poorer families to struggle with the policy contradictions and to face the unavailability of day care.

How can training be coherent when faced with such incoherence of provision? Education officials stress the need for 'preschool education' and see the child as primarily a learner getting ready for the competitiveness of schooling; social workers see the child as vulnerable and damaged and in need of care and surveillance; employment officials consider the child of little consequence, needing to be warehoused as soon and as cheaply as possible in order to enable her mother to work. If these contradictory views of the child and the state's responsibility towards families and children co-exist, what are students to make of it? In the survey quoted above (Penn and McQuail 1997) students chose to work, not on the basis of what kind of work was being done with children, but where they would have the most job security and the best pay prospects, namely in the local authority sector. Nannying, childminding and private day nurseries were a poor second to local authority work as a career choice:

> 'Nanny, that's even lower [than a childminder], its like a hairdresser or apprentice hairdresser, a Saturday job, cook.'

> 'What, go on a course and become a childminder!'

Similarly, the providers we interviewed, whatever their background in a day nursery, playgroup or nursery school, recommended nursery teaching as a career over and above any other work, because of the enhanced pay and conditions.

> 'I don't know about a young girl, I would say maybe they would like to go into nursery teaching. The job I do is more suitable for a mum. If I would have gone into this career when I didn't have children I would have gone into teaching . . . I am lucky because I have had a partner to support me. If I didn't have a partner maybe I would have gone further.'
>
> (Playgroup supervisor)

Just as there is a hierarchy of provision, with some workers achieving much better pay and conditions than others, so there is a hierarchy of training, and certainly with hindsight, whatever their own route, all our providers recommended the training route with the best career prospects, namely teaching. However, teaching itself at present contains all kinds of contradictions, not least that children do not appear to exist before the age of three years, and training is aimed at 3–8 years or 3–11 years, in one setting only, the classroom (Penn 1997a).

Training, then, has to make sense of these contradictory career job opportunities, and to prepare students for the world outside college. Can – or should – one training cover all these options? This is a question discussed at length in Moss and Penn (1996). In the chapter on training in this book we argue for a comprehensive modular training for all those working in the field of early childhood services, on the Spanish or Danish model, where qualifications are completed and/or added to *after* beginning work; but our argument presupposes that there will also be a reform of provision, with services becoming more coherent, particularly as regards working parents, and with the state taking responsibility for overseeing such coherence. The training then becomes a meaningful and continuous affair, with as much time devoted to in-service training as initial training, and the latter being seen as the *beginning* of a process of reflecting and learning on the job.

The organization of the workplace

Training for work in early childhood services is practical; it is intended to prepare students for the workplace. In the section above I argued there were many different kinds of workplaces, where different kinds of work was being undertaken, and where the expectations of what workers would do, and how they would be remunerated, was very different. In this section, I want to look at a particular and fundamental aspect of the workforce, the notion of management and hierarchy.

In the Anglo-American literature, the concepts of management and leadership are so embedded in the understanding of the organization of work that it is almost impossible to envision an alternative way of thinking about how tasks in a work setting can be identified, prioritized, distributed and undertaken other than by having a hierarchical system in which managers or leaders direct and control (and perhaps inspire) the flow of work. Most of the rhetoric about management and leadership omits to mention money and status. Managers get paid more, and have more power over decision-making; the other side of the coin is that non-managers get paid less and have less power over decision-making. Non-managers have to defer to managers; they are subordinate to them, and their status and remuneration are less. The pathways to becoming a manager are embodied in the notion of a 'career structure' that is a delineation of the steps – promotion – towards the goal of becoming a manager. This career structure, the possibility, rather than the promise, of gaining more control, more prestige and more money in a work setting is held out as an incentive towards doing your job well. If you perform well, you can think about applying for promotion, although of course you may not get it and may become embittered if you do not.

Within early years in the Anglo-American literature, these concepts of management and leadership have been adopted uncritically. The literature assumes that hierarchical management is a 'given' and focuses instead on what attributes successful managers possess. Richman and McGuire (1988), for instance, suggest that successful managers are those who involve themselves directly in day-to-day activities, and who are seen to be expert practitioners. Jorde-Bloom (1988) has produced an Early Childhood Work Environment Rating Scale. She delineates ten areas in which staff can rate the nursery in which they work, but implicit in this scale is the notion of a manager or director. Rodd (1994) has written a book *Leadership in Early Childhood* and looked at nurseries in Australia. She also concludes that:

> The development of leadership skills is a vital and critical challenge for early childcare professionals . . . if the provision of socially and culturally responsive services for young children and their families is to be successful in the next century.
>
> (Rodd 1994: 14)

In a number of European countries, however, there are enduring and long-standing cooperative traditions in nurseries. Saraceno (1977) considers that these derive from the radical experiments of the 1960s, but there is also evidence that the traditions are much older and more culturally widespread (Corsaro and Emiliani 1992).

As part of a comparative study of day nurseries, I investigated and compared the organization and management of day nurseries in Spain, Italy and the UK (Penn 1997b). Many nurseries in Spain and Italy are organized as collectives, that is all teacher/care staff are paid similar rates, no-one is in charge and decision-making is collectively undertaken. In Spain, for example, the nurseries I investigated were responsible for their own administration, their own training and development plans and their own professional standards. They elected a supernumary member of staff as a secretary to deal with all administrative issues, but when I asked about their work these secretaries were at pains to point out that they were in no way 'in charge' and decision making was firmly collective. The collective way of working meant that the activities and professional development of the nursery were conceived of as a whole for the nursery. The nursery itself was viewed as a functioning organism, as opposed to a collection of individuals in the same place. Rather like the way in which hierarchy was viewed as implicit in the Anglo-American context, collectivism was taken for granted in the Italian and Spanish contexts. It was not problematic *per se*. The view was that relationships between staff were an important model for children's relationships with each other, and the more egalitarian the relationships between staff, the more the children would develop reciprocal friendships and cooperation among themselves. The Spanish staff were thoughtful and volunteered many comments about their collective way of working.

> 'I have the good luck to be in a team where I have observed few conflicts, where people talk about things, a kind of dialogue which makes conflict unnecessary. Also we have a lot of freedom within the group rooms and within the framework set by the nursery.'

> 'Even if I didn't like the work I would still like my colleagues. Bad relationships with colleagues would spread to work with the children.'

> 'I'm in agreement with the structure and organization of the centre although from a practical point of view, working and deciding as a team takes longer, and things get done more slowly. Even so, I would not

change it even if certain aspects of punctuality and organization are lacking.'

'Working in a team is positive but difficult – you have to take account of a range of views and arrive at the best compromise agreement.'

'We need to find a form of organization that recognizes all aspects and all the diversity of a team.'

'We have differences but they are not sources of conflict. Perhaps the fact that we have enough autonomy and we have friendships within the group facilitates the work means we have very few conflicts.'

In the UK, however, the nurseries were hierarchically organized. There was an officer in charge (O-I-C) and her deputy, both supernumary. Then there were a number of graded or senior posts, and the remainder of the staff were employed on basic grades – altogether nine grades of staff, each grade carrying a different status and remuneration. The officers-in-charge in turn deferred their decisions to a nursery manager, who in turn deferred her decision to an assistant director of social services whose main function concerned residential services to the elderly. Decision making was continually referred up and down the system by means of written instructions.

Yet there was considerable rhetoric about inclusive management and management skills. The officer-in-charge was very much in charge, and there was no question about the decisions of the officer-in-charge being overruled. Often they were not even discussed. Since the nurseries were open throughout the year, rotas had to be continually re-organized to allow for cover of staff who were absent on holiday or away sick. This meant that the whole group of staff were rarely present, and organizing meetings was still more difficult. Instead of any group discussion of professional progress, there was a system known as 'supervision' in which each member of staff was allocated half an hour every fortnight or so to talk with a more senior member of staff about the problems she was encountering in her daily practice. Again, there was no explicit rationale for this practice; it was something that everyone did without it being made clear why or what it was intended to achieve, and because it was embedded, it was difficult to explain to an outsider. However, staff airing their personal problems put themselves in a difficult position in relation to their boss, because the person to whom they were airing their grievance may also have been the person who had caused it. Moreover, any problem or grievance was first perceived as a personal rather than as a collective problem.

Given these inherent and sometimes irreconcilable tensions of management, even in the best of circumstances things go wrong. What can followers do about it? The problematic nature of these unequal hierarchical relationships are articulated by trades unions, and there is some protection for subordinates enshrined within employment law, but otherwise hierarchy is usually seen entirely from the point of view of managers. The hierarchical nature of these nurseries was not only unquestioned but reinforced at every turn, and the only protection the more junior or subordinate employees had against unjust decisions was through union action. Consequently, the managers were very antagonistic to the union because it challenged their point of view. The woman who was the union shop steward for the nursery nurses was described to me in very derogatory and half-fearful tones as 'a trouble-maker', because she voiced a point of view about procedures which was not acceptable to those in charge.

In both Italy and Spain an egalitarian way of working was seen as unexceptional, and drew on much wider historical and cooperative traditions. It was not seen as unusual, and no special skills or training were required to work in this way. It was simply how the nurseries were organized. Because collective practices were normal, there were no obvious informal leaders or power struggles as has happened with the few fraught experiments with collectives in the UK in the 1960s and 1970s, where breaking away from a hierarchical system proved extremely problematic (Stanton 1989).

In Italy and Spain, collective working was a well-tried way of working with who staff felt comfortable. It was reinforced by social practices – daily communal meals and frequent outings and celebrations. In the UK, by contrast, there were no social practices which could counteract or mitigate hierarchy – no communal mealtimes or communal outings. The friendships of the nursery rarely spilled over into non-working time.

These organizational aspects of the workplace, although so powerful and determining of daily practice, are not seriously considered as an aspect of training, either in childcare training or in teacher training. Instead, there is a loose rhetoric about 'teamwork' which glosses over all the differences of power and remuneration, and assumes that people will be nice to one another and choose to work together whatever their differences in status, which in the confusing field of early childhood services are particularly marked. Where hierarchical systems exist and so much power is invested in individual managers, then the quality of the management is important. A good manager, who works democratically with her staff and is an experienced practitioner, can influence the practice in the nursery. A poor manager, by the same token, has an adverse effect. But the possibilities of more cooperative and less hierarchical organization remain largely unexplored. 'Teamwork' is yet another area where clearer argument is necessary, and the lessons from practice need more profound analysis.

Conclusion

In this chapter, I have tried to highlight some of difficulties and inconsistencies in current training for work in early childhood services. I have not attempted to provide answers here, although I have done elsewhere (Moss and Penn 1996). However, as the chapter illustrates, I consider there are some fairly fundamental difficulties in training for work in early years which have yet to be faced. I hope this chapter proves a vehicle for addressing them.

Note

1 Rather than use the expression 'Third World' or 'Developing World', instead I use the term 'Majority World'. Similarly, I use the term 'Minority World' instead of 'Westernized' or 'Developed World'. These terms 'Majority World' and 'Minority World' are increasingly used in the literature to highlight the imbalance of resources between the two.

Early years educators: skills, knowledge and understanding

Barbara Thompson and Pamela Calder

The context: editors' comment

Recent developments in early years training have led to a wide-ranging debate among those responsible for training at all levels with regard to the content of courses and the kinds of knowledge and attributes which workers should possess. The differences in types and levels of training, length of course and prior experience and knowledge of applicants, has caused widespread concern and generated heated discussion among trainers and course developers.

This chapter arises out of one such debate among members of the Early Years Training Group who have contributed to this book. This debate, which was lengthy and extremely interesting, was taped and transcribed – no mean task! Members of the group were then invited to respond, having had time to reflect on their position and following discussion with those whose interests they represent.

Barbara Thompson, training officer with the Pre-School Learning Alliance, took on the daunting task of writing from her perspective both as an academic and one who is involved in the planning and development of training for playgroup staff. It is just one perspective but it is intended to generate thought and discussion.

It will certainly challenge, for what it does not do is offer any simple solutions or checklists of content. A curriculum framework for training, again for discussion within specific course contexts, is offered as an appendix to this book. The intention of this chapter is to provoke reaction and to encourage the reader to examine the most recent thinking about child development, to challenge old assumptions and to respond by re-examining what it is that early years workers, at all levels of training, should know and what kind of people they should be.

Proof that Barbara Thompson's perspective provoked a response within the group is provided by Pamela Calder, who as someone involved in the new integrated degree courses in Early Childhood Studies, challenges some of the issues raised. Theirs are just two perspectives on what is a complex, fairly contentious but nevertheless critical area.

As this chapter illustrates, course content is only one aspect of early years training. Ability to think critically and to analyse and reflect on practice is crucial for all early years educators if appropriate experiences are to be provided for children. But as Thompson asks, how is critical thinking developed?

This is a thought-provoking chapter and one which does not sit easily with the view that a syllabus or list of modules is all that is required to run a course. 'Teaching young children is a complex and demanding task' as the National Commission on Education states. So too is the education and training of those who work with them!

Barbara Thompson

A diversity of forms of provision and qualifications

Among those involved with early years education, there is concern about the existing diversity of forms of provision and about the accompanying diversity of qualifications for early years educators. Within the training group's debate, several proposals were made for addressing the diversity of qualifications. Some members proposed the creation of a climbing frame of qualifications for early years workers which identifies the level of particular qualifications and allows comparable qualifications to provide progression routes to further qualification. Others argued for existing qualifications to be encompassed in Early Childhood Studies degrees. These issues are addressed more fully in Chapters 5, 6, 7 and 8.

The knowledge base of existing qualifications

Examination of the knowledge base of the existing qualifications for early years educators reveals common areas of knowledge which are covered by all of the qualifications. As the Rumbold Report (DES 1990) identifies, there are variations in the depth in which these are covered and the emphasis which is given to specific areas. The report's description of the knowledge, understanding, skills and attitudes required by early years educators cover the areas which Bruner (1974) argued are important for all educators, that is knowledge about learning, about teaching and about knowledge. Each covers a range of skills, knowledge and understanding.

Knowledge about learning

- Child development – the range and stages of acquisition of the behaviours and abilities acquired by children between 0 and 8 years.
- The processes through which children construct meaning from their experiences, including how they use language in this construction.

Knowledge about teaching

- How to apply a knowledge of child development to providing a range of activities and resources to promote children's learning and development, including the implementation of a broad and balanced curriculum which provides continuity with the National Curriculum.
- How to communicate and interact with children in ways which build on and extend their existing knowledge and abilities.
- The organizational and managerial understanding and abilities needed to work as part of a team.
- Observational skills and their use in the assessment and monitoring of children's progress.
- Creating good relationships with parents and other professionals.
- Personal qualities in terms of sensitivity and the holding of high expectations for oneself and others.

Knowledge about knowledge

- Human culture – an understanding of the ideas and skills which provide a foundation for children in science, mathematics, literature, art, music, history, geography, politics.
- Human values – an understanding of the experiences which will arouse children's awareness of environmental issues, and what it means to belong to and contribute to society, democracy.

While a common knowledge base for existing qualifications for early years educators can be identified, there are differing views about what constitutes appropriate knowledge in the areas which have been described. These differing views are themselves part of wider debates about the nature of knowledge and how it is constructed.

The debate about the nature and construction of knowledge

The focus of debates about the nature and construction of knowledge has been the ways in which both are influenced by culture, and what the implications of the recognition of this influence might be for the authority of knowledge. Knowledge has been created from humankind's attempts to describe and explain the world around us.

As Polanyi argues, the creation of these descriptions and explanations involves us in thinking about what was created and how it was created:

> Man [*sic*] must try for ever to discover knowledge that will stand up by itself, objectively, but the moment he reflects on his own knowledge he catches himself red-handed in the act of upholding his knowledge. He finds himself asserting it to be true, and this asserting and believing is an action which makes an addition to the world on which his knowledge bears. So every time we acquire knowledge we enlarge the world, the world of man, by something that is not yet incorporated in the object of the knowledge we hold, and in this sense a comprehensive knowledge of man must appear impossible.
>
> (Polanyi 1959: 11)

For Polanyi, our search for knowledge should be a pursuit of objectivity, that is an attempt to use impartial observation and analysis, in order to describe and explain the world and its behaviour in terms of general principles, which are applicable to a range of situations and circumstances. He argues that this search involves reflection on the process of knowledge creation and the ideas created. It is from the examination of this process that questions regarding the influence of culture on the construction of knowledge have arisen. The source of these questions has been the recognition that the examination of how knowledge is created cannot escape consideration of who creates it.

This examination has posited that any creator of knowledge brings to the activity of observing, analysing and the building of descriptions and explanations, a set of values which arise from the society in which s/he functions. (The quotation from Polanyi provides an example of someone operating in an era when the use of the generic term 'man' rather than one which indicated the inclusion of both females and males, was less likely to be questioned than it is today.) In the areas of knowledge covered by early years qualifications, these values include beliefs about the nature of adulthood, childhood and society, what constitutes knowledge, and the purpose of education. A further consideration is that the adults, children and societies who are the subject of study, are themselves in some measure culturally constructed. Bruner, in comparing the activity of knowledge creation in the physical sciences and the humanities, recognizes that the creator of knowledge is not able to take a completely independent and objective position in either discipline. However, in the case of science the objects of study are not themselves part of a sociocultural context.

> Science attempts to make a world that remains invariant across human intention and human plights. The density of the atmosphere does not, must not alter as a function of one's ennui with the world. On the other hand, the humanist deals principally with the world as it changes with the position and stance of the viewer. Science creates a world that has an

'existence' linked to the invariance of things and events across transformations in the life conditions of those who seek to understand – though modern physics has shown that this is true within very constrained limits. The humanities seek to understand the world as it reflects the requirements of living in it. In the jargon of linguistics, a work of literature or of literary criticism achieves universality through context sensitivity, a work of science through context independence.

(Bruner 1986: 50)

The debate about knowledge and the knowledge required by early years educators

What are the consequences of the debate about the nature and construction of knowledge for the knowledge required by early years educators? The researchers and theorists responsible for its construction have sets of values and expectations arising from the societal contexts in which they have developed and operate. These have affected their descriptions and explanations of how children develop and learn, and the environments which are most advantageous to this development and learning. For example, Riegel has said of Piaget, whose theories have informed much educational practice in Britain, Europe and America during the latter half of this century, that his stages of development in thinking patterns describe the modes of thought required by the objective-scientific thinking valued by European and Anglo-Saxon societies.

For all these reasons, Piaget's theory describes thought in its alienation from its creative dialectical basis. It represents a prototype reflecting the goals of our higher educational system that, in turn, are reflecting the nonartistic and noncreative aspects in the intellectual history of western man [sic].

(Riegel 1979: 50)

Further, the children who have been studied and the social settings in which these children functioned were to some extent culturally constructed:

Human culture, of course, is one of two ways by which instructions about how humans should grow are carried from one generation to the next – the other being the human genome. The plasticity of the human genome is such that there is no unique way in which it is realised, no way that is independent of opportunities provided by the culture into which the individual is born.

(Bruner 1986: 135)

Should the response to this position be to see all knowledge as culturally situated and, therefore, only applicable within the context from which it arose? Does this mean that knowledge about children which has been derived on the basis of a particular set of cultural values is inapplicable to children living and learning in other cultural settings? As Stott and Bowman argue:

> Research and theories of child development focus on change in the organism over time. They seek to provide a description of development and to offer a general set of principles or rules for change in the course of development. These principles have been called into question for a variety of reasons. One is their adherence to natural science methods and concepts, including the notion that knowledge is impersonal; in fact, its objectivity is taken as a virtue. Theories of development have been criticised for their ethnocentric bias and notions of universality in their specific social, historical and cultural contexts. . . These criticisms, however, need not lead to an abandonment of child development knowledge in our training programs. We agree with Geertz (1973), who said, 'I have never been impressed by the argument that, as complete objectivity is impossible in these matters, . . . one might as well let one's sentiments run loose.'
>
> (Stott and Bowman 1996: 171)

A way forward is provided by the arguments which they move on to make. These are that the changes in theories and their implications for practice can be the object of study, as can the social contexts in which children exist, the aims which underpin different approaches to education and the values which underlie theory. Thus, the cultural contexts which influence the construction of knowledge themselves become a focus for study, and we are able to operate beyond the constraints of cultural background. This latter would seem to be an important area of consideration for early years educators. It suggests that we have the ability to examine different value systems and to operate from the basis of more than one system. Donaldson sees this ability as one of the defining characteristics of humans:

> One of the most striking things about us is that we are highly prolific 'intention generators'. We set goals for ourselves of the most diverse kinds . . . The devising of novel purposes comes readily to us because we have brains that are good at thinking of possible states – at considering not merely what is but what might be. We exist in a world of 'hard fact', but we can imagine it as changed; and from a very early age we know that, within certain limits, we are able to change it. It matters very much to us to find out how these limits are set, an activity closely related to the general purpose of understanding what the world is like.
>
> (Donaldson 1993: 7, 9)

In making the ability to move beyond the constraints of any particular value system a defining human characteristic, Donaldson makes its promotion a key feature of human development. For those who accept this argument, it will be a crucial ability to foster in young children, and how to promote it will be an important part of the knowledge which underpins the practice of an early years educator.

The content and process of training for early years workers

What are the consequences of the influence of cultural background on the construction of knowledge for the content and process of training for early years educators? It suggests that their training should give early years educators an awareness of the epistemological foundations of the subjects which they are studying, that is, the assumptions about what is held to be valid knowledge and appropriate ways of creating it in these subjects.

Current practice believes that early years educators need to be capable of planning, implementing and reviewing their work with young children and their families through applying their knowledge about:

- Child development
- The ways in which young children learn
- The process of teaching
- Health
- Working in partnership with families
- Functioning as part of a team of professionals
- Legislation affecting early years provision
- The organizational structure of different forms of provision
- Policy for early years education and care

The study of each of these needs to help students to examine the constructivism of this knowledge and the processes involved with its construction.

In order to be more specific about how this might be achieved, perhaps it would be helpful to examine knowledge about child development in more detail. The constructivism and the values which have determined the propositions of theories of child development will need to be made explicit to students.

Just as the values which underpin theories of child development arise from cultural contexts, so the lives of children take place within cultural settings which contribute to their experience, the meaning which they give to this experience, and to their response to the provision of care and education made by early years settings. For example, children from backgrounds which prize logical thought and a search for reason, within any experience, will have expectations of finding order and explanations of why in their experiences, and will be looking for these within the activities which are made available to them. In order to be able to respond to children in ways which are sensitive to their cultural background, but which help them to realise the human potential of engaging with a variety of cultural perspectives, it will be important, in their training, for early years workers to explore cultural contexts. This exploration will be relevant to the awareness and understanding required by early years workers in order to work as part of a staff team and in partnership with children's parents. It will involve examination of how cultural contexts arise, how they are maintained and their influence on children. Students' ability to make this exploration will be constrained by the perceptions stemming from their own sociocultural background. Consequently, they will need to develop the ability to explore and question their own values and expectations, and the sociocultural roots of these. Values determine the construction of theories of child development, they also determine the purposes of the approaches to education within which early years workers apply these theories. It will be important, therefore, for their training to enable them to examine the purposes which underlie different approaches to education and the consequences of their adoption, and to evaluate these consequences.

Training for early years educators should, therefore, enable them to engage with its content in ways which promote an open and questioning attitude towards different perspectives and modes of operating. This is the position which Bruner describes in arguing that cultural relativism is not an inevitable concomitant of cultural psychology:

> . . . one further reason why I believe that a cultural psychology such as I am proposing need not fret about the spectre of relativism. It concerns open-mindedness – whether in politics, science, literature, philosophy, or the arts. I take open-mindedness to be a willingness to construe knowledge and values from multiple perspectives without loss of commitment to one's own values . . . I take the constructivism of cultural psychology to be a profound expression of democratic culture. It demands that we be conscious of how we come to our knowledge and as conscious as we can be about the values that lead to our perspectives. It asks that we be accountable for how and what we know. But it does not insist that there is only one way of constructing meaning, or one right way.
>
> (Bruner 1990: 30)

How is this questioning and openness to be encouraged, and is it possible throughout the levels of qualifications which are accessed currently by early years educators? In order to answer these questions, it is helpful to examine more closely what contributes to an ability to question and to be open.

The extent to which students will be willing to question knowledge, and be open to the possibility of different perspectives leading to differences in its construction, will be influenced by their conceptions of what constitutes knowledge. If these conceptions are of knowledge as a construction through which we seek to understand the world, and which is continually being changed, added to and created, then they will be more likely to perceive it as something which can be questioned, and which requires an open-minded response. It is from our learning experiences that conceptions of knowledge arise. Therefore, learning experiences for early years educators will need to help them to engage with knowledge in ways which reinforce constructivist conceptions. These can include the following:

- Enabling students to explore the societal and historical background of particular theorists, and the links between these and the methodology through which their theories were established – for example, the influence of Piaget's background, as a geneticist at a time when objective scientific thought was valued, on his belief that it is a universal attribute of the human mind to use the patterns of thought which he described, and his favouring of test-type situations with a limited number of children for the observations on which he based his theories.

- Helping students to understand the relationship between concrete situations and the propositions of theory, and the ways in which propositions are formulated and tested. For example, by providing a practical problem, such as a set of different objects falling through the air, and giving students the task of creating and testing a theory to explain their behaviour, the processes experienced by the students can be used to examine those used by researchers.

Their past learning experiences will have given students a set of conceptions about the learning process which will affect their ability to question and be open-minded about knowledge. Students will not always be conscious of these conceptions, and it may be necessary to raise students awareness of them and to adjust them. This will be assisted by:

- Helping students to examine the conceptions of knowledge which are likely to arise from particular styles of learning experience. For example, students can be given the opportunity to describe how they see knowledge and to link this to the ways in which they were taught in the past.
- Providing learning experiences which are supportive of a questioning and open-minded attitude towards knowledge.

Both of these approaches can be realised through the employment of participative methods and helping students to reflect on how they are learning. Participative methods allow students the following opportunities:

- To discuss the ideas presented to them – for example, asking students what they think that Donaldson (1978) is saying when she argues that in situations which are meaningful to them children are able to conserve number.
- Compare these ideas with their own and others' experience – for example, share their experiences of children's actions, comments and questions during counting activities, their comments, and compare these with Donaldson's arguments.
- Draw conclusions – for example, consider what Donaldson's arguments and their own experiences indicate about the processes through which children develop the ability to conserve number.
- Reflect on the application of these conclusions to practice. For example, think through what their conclusions suggest about the counting activities which should be provided for young children and the questions which adults might ask children as they engage with these activities.

The development of an understanding of how they are learning can increase students' awareness of the strategies which help and hinder their learning, and can encourage them to be active engagers with knowledge rather than passive recipients of it. Such an awareness will be promoted by:

- sharing with students the reasons for the choice of the learning methods which they are experiencing;

• asking students questions which help them to reflect on their engagement with the learning process – for example, how they participated in the learning methods used; the effect which this participation had on their learning; changes which they might make their participation in order to help their learning.

Each early years training programme is predicated upon an approach to education and its accompanying set of values. These are not always made explicit to learners. However, if the approach and accompanying values of any particular programme are shared and explored with the participants, it will provide an opportunity for all of those involved with the programme to be encouraged to think critically about the approach and its values.

Designing learning experiences so that thought is given to the conceptions of knowledge, the learning process and the purposes of education which they promote should be capable of application to training for early years educators, whatever the extent and depth of the knowledge covered. What is being described is a specific approach to the learning process and, as Stott and Bowman argue, one which need not be tied to particular levels of qualification:

> At the undergraduate (and often high school) level, it seems as if all too often simplistic forms of theory and research are represented in a 'trickle-down' style. This suggests that teacher education is a process of transferring little parcels of information from one person to another rather than one that engages and enflames a student's individuality and desires within the framework of some purposive community of learning (Douglas, 1955). We believe that the goal of education at all levels should not be to give students a specific kind of information, but rather to provide a framework, the glue, to hold together the information they do possess. The framework is at one and the same time something that students create for themselves and a set of shared values, a disposition to understand, evaluate, and be open to the ideas of others (Douglas, personal communication, March 1995).
>
> (Stott and Bowman 1996: 180)

The suggestion that the modes of thinking which engender questioning and open-mindedness, that is those of critical thinking, are appropriate for all levels of qualifications for early years workers raises the question of when in the educative process the encouragement of critical thinking should begin?

The development of critical thinking and the early years curriculum

In terms of the educative process, learning in adulthood takes place when significant parts of the process have already taken place. Several approaches to the provision of adult learning perceive the promotion of the ability of adults to be self-directed learners and to think critically, as valuable for enabling them to be participative and contributive members of society. An examination of these approaches would seem to offer useful material for considering when the encouragement of self-directedness and critical thinking should begin.

The common experience of the providers of such approaches to adult learning has been that, when placed in learning situations, most adults display a distinct lack of propensity towards self-directedness and critical thinking. From his work with adult returners to education, Mezirow (1981) linked this situation to their sociocultural perspectives of themselves, as both adults and learners. He found that these perceptions which often had their roots in earlier learning experiences constrained the adults' ability to learn, and to do so in ways which promote critical thinking. My own experience with a group of adult learners of using an approach to learning in which the basic assumption is that adults have the potential to be the originators of their own thinking and feeling (Nottingham Andragogy Group 1983) was that their ability to exercise the critical thinking and open-mindedness, required by the approach, was influenced, often detrimentally, by their school experiences.

An examination of approaches to adult learning which seek to foster adults' ability to think critically and to be open-minded seems to indicate that these should be a theme of the educative process from its beginnings in the early years. Earlier in this chapter knowledge about how children learn and knowledge about what they are learning were recognized as being important for early years educators. Each early years setting offers a curriculum, in that there is a content and process to the learning which it provides for children. The training of early years educators must help them to consider the role of the early years curriculum in supporting the above theme. This will involve their considering how to introduce children to the content of human culture through a process of questioning, posing and solving problems, and being adventurous in their approaches to problem posing and solving.

Earlier in the chapter, the need to introduce children to the scope of human culture and values was identified. This incorporates the following:

- Science – discovering and thinking about how the natural world is made and works.
- Mathematics – finding out about quantity and measurement.
- Literature – deriving interest and pleasure from books and poetry, and being able to respond to and use the written word.
- Art – expressing ideas and feelings using a range of materials and tools, and developing the skills required for their use.
- Music – responding to and expressing feelings through instruments, and live and recorded music.
- History – awareness of the past and its links to the present.
- Geography – an understanding of place through awareness of the features of one's locality and the world beyond it.
- Politics, democracy, and belonging and contributing to society – awareness of the effect of our behaviour on other people and having a responsibility

towards others; involvement in making decisions about what should be done and how it should be done.

- Environmental issues – awareness of the need to and how to look after the world around us.
- Personal and social – being aware of and responsive to our own and other people's feelings; awareness of our involvement in the different groups to which we belong/in which we participate.

In each of these areas of learning, early years educators' own appreciation of and conceptual knowledge about the area will be crucial to their ability to introduce children to the ideas and experiences belonging to it. Their training must confirm this appreciation and conceptual knowledge, help them to identify the knowledge from each subject which they should be making available to children, and enable them to do this in ways which help children to begin to use the modes of thinking which encourage the development of critical awareness. If early years provision is to play its part in the development of critical thinking in young children, then critical thinking will need to be valued both by early years educators and those responsible for their training.

Curricula for early years educators and young children

In exploring the content and process of the curricula for both early years educators and for young children, I have argued for the process to employ methods of learning and teaching which encourage critical thinking. The character of such methods will involve both learners and teachers in an ongoing examination and questioning of knowledge, and the processes through which it is developed. I have argued for the content to make available knowledge with which the learner engages this critical thinking and as a result extends their knowledge. Attention to this extension of knowledge, that is, the products of the learning process, is important. The argument being made is that for both curricula learning should be seen as a dialectic between process and products, that neither should be promoted at the expense of the other, and that both should promote learners' ability to engage with knowledge constructed from a range of cultural perspectives.

Pamela Calder

Barbara Thompson and I began working on this chapter together after a debate among some of the contributors to this book about whether there was a 'nugget' or core that should be taught to all early childhood educators. We agreed that what was needed was a critical approach, and one that needed an understanding of process as well as content. We also believed that there were many existing lists of what should be in provided as content, for instance Rumbold (DES 1990: 47), Edwards and Knight (1994), Alexander (1992: 46), Kellmer-Pringle (1980) and we wanted to first explore what a more critical stance would entail. However, as we worked on the chapter it became clearer that there were disagreements between us as to how we were interpreting words such as 'culture', 'cultural' and 'cultural context', and that we differed in the weight we were giving to organizational frameworks and the way in which we wanted to deal with competing value systems. These disagreements could perhaps be characterized by a debate between a modernist and a feminist postmodernist approach. Barbara argued that she agreed with Habermas, in taking the approach of critical theory rather than a relativist position. As we worked together, it became clearer that there were a number of ways in which I wanted to diverge from the argument being made or wanted to challenge what was written.

A postmodernist critique argues that it is important to see theories as socially and historically located, that is located in time and space. I read this as that one should also locate oneself in what one writes, and not take what has been called 'the view from nowhere' (Assiter 1996: 95) which can be seen as what happens when one writes impersonally, in the third person. In the discussion of Rumbold above (DES 1990), it seems to me that not all possible areas are covered in relation to Bruner's (1974) discussion of knowledge about teaching, learning and knowledge. For instance, Rumbold has little to say about the importance of organizational context. Nor in the quotation from Bruner, is enough recognition given to the implication in his work that different competing, or conflicting (cultural?) values may permeate through knowledge about teaching, and learning. Bruner (1974) recognises that value choices underlie our aims and purposes in teaching and the goals we have for what should be learnt.

Accepting different statuses and roles among early childhood educators as we do in the UK and the USA, leads to an acceptance of courses and training at different levels in which both different content, and different depth of content is also accepted. It seems to me that Barbara Thompson's contribution has not recognised the full force of the challenge to current practice and to the way in which child development is often regarded as a value-free scientific base for practice.

Moss and Penn (1996) have pointed to the wider policy context influencing the values of society and the different aspirations and values that societies hold for their children. Calder (1996a) has discussed how research tools such as the Early Childhood Education Rating Scale (ECERS) omit evaluations of practices associated with values that were not shared by the North American construction of the scale, but which are considered important in the other European countries, for example Sweden's emphasis on outdoor skills and care for the environment, and Italy's emphasis on the aesthetic. She has also discussed competing values and their relationship to early childhood education practices in the context of the re-unification of Berlin (Calder 1996b). The unease which has been apparent in a European context may stem from some of the conflict produced when trying to develop a multicultural society where deep values may not be shared. It is the different routes which have been taken by those trying to solve the problem that has helped contribute to a sense of lack of certainty and to some reflection.

A fear of relativism has led to different positions and solutions. Two ways out of the dilemmas produced have been taken. The first is to take an assimilationist stance. This is to assume that there are core mainstream values to which other dissenting groups should conform, usually the beliefs and values of the national society. This approach is the one often taken by dominant groups, sometimes unquestioningly. An approach which argues for a universal 'rationalism', as Barbara Thompson tends to do, is in danger of leading to this position. The second way is to go for a different kind of universalist approach. But this universalist approach will be based on a democratic agreement, for example, to aim for antiracist practice. Policy statements of what this entails can then be developed by democratic discussion. Those who take part in, work in, or use the system are then asked to agree to antiracist practice and principles and to the agreed policy statement. However, it will also be accepted that the way in which these principles are to be translated into practice continues to be open to democratic debate; that policy statements need to be drawn up, by which practice can be regulated and evaluated; but that it is accepted that these remain essentially provisional. They can be changed by democratic agreement.

Alison Assiter has tackled this. She argues:

an epistemic community, I suggest, then, will be a group of individuals who share certain fundamental interests, values and beliefs in common, for example, that sexism is wrong, that racism is wrong, and who work on consequences of these presuppositions.

(Assiter 1996: 82)

She quotes Sandra Harding on *Strong Objectivity*, who:

argues persuasively that 'objectivism' – dispassionate, value-free science – is just the mirror image of epistemological relativism. Instead, she suggests, true objectivity requires both cultural relativism, and maximally liberatory social interests.

(Assiter 1996: 83)

The outlook I have described, although quasi realist, does not assume the enlightenment realist 'view from nowhere'. It does not assume a non-located, non-contextual, non-value-laden God's eye perspective from which 'the truth' is revealed. Rather the epistemic community is historically located, its beliefs and its experiences are inflected by the values that it holds. However, the nature of the values upheld by any one community are such as to undermine claims to 'the truth' made by other communities. The claims of any one community are not true for all times and in all places; rather they are open to constant revision by other communities.

(Assiter 1996: 95)

In the USA a form of this debate about postmodernism, relativism and deconstruction has surfaced in the *Early Childhood Research Quarterly* (1996). A recent edition has been devoted to exploring the implications of the argument that all human knowledge is a social construction, and that knowledge that is socially constructed can vary because of the nature of such social constructs. For example, different languages incorporate different concepts of the world in the way their words are used to break up and classify reality. Languages vary in their conception of the world. Social structures which pre-exist the birth of the child such as education and the law, are also humanly constructed (Berger and Luckman 1967) and vary within and across cultures. Lilian Katz (1996) has realised that issues which are being raised about the relativity of values threaten the search for a universally agreed set of principles concerning the nature of developmentally appropriate practice. Sally Lubeck (1996), in the same volume, shares this unease. Lilian Katz discusses changing her mind about the significance of child development as a positivistic, research-based 'scientific' way of determining developmentally appropriate practice.

The debate in the USA has become a critical debate about Bredekamp's (1987) notion of developmentally appropriate practice. In this country, a theoretical debate about the nature of theory and scientific practice in developmental psychology has also been taking place (Burman 1994; Morss 1996). In psychology, these issues have been debated under the heading of social constructivism and by Rom Harre (Gergen 1985; Parker 1989; Shotter 1993; Smith *et al.* 1995) and others under the headings of discursive psychology and critical social psychology. Erica Burman (1994) has raised it for developmental psychology, in her book *Deconstructing Developmental Psychology*. Are there, for instance, universal needs? Martin Woodhead (1988, 1996) has discussed the role of cultural construction in identifying 'needs'. An example of how the ostensibly same practices can have culturally different meanings is illustrated by the research of Chao (1994). She has described how a child-rearing practice which most British and US psychologists would believe is harmful, an authoritarian parenting style, can have quite a different meaning for children in a Chinese context.

Thus, developmental psychology itself changes. Currently, many people in the field are stressing the relativity of values. The other current change is one of emphasis towards cultural context (Cole 1996) and a consideration of the relationships between people and of how the culture is acquired and constructed (what Gunilla Dahlberg in her current writings is referring to as 'co-construction'; see for example Dahlberg and Åsén 1994). This is a paradigm shift that is occurring in the discipline and has not yet been fully incorporated into practice. It allows for a new focus on relationships, on considering children's friendships, for example. But taking context and reflexivity into account is challenging. How do we incorporate meaning into our analyses of empirical research on child-rearing, for instance?

One outcome of these kinds of concerns is that, although for educators it may be useful for the discussion or search for developmentally appropriate practice to continue, this should be done in such a way that those using such guidelines should be aware of both the provisional nature of knowledge and also of the way in which all studies in the social sciences (including the study of child development and developmental psychology) are necessarily implicated in value positions. This is the position which I believe is taken by Bruner, when he argues that there is no need for the kind of cultural psychology that he proposes to 'fret about the specter of relativism', since it concerns 'open-mindedness' which he takes to be 'a willingness to construe knowledge and values from multiple perspective without loss of commitment to one's own values' (Bruner 1990: 30). Thus Bruner (1990), like Assiter (1996), tries to resolve the apparent dilemma of relativism by arguing for a stance close to my second position, that is provisional agreement to values to which one tries to persuade others, on the grounds that these values provide the best fit to an end that we can currently achieve; and that each one will hold to their values and views while providing the best evidence available to support them.

This position assumes that one can only work with those who share some overall values or overarching principles. Such principles and values may be about what philosophers have called the general good, and perhaps there has often been reasonable agreement about what this might be. For example, many countries have signed up to the United Nations Convention on Human Rights (1948) and the European Convention on the Rights of the Child. However, real debate comes while trying to put such principles into practice. Even when there is agreement about values, this does not determine how they are interpreted or how they may be put into practice; however, it makes possible the coming to some agreement. This position provides the basis for dialogue and possible agreement.

We can explore what it might mean to take particular value positions. For example, if we consider children as citizens being introduced to human culture, what are the implications for those who are to be the educators? We can examine what the educators might need to know. For example, knowledge about knowledge could include:

- 'being';
- developmental psychology;
- the reflexive nature of knowledge;
- the educators themselves.

Knowledge about human culture could include the following:

- What we call subjects, or disciplines, but also of how to teach such 'subjects' to very young children including babies (for example, babies in Catalonian nurseries being introduced to Mozart; see Penn 1997b).
- Being skilled, being an expert (the educators may need skills of teaching, inspiring, educating, caring and being sensitive, for example).

We can use Bruner's categories to think about what might be needed.

Knowledge about teaching

- The ecological content in which teaching takes place, at the level of the society (the laws relating to child and family welfare) and also to society's values (democracy, solidarity, economic wealth creation, etc. for instance).
- The family: knowledge relating to parents, fathers as well as mothers, to siblings, to grandparents.
- The organization: the school, the nursery, the class; and of other organizations, such as those involved in health, welfare and social work.
- About how to teach: for example, praise, punishment, modelling, encouragement, motivation, discipline, theories of pedagogy.

Knowledge about learning

- A critical analysis of child development and developmental psychology.
- The details of language development.
- Special needs, recognizing handicap or brilliance.

Knowledge about knowledge

- What do we want children to learn?
- Being and becoming and also knowledge about . . . for example, the working artist with studio/workshop Atelier in Reggio Emilia (Gura 1997); the babies in Spanish nurseries being shown Miró paintings (Penn 1997b). We may also need to think about skills and the relationship with practice.

However, these categories of Bruner tend to lead to an emphasis on learning as 'becoming' rather than on 'being'. There are other aspects, such as children's enjoyment, their safety, their health, their comfort and their friendships with other children, that tend to be obscured by an emphasis on learning.

The argument I have been making leads me to explore the implications of my own values. If I explore my personal position, I would want those looking after my children to share my values. Thus I believe what is essential for people working with children is that they share the following.

- Feminist values, meaning that I believe children are currently brought up in a society that discriminates against and oppresses girls; similarly anti-racist values, since in our society I believe non-white people are discriminated against.
- Democratic values. I believe that where people disagree the best approach to dealing with differences is through discussion to try to see if a consensus can be reached. If not, one may have to continue holding one's own values and continue trying to find supporting evidence which will convince others.
- I want children brought up to feel their lives are worthwhile. Thus it is important to try to give them confidence, but also to show them that

people need to feel valued by others to have a fulfilling life and that the relationships one makes with other people are important throughout one's whole life. Therefore generosity, empathy, emotional skills and intelligence are as necessary as intellectual skills (Goleman 1996).

• The attitudes, feelings and emotional empathy of those who work with children in any role is also important. Even those managing services should be able to understand this dimension or they are likely to have different priorities in developing and administering an early childhood service. This will also have implications for the kind of curriculum considered important (Calder 1990).

• This should lead to increasing the self-esteem of children, including that of girls, and of course children from all backgrounds. This has sometimes been called 'equal opportunities' but should be more than this, since equal opportunities implies opportunities for achievement in the future but does not necessarily imply making people whole or happy with themselves. Tricia David argues for a holistic approach.

There will be differences in in-service and undergraduate education because students who are in work will already have personal examples of practice which they can analyse. This points to the importance of observational studies where students are not already in a workplace setting. Observation can allow them to understand in context their own personal feelings about a situation, particularly when they are able to share the interpretations of others about the same observations, so that they may both relate their own history and experience to that of others and to theoretical perspectives and to other studies. Any such statement of values, however, I would expect to be a starting point, from which we could begin to have a dialogue with each other, to see where we could reach agreement in putting our values into practice. Thus any lists would not be final. They would continue to be open to revision.

⑤ | Teacher training for the early years

Lesley Abbott and Ian Kane

This chapter addresses the implications for teacher training of recent changes in national early years provision: there is a new Labour Government (since 1997), a new White Paper and a new National Curriculum for initial teacher training. Ironically, it is already in need of radical revision if the Government's plans for *Excellence in Schools* (DfEE 1997a) are to be delivered. More recently still, the Dearing Inquiry into Higher Education (1997) has delivered its report. Several issues interconnect. Those which this chapter addresses include:

- the importance of a properly qualified multi-professional workforce;
- difficulties in defining the term 'early years';
- the status of early years providers and workers;
- the semantics of 'choice and diversity';
- the challenges of revising course structures and admissions requirements;
- 'competences' and the content of training.

The chapter concludes with some proposals for further discussion.

A clear message

The newly established Early Childhood Education Forum in 1993 brought together forty national organizations working with and for young children. The training of early years workers including teacher education was a central concern. There is an argument that such professionals should be graduates.

> Diversity in early childhood services means that individuals need to be confident and competent in their role within those services, i.e. they should be appropriately trained. . .
>
> (Early Childhood Education Forum, October 1995)

Well in advance of the 1997 General Election, *Early Excellence – A Head Start for Every Child* emphasized the requirement for:

> The involvement of a qualified teacher in both the planning and delivery of all education services.
>
> (Labour Party, November 1996: 13)

Following the General Election, an early move towards fulfilling this promise was a circular (DfEE 1997c) outlining the Government's medium-term aims along with the principles which would underpin Government policy. This document confirmed the above commitments and recognized, in line with *Early Excellence*, that:

> High quality provision, suited to the particular needs of the age group, is crucial in the early years.
>
> (Labour Party, November 1996: 11)

Subsequently another DfEE circular affirmed:

> A Qualified Teacher should be involved in all settings providing early years education.
>
> (DfEE 1997f)

In July 1997, the Government White Paper, *Excellence in Schools*, in its early years section 'A Sound Beginning' affirmed:

> If they are to have an education that matches the best in the world, we must start now by getting integrated early years and childcare, and primary education right.
>
> (DfEE 1997a: 15)

Defining early years

It has not been easy to find an appropriate definition of 'early years' within the recent political, social and educational context. Various definitions have included 3–5 (DES 1990; Ofsted 1995b; SCAA 1996), 0–6 (Ball 1994) and 0–8 years (DoH 1991), the last being the age range covered by the Early Childhood Education Forum. In DfEE Circular 10/97 drafted by the Teacher Training Agency (TTA), opportunity is offered to make separate provision for training for the age range 3–5 years.

This variable designation has been an influence on provision for the early years in teacher education courses. For many the early years age phase was accepted as 3–8 years, occasionally 4–8 years. For accreditation purposes, 3–8 was used by the Department for Education and Science. The Rumbold Report (DES 1990), while accepting the importance of the 0–3-age range, regarded 3–8 as an appropriate age span. In 1995 *The Framework for Inspection of Nursery and Reception Classes* (Ofsted 1995b) adopted the 'early years' as standard terminology for children below statutory school age, by which they meant the 3–5-age range, signally ignoring the under-threes and the rapidly increasing numbers of 4-year-old children in the primary school system. The problem was exacerbated by the Nursery Voucher Scheme (DfEE 1996a). Although short lived, it set a precedent for very young 4-year-olds to be admitted to reception classes. To protect young children and to raise the status of the early years and hence of the teachers working at that stage, the RSA *Start Right* report (Ball 1994) suggested revision of the age of entry to statutory schooling, while Sir Christopher Ball (*The Guardian* 1995) proposed that the school starting age should be raised to 6 years and that the 0–6-age range should be designated Key Stage Zero! This suggestion was warmly welcomed by Peter Moss, Convenor of the European Childcare Network, who believed that such a change would bring the UK in line with most of its partners in the European Community (Moss 1997). Ball, Moss and many others have also strongly argued for the development of more and better nursery facilities, linked to children's learning needs, and family childcare requirements. *Desirable Outcomes for Young Children's Learning* (SCAA 1996a,c) and recent developments in baseline assessment (DfEE 1997a) do not sit easily within this concept, although it is encouraging that the TTA recognizes the importance of a broad base of knowledge for early years teachers.

Professional status

Despite European recognition that working with young children is important, the UK remains one of the few countries worldwide where all nursery teachers are fully qualified teachers, able to teach, with the agreement of schools and LEAs, throughout the education system. A review of training across Europe (Oberhuemer and Ulich 1997; see also Chapter 11) points out that other countries are gradually moving towards graduate level qualifications for all early years workers, not just teachers. Ironically, the previous Tory Government's policy and Teacher Training Agency (TTA) implementation have seemed to seek progressively to move teacher training away from higher education, against the grain of European development, which makes it even more important that professionals in the UK hold the line on the value of graduate qualifications.

While the Rumbold Report (DES 1990) and the National Commission on Education (1993) both acknowledged teaching young children to be a highly complex task, those responsible for the accreditation of early years training courses, for example, Council for the Accreditation of Teacher Education (CATE) and subsequently the TTA and those 'on the ground' have found it increasingly difficult to establish the kind of support required, resulting in hard fought battles to safeguard the rigour and relevance highlighted by Rumbold. Watered-down provision has been nodded through, with all parties anxious to concentrate on their shared perception of 'mainstream' education – better known, better understood, usually better resourced, and uncomplicated by any need to locate the education of children and the training of teachers in a serious multi-professional context. Dearing (1997) falls into the same trap. In a passage critical of the BEd degree's capacity to provide intending teachers with adequate subject knowledge, in Report No. 10, Sir Stewart Sutherland writes:

> I believe that the present Bed route will continue to be an appropriate route for early primary teaching, particularly KS1, and that it provides knowledge about teaching young children and how children learn which is unlikely to be provided through other courses.
>
> (Sutherland 1997 para 33: 10)

So, a nod for the early years but not so much as a wink in the direction of multi-professionalism! Perhaps more worrying still is the absence of any suggestions that the PGCE route could offer a route for early years teachers. We shall argue strongly later that it is a crucial route if valuable recruitment opportunities are not to be missed.

Benign, albeit patronizing neglect, has been compounded by unintended consequences. Recent reform of primary education has had a major impact on early years teacher education as the schools' National Curriculum has required that intending teachers focus their efforts on the core and foundation subjects, taking attention and time from a study of children and childhood.

The newly established CATE placed a requirement upon all teacher training establishments to meet stringent criteria from the Secretary of State. Concerns of those committed to early years training were the tokenistic representation of the early years on the Council, the lack of awareness of the distinctive nature of work with very young children and the failure to recognize the wider context of early education. DFE circular 14/93: *The Initial Training of Primary School Teachers* (DFE 1993) set out the knowledge and skills needed by newly qualified teachers and prescribed a greater role for schools. It supported the case for a variety of routes into teaching, including a six-subject, three-year BEd degree to prepare primary teachers to work across the curriculum, a significant watering down of standards, a blow to status and a totally illogical approach to remediating the oft-claimed weakness of teachers' subject knowledge, for example, as set out in the report of the so-called 'three wise men', Alexander, Rose and Woodhead (1992).

However, the circular did encourage the use of the accreditation of prior learning (APL) and prior experiential learning (APEL) to widen access to teaching – a welcome move. It also proposed new courses to prepare classroom assistants to support basic skills work. The resulting Specialist Teacher Assistant (STA) programmes were viewed by some as threatening and a 'back door' entry for the 'mums' army'! Their impact on schools has been evaluated in a national research study. The findings are fully discussed by Moyles and Suschitzky (1997a) and further in Chapter 10. It is important to keep the programmes for STAs under ongoing scrutiny. For some, the notion of the 'mums' army' still lives. As Lord Pearson of Rannoch said, as recently as February 1997 in a seminar sponsored by the Universities Council for the Education of Teachers (UCET):

> I cannot understand why the education establishment opposes the concept of mums' army. Intelligent women with good 'A' levels who

have successfully brought up their own children are, to my mind, obviously well-suited to teach, after perhaps a short course of some months at most. I have to say that at the moment I would not entrust those courses to Departments of Education.

(UCET 1997)

The danger in the introduction of STAs and in defining only the 3–5 age range as early years, is that training could be seen as quite separate from primary education as a whole, and could deny students the opportunity to practise in a range of schools and age groups and to consider issues of continuity, transition and coherence with Key Stage 1. There is a long-established consensus that primary schools in general need staff who have an understanding of the ways in which young children learn, grow and develop and of the foundations on which later learning is built. No significant assessment has been made of that consensus. What we would argue is that such a condition is necessary but not sufficient. So much is this crucial issue determined by the attitude of head teachers that the serious omission of early years issues from the TTA's Headlamp and National Professional Qualification for Headteachers (NPQH) provision, seems a weakness.

The strength of present teacher-training courses is that many claim to provide both a generalist primary and specialist early years experience. Weakness occurs when insufficient time is given to the early years. Any change in definition of age range could result in compartmentalized training, for example, Early Years, Key Stage 1, Key Stage 2. The non-statutory nature of under-fives provision and the redesignation of the early years age range could provide a loophole for those who do not consider it important that young children are entitled to appropriately trained graduate teachers. There is always the danger that this area of work could be seen as the domain of further education rather than higher education. Such an eventuality would be a blow to status, decoupling the early years 'profession' from higher education. It would also be illogical since it is universities which are best able to contribute the expertise necessary for multi-professional training drawing on departments of nursing, law, or social work in which both professional training and research are based.

The myth of 'choice and diversity'

In her first-year review, Anthea Millett, on behalf of the Teacher Training Agency (TTA 1995: 2), reaffirmed the major aim 'to secure a diversity of high quality and cost effective initial training which ensured that new teachers had the knowledge, understanding and skills to teach effectively'. Unfortunately it did so as part of its commitment, not to mainstream provision, but rather as part of its mission to promote School Centred Initial Teacher Training (SCITT), whereby teacher training would become the responsibility of the school rather that higher education. In practice, this diversity has included not only the encouragement of SCITT consortia but also new employment based routes whether 'graduate', 'licensed', 'overseas' or more recently, and for extended consultation, 'registered'. The SCITT schemes are favoured by TTA officers, a view which was shared by Tory ministers, and have received high-profile praise – notwithstanding their poor performance on the evidence of Ofsted reports (1993–4) including very recent (1997) ones (see, for example, Report Numbers 17/97 ITTSP or 41/97 ITTSZ).

In claiming that through all its work it will promote choice, diversity, efficiency and accountability, the TTA has laid itself open to multiple criticism. Evidence of widespread client dissatisfaction with the working of the TTA is to be found in Mahony and Hextall's (1997) study of the operation of the Agency which records a mere 30 per cent satisfaction rating. Dissatisfaction was recorded no less among LEAs than higher education establishments and it is worth speculating that had the TTA made a bold early years initiative as high a priority and as high profile as, for example, National Professional Qualifications (NPQs) or student profiles, the response of some clients might well have been more positive. Certainly it is LEAs which have borne the brunt of maintaining, supporting and expanding nursery provision. 'Choice and diversity' have a hollow ring where there is little of either in terms of provision, and little choice for head teachers in some parts of the country when selecting staff to work in early years settings. In a national survey of qualifications, Blenkin, Rose and Yue (1996) found that two-thirds of teachers working with under-fives had no specific training to work with this age group.

'Choice and diversity' were reasons highlighted for the introduction of the Nursery Voucher Scheme (DfEE 1996a). Even at the pilot stage the lack of either was evident. These are two overused words. 'diversity' has been described as 'a disgraceful patchwork of provision' (Hevey 1995: 8) while 'choice' is non-existent for many parents. The same two words when applied to teacher education are equally hollow. When faced with the necessity to squeeze a quart into a pint pot, it is the 'early years' which frequently suffers. Its non-statutory status in school is often translated into its low status within training institutions and, moreover, reflected in the new National Curriculum for Initial Teacher Training as will be discussed below.

The challenge of multi-professionalism

What precisely is 'different' about early years provision? In a review of the distinctive nature of early years training and in particular the personal, social and professional knowledge and skills required by early years teachers, Hevey and Curtis (1996: 224) outlined areas of knowledge as:

- a sound knowledge of child development and educational theory;
- the ability to develop strategies to transmit knowledge to others;
- a deep understanding of the subject in the early years curriculum and the value of play;
- a knowledge of and respect for cultural and social similarities and differences;

- observational skills and knowledge and ability to assess and evaluate, not only the programmes they offer and the children's progress, but also themselves;
- a knowledge of the laws relating to families; and
- a knowledge of policies and their underlying philosophy.

While these matters are not entirely missing from the new TTA-led requirements, it is necessary to strain very hard to find some of them.

The status of particular forms of knowledge and the resulting perceptions of career development are real issues for early years trainers and students. It is regrettable, therefore, that in critical documents, for example, the Ofsted framework (Inspection) and the Ofsted/TTA framework (Quality Assessment, 1997) and subsequently Circular 10/97 (National Curriculum) specific requirements are not drawn out. What emerges instead is a belief that teaching and its assessment derive from generic factors. The impression given, for example, at TTA consultative conferences is that 'early years' is seen as a 'lobby'. Providers regret the manner in which the undefined term 'early years' is casually tossed about and more often than not lumped in with 5–19 provision. People who would not dream of asserting that protagonists of post-16 education are just a 'lobby' thoughtlessly fail to recognize that there are early years skills and much knowledge which is non-generic.

As with officialdom, so sometimes with providers the multidisciplinary nature of the work of the early years teacher has often been largely ignored. New degrees in Early Childhood Studies, which provide an excellent career foundation, now offer a natural progression for graduates who want to teach via a postgraduate certificate course (PGCE). Arguably, the content of the early childhood degrees is, in an ideal world, what most early years teacher trainers would wish to see included in a 3- or 4-year BEd and is certainly what the Government would appear to be looking for in its support for multi-professional training. It is a point, however, that Dearing Report No. 10 rather missed.

Multi-professional provision offers the exciting opportunity to tap in to a pool of aspirant part-time students who can use their workplace as a focus for practitioner enquiry and can bring to initial teacher training an individual and a collective multi-professional dimension. There is a need for part-time PGCE courses which acknowledge prior experience and/or learning, sufficiently flexible to meet the needs of a new type of student. Such opportunities do not exist beyond the Open University, where isolation and distance from a learning community remain obstacles. It did appear in mid-1996 that such opportunities might arise as the TTA announced it would protect part of its primary growth allocations for early years developments. The pensions regulations row of late 1996 and the consequent abandonment of the TTA targets, themselves only months old, shattered these hopes. They were happily resurrected in August 1997 when TTA specified its priorities for the allocation of future numbers raising optimism that within the TTA there is a will to address the needs of young children. If there is to be a 'lobby' for early years provision, then who better to lead it than the TTA?

Such a notion begs a further question. The most recent data collection exercise required by the TTA is very specific in requesting the specialist subjects of students on PGCE and BEd courses. The explanation informally offered is that the information is needed to facilitate the reduction of allocations to those courses which feature primarily subjects which appear overstocked. While acknowledging the importance of students having knowledge and expertise in a specific area, continued overemphasis on a primary subject for entry to PGCE courses and lack of recognition of the broad base of knowledge and skill which graduates from early childhood studies degrees possess, could deprive schools of knowledgeable and proficient early years teachers. It could also drive would-be early years practitioners towards the more lax standards of the BEd degrees where the standard of specialist subject to be achieved is expected to be approximately 'A' level (DfEE 1997b: Circular 10/97). There are mixed messages here. Does subject knowledge matter? What is subject knowledge in terms of early years provision?

The need for flexibility

Courses of initial teacher training need to reflect the knowledge and skills which students bring as well as the standards required on completion. Mature entrants without conventional qualifications frequently bring a body of experiential knowledge. Matching mature students to courses of appropriate length and design will often depend on the Accreditation of Prior Experiential Learning (APEL). APEL procedures seek to assess the knowledge and skills developed through each individual's combination of formal education and experience, and need to be clear and consistent. Higher education institutions' approaches to the APEL to widen access to initial teacher training are particularly important in the light of the increase in multi-professional courses and in the present political climate where targets for the expansion of early years educational provision generally and the reduction of class sizes (5–7) must be met. As the White Paper *Excellence in Schools* affirms (DfEE 1997a, para 16): 'Our pledge to reduce class sizes for 5-, 6- and 7-year-olds will be a key factor in improving standards in primary schools.'

There is, in addition, scope for the Assessment of Prior Learning (APL). Vocational courses (for example, BTEC in Nursery Nursing or NVQ in Health and Social Care) lay an excellent foundation for professional aspects of a BEd course, but difficulties can arise when students are selecting a main subject. 'Diversity' should be made meaningful. Students should be able to argue for the main subject of their choice in ways which might include a significant subject focus within the modules taken on their BTEC course or via NVQ assessment; or by taking an 'A' level in their chosen subject alongside the other forms of assessment; or on the basis of other qualifications or proof of attainment relevant to their chosen subject (such as for art, a portfolio of artwork; for music, membership of an orchestra; for drama, involvement in theatre in education or other drama groups). Flexible procedures such as the above constitute one way in which the resource consequences of nursery expansion and class size can be addressed, without recourse to 'mums' army'-type solutions.

The link between vocational and academic qualifications and the view that a range of skills and experiences gained in other contexts could benefit students was assisted by the publication by the Committee of Vice Chancellors and Principals (1993) of a *Strategy for Vocational and Higher Education*, which pointed to the perceived divide between 'academic' and 'vocational' and the lack of parity of esteem. While there may be clear differences between 'pure academic' and 'vocational' approaches, there is, the report argues:

> Increasing convergence in the middle reaches of what must be now surely accepted as more like a continuum than two separate areas.
>
> (CVCP 1993)

The establishment of the new Qualifications and Curriculum Authority, while raising issues concerning funding and course location, is nevertheless a step in the right direction. Meanwhile the debate which generated the Dearing Inquiry into Higher Education (1997) and the Kennedy report on further education (1997) and their mutual connections, continues. The increase in multi-professional degrees in early childhood studies preceded by a range of possibilities for workplace assessment and a 'climbing frame' of training opportunities, makes even more important the process by which 'academic' and 'vocational' training are brought closer together. While NVQ level 3 in childcare and education has provided an important stepping stone on the route towards higher education for those students wishing to pursue teaching as a career, a barrier has been created by the lack of opportunity for assessment at levels 4 and 5. It is therefore crucial that higher level NVQs are fully developed and their relationship within and between further and higher education made clear.

However, there are reservations concerning the concept of 'occupational competence' when applied to teaching in general and working with young children in particular. The contributions to competence of knowledge and understanding of how young children learn, grow and develop, of curriculum content and its application and of the role of the early years teacher, must be made explicit. Opportunities for reflection on, and analysis of practice, are essential components of teacher education and are in danger of being overlooked in a system where too much reliance is placed upon occupational competence and performance. A checklist approach to teacher training will never be appropriate. While workplace experiences and assessment are key elements, the debate and engagement with trainers at higher education level must continue to be the hallmark of quality.

Competencies and course requirements in initial teacher training

In some universities and colleges, specific under fives' competencies were included in the assessment of student competencies additional to those required by government circulars (e.g. DfE 1993). Again this is necessary but not sufficient. The debate must be widened to include 'multi-professional competencies' now highlighted by the Government's aim to develop multi-professional early years centres (DfEE 1997c) which have emerged as Early Excellence Centres in the White Paper (1997a).

Questions regarding the distinctive nature of the competences, skills and knowledge required by the early years teacher were addressed at a meeting (July 1996) of early years trainers and the TTA. Answers were summarized by reference to a statement made by members of the Early Years Training Group to the RSA Early Learning Inquiry and recorded in the subsequent report (Ball 1994):

> The professional preparation of teachers is complex because teaching itself is complex. This is true for teachers at all stages. But it must be argued that early years teachers require a breadth of knowledge, understanding and experience which is not required by those training to teach other children. The early years constitute a crucial stage in which the foundations for later learning are laid. A vast amount of learning and development takes place during these early years and teachers must be fully equipped to capture the unreturning moment. They must have mastery of the curriculum context as well as having a sound knowledge of child development including language acquisition, cognitive, social emotional and physical development. They are required to lead and plan for a team of other professionals including parents, nursery nurses, students and others including speech therapists, language support teachers, psychologists and social workers. They are responsible for the assessment of children and for monitoring progress and ensuring continuity and progression between stages and establishments. It is widely recognised that the quality of children's education depends on the quality of the teachers and the effectiveness of their training and development and that training for teachers in the early years should not be any less rigorous or demanding than that of any other teacher.
>
> (Ball 1994: 58)

The TTA assumed responsibility for funding initial teacher training in 1995. The requirement that the TTA should work closely with Ofsted in gathering evidence about the quality of teacher training to inform funding decisions resulted in an inspection sweep of all primary providers. Given Ofsted's reluctance to publish the anticipated overall report on the Primary 'Sweep', the only substantial account remains UCET's Occasional Paper No. 6 1996. While HMI found most existing provision at least 'good', there were nonetheless weaknesses identified and these weaknesses carried messages regarding the status of Key Stage 1 vis-à-vis Key Stage 2 provision. For example: 'There is variation in practice in relation to the challenge of differentiating between KS1 and KS2' (mathematics); 'More attention could also be paid to progression from KS1 to KS2' (English); 'In most courses, students receive "primary" training covering both KS1 and KS2. While this is generally effective, there is room for improvement in considering how the two stages interrelate in practice' (English). The question to be asked about courses which span some or all of both key stages is, when there is a blurring of the necessary conceptual framework, what becomes of that part of training which lies outside the two key stages? What price Key Stage Zero? A solution is to take advantage of the licence in Circular 10/97 (DfEE 1997b) to offer courses concentrating on age 3–5. While this solution would certainly give the sharp focus desired, it nonetheless begs the question of 'before and after' and raises again the issue with regard to an appropriate definition of 'early years'. Alternatively, if 3–5 is the chosen designation, what requirements need to be set out for the necessary knowledge of before and after? Indeed, a recent research study *Educare for the Under Threes* (Abbott and Gillen 1997), points to the importance of the 'pre-three' experience in preparing children to benefit fully from nursery education 3–5.

An emphasis on standards and competencies also permeates the most recent documents on the future of teacher training. Circular 10/97, which sets out the Requirements for Courses of Initial Teacher Training (DfEE 1997b) replaces the pre-existing criteria set out in DfE Circulars 9/92 and 14/93 and DfEE Teacher Training Circular Letter 1/96. Early years students will be required to cover all the areas covered by general primary students and early years specific requirements. Once again, those early years 'specifics' such as multi-professional work, management, team leadership, working with parents and carers, community involvement, transition and continuity and the centrality of child development, are still not recognized and acknowledged. They appear neither as competencies nor content, nor are they implicit in the standards set out for the award of qualified teacher status. In the light of recent Government directives regarding the widening of opportunity, and indeed the necessity for qualified early years teachers to work in a range of settings other than classrooms, the lack of recognition in the above documentation is of concern. Nor is much said about training, in more than general terms, in the circular issued by the Government on post-voucher developments (DfEE, 1997c).

Specification is made in Circular 10/97 (DfEE 1997b) of the minimum amount of time to be spent in school but no requirement is made for early years students to experience the wider context of community nurseries, family centres, day care, social services and private and voluntary sector provision, all of which can and, in the light of Government proposals, should employ trained teachers. More significant still, should early years intending teachers now gain experience in the early excellence centres proposed in the Labour Government White Paper (Dfee 1997a)? Indeed, can the definition of 'partnership', the cornerstone of current initial training, now be extended to cover early excellence centres? If specific skills are recognised as a necessity in terms of working with early excellence centres, then should not these be set out not only in some rapid revision of Circular 10/97, but also should there not be a substantial retraining programme, for example, in Headlamp or NPQH, for those serving early years teachers whose skills lack the multi-professional dimensions, which are now emerging prominently? There is a clear need to revise the Ofsted/TTA *Framework for the Assessment of Quality*

(Ofsted 1997a). What an anomalous document that appears when set against the White Paper's vision of 'a sound beginning' (DfEE 1997a)! It is totally unclear how the cells relate to multi-professional training or the contributions of early excellence centres. Requirements regarding assessment, recording and reporting look equally incomplete. Proposals for baseline assessment (DfEE 1997a) will need well-trained early years practitioners able to administer procedures effectively. The induction of trainees into diagnostic and observational skills needs strengthening.

Conclusion

To conclude, we would recommend the following:

- The years 0–8 should be seen as a continuum.
- Courses should seriously address ways in which students can be fully equipped to work in early years settings.
- There is integration of the induction programme with initial training as a requirement of continuing professional development whereby early years teachers would study the 0–3 and 5–8 age ranges via modules 'wrapped around' the core 3–5 programme in initial training. The need for such integration is addressed in the (Dearing) NCIHE Report No. 10 (1997).
- The curriculum for teacher training should be reviewed alongside the National Curriculum and the *Desirable Outcomes* (SCAA 1996) in a genuine attempt to provide appropriate national standards for early years as outlined in *Excellence in Schools* (DfEE 1997a).
- Partnerships should extend beyond those forged between higher education and schools to include the centres of excellence, community nursery centres and multi-disciplinary provision in general. Partnership and collaboration are key words in both *Early Excellence* (Labour Party 1996) and *Excellence in Schools* (DfEE 1997a).
- The establishment of a rolling programme of mentorship should be established in the above. Mentoring and supervision of students in training will provide additional staff development opportunities and could be accredited against award-bearing courses.
- New 'partnerships' should be quickly established and centres of excellence staff be involved in course processes. Centres of excellence will have a particularly important role to play in providing opportunities for retraining via 'multi-professional' experiences alongside support provided by higher education.
- The new local authority early years partnerships should also include teacher trainers among their members. This will ensure that the demands of teacher supply are addressed at all levels if the aim to provide 'a comprehensive and integrated approach to preschool education and childcare' (DfEE 1997a) is to be achieved with the involvement of teachers in all centres.
- There should be a rapid review of course content and structure; to meet the

demand for appropriately trained staff innovative ways of addressing the specific needs of early years teachers should be found as a matter of both content and status.

If the new Labour Government's aim for the involvement of a qualified teacher in the planning and delivery of all early years education services is to be achieved it is hoped that, as Webb (1972: 182) urged in response to the last promise of an expansion of nursery education, 'that those responsible for teacher education are prepared to take centre stage' and 'to give the performance of their lives before someone announces the next Act!'

Addendum

Since this chapter was written, Circular 4/98 has been published by the DfEE (May, 1998). Paragraph 2.3.1 states:

3–8 courses

These courses must include specialist training for Early Years (nursery and reception); the core subjects across Key Stage 1 and Key Stage 2 as specified in the ITT National Curriculum, and either at least one specialized subject across Key Stage 1 and Key Stage 2, or an additional advanced study of Early Years.

This is encouraging in that recognition is given to the Early Years as a specialist area. It is particularly welcome in its acceptance of the Early Childhood Studies degrees as appropriate for application to PGCE courses providing other standards are met.

The development of quality services through competence-based qualifications

Maureen O'Hagan, Sue Griffin and Pat Dench

Since 1992, competence-based National Vocational Qualifications and Scottish Vocational Qualifications (S/NVQs) have been available to early years care and education workers. This development represented a radical change in the way that candidates would be able to gain qualifications. No longer would they need to give up work in order to take a full-time college course: for S/NVQs they would be assessed on their competence in the workplace, with the knowledge and understanding which underpins performance being gained through distance learning, short courses, or any other method the candidate found the most convenient for their particular situation.

In this chapter, we seek to explore:

- the contribution of S/NVQs to the development of quality in early years services;
- some of the difficulties encountered in implementing these qualifications;
- the way these qualifications link to other training and awards in early years work;
- some indicators of desirable future developments.

It should be noted that we apply the word 'training' to all aspects of the learning or education necessary to prepare someone for a work role. This includes acquiring new information or knowledge, developing new practical skills, and developing or extending perceptions of values and underlying principles.

In examining the contribution of vocational qualifications to developing quality services for young children and their families, we start from the premises that:

- early years work requires a broad range of complex skills and an extensive knowledge base;

- all training and all qualifications for early years workers must reflect this demanding skills and knowledge requirement.

These premises contrast with the low status which society in the UK accords to early years work, and the level of pay usually received for the work. Inadequate attention and resources have been devoted to training (educating) and assessing those who take on the responsible and complicated work of caring for and educating our youngest children. The official Sector Occupational Codes (SOC) used by the Office of National Statistics to classify types of occupation portrays the work as low level and low skill. It is also perceived by many as mechanistic, composed of discrete simple tasks which require little intellectual capacity to learn, little ability or personal maturity to put into operation and no significant knowledge base to sustain practice. Yet the very nature of young children (unpredictable, ever changing in their development and behaviour) and of their parents (encountering new and even daunting responsibilities and roles, in need of support derived from experience) means that just the opposite is the case.

The contribution of S/NVQs

We maintain that the advent of S/NVQs to the early years field has brought the potential:

- to contribute to the development of a more accurate picture of the complexity of early years work by defining more precisely the skills and knowledge needed in various work roles and settings;
- to give practitioners recognition of the skills and knowledge they have already acquired through previous learning and experience, while highlighting specific remaining needs for additional training and experience;
- to encourage practitioners to develop a reflective approach to their customary work and to extend their knowledge and skills towards attaining defined standards;
- to make more explicit the values on which the work must rest and be inspired by, interpreting broad principles into the detail of daily work and specific interactions;
- as a result of all the above, to make a major contribution to the development of quality early years services which meet the needs of young children and their families.

These assertions lead us to be advocates of the S/NVQ approach to training and qualifications, and support our own professional involvement in these qualifications. While we are not blind to the shortcomings and difficulties so far encountered, we continue to strive to make contributions to the refinement and improvement of these awards, as our part of working for better early years provision.

Background information on the development of S/NVQs in Early Years Care and Education can be found in Hevey and Curtis (1996).

The accurate picture

The methods used by the Under Sevens Project of 1989–90 to develop the National Occupational Standards (on which the S/NVQs were based) focused on the real work carried out by real early years workers in real work situations, using processes known as 'functional analysis' and 'occupational mapping'.

Functional analysis consisted in asking those who undertake work with young children and their families to describe what it is they do in their work. The process started with groups of practitioners agreeing a statement about the overarching purpose of their work. This involved much exploration of basic philosophies and motivation. The next step was to analyse, at a broad level, the aspects of practice which contribute to achieving that aim, and then moving on to a process of breaking down the main categories of work into the fine detail and the quality indicators which produced the Standards.

Thus, the Standards represent the reality of everyday work, but are also overlaid with considerations of aspiration to develop and improve practice, to make daily work more effective in meeting the needs of children and families.

Occupational mapping took the functions derived from the analysis process and questioned 1,000 practitioners across the UK in many different work settings about which of these functions they regularly or rarely undertook in their daily practice (Hevey and Windle 1990). This enabled the clustering of functions into groups which reflected customary work patterns at various levels of work, identifying what was common to various settings and roles.

We have described the processes of developing S/NVQs in order to support our assertion that the National Occupational Standards are an accurate reflection of the complexity and high level of skills and knowledge necessary in early years work. We present this evidence to refute any remaining doubts about whether or not this is an area of work for people with abilities to acquire a broad knowledge base and operate diverse skills independently. We consider that this in itself supports the status of early years work.

No level 1 S/NVQs emerged from the development process because there are no early years work roles in which discrete, simple tasks are carried out routinely under close supervision. It is of utmost importance that, if these codes are to be used as the basis of policy, the Office of National Statistics seriously considers the need to amend them.

Identifying training needs

S/NVQs have been the focus of new concepts, and have had the effect of sharpening perceptions about the nature and interrelationship of training and qualifications. S/NVQs are competence-based qualifications, whereas most preceding qualifications were knowledge based. In order to gain an S/NVQ, a candidate has to be assessed as both having knowledge and understanding about what is involved in her/his work, and also being capable of operating to defined standards in real work situations. Competence-based qualifications take a step on from knowledge-based ones, in that they require candidates not only to show that they have a sound basis of knowledge about their work, but also demand evidence that this knowledge can be drawn on and used to produce and sustain consistently effective day-to-day practice.

There is a difference between training and qualifications, and S/NVQs make more explicit that training is the means to preparing candidates for assessment against the Standards, while successful assessment is required to claim the qualification.

The Standards and the assessment which give access to the qualification are constant, but there is no one single required path of preparing for assessment. Each candidate can develop readiness for assessment through individual combinations of formal training, informal learning, experience and growing personal maturity. This challenges those who design and deliver training to do so in a more flexible and open way, offering opportunities for learning which can be tailored to suit individuals' needs. Some training providers have responded imaginatively to this challenge, but others still pressurize potential candidates to work through training courses, even when this involves covering ground with which the candidate is already familiar.

Many mature early years workers (paid and unpaid) are returning to training after a gap of many years, and some bring with them negative experiences of previous learning which may deter them from embarking on a qualification. S/NVQs supports such workers in simultaneously giving them credit for what they have already learned from previous training and experience, but also presenting them with indicators of where the gaps in that learning lie – and what training they must yet undergo before they can reach the Standards and gain the qualification. The opportunity to be assessed in a workplace where they feel at ease and confident gives access to further steps on the qualifications ladder or 'climbing frame'.

The reflective practitioner

It is widely agreed that one of the hallmarks of the professional worker is someone who frequently considers her or his style of work and, by drawing on new information, ideas and opinions, is able to adapt and develop new ways of working. S/NVQ encourages this approach – partly through the process of revealing skill and knowledge gaps as indicated above, and partly through the process of assessment itself.

S/NVQ assessment starts with candidates examining the Standards and comparing their usual work practice to them. If they normally work in the ways and to the quality reflected in the Standards, they move on to considering what evidence they will be able to bring forward to demonstrate that this is the case. One favoured form of evidence is the 'reflective account' which involves candidates reporting on their practice, identifying the ways in which it meets the Standards.

They must also examine the knowledge requirements, and identify the aspects for which they will not be able to produce evidence of sufficient breadth and depth of understanding. For some mature candidates whose practice has been developed mostly through experience, this may be the first time they have identified and articulated the knowledge base which they draw on for their practice. If they and their assessors form the judgment that their practice and knowledge as yet falls short, they must develop strategies for raising their practice and extending their knowledge.

Again, the nature of S/NVQ prompts development of good practice to the benefit of children and families.

Values and principles

Besides the skills expressed in the Standards, and the knowledge also set out, S/NVQs incorporate a strong value base. Principles have been defined and are embedded in the Standards. During 1996–7 the S/NVQs were reviewed and revised. One outcome of this review is a more clearly expressed and detailed set of principles, which we consider it worth quoting in full (see Box 6.1).

Box 6.1

Early Years Care and Education S/NVQs

Statement of Underlying Principles

These principles draw on both the UN Convention on the Rights of the Child and the Children Act 1989, and also take into account the delivery of the School Curriculum and Assessment Authority (SCAA) *Desirable Outcomes for Children's Learning*. They are based on the premise that the earliest years of children's lives are a unique stage of human development, and that quality early years provision benefits the wider society and is an investment for the future.

1   *The welfare of the child*
The welfare of the child is paramount. All early years workers must give precedence to the rights and well-being of the children they work with. Children should be listened to, and their opinions and concerns treated seriously. Management of children's behaviour should emphasise positive expectations for that behaviour, and responses to unwanted behaviour should be suited to the child's stage of development. A child must never be slapped, smacked, shaken or humiliated.

2   *Keeping children safe*
Work practices should help to prevent accidents to children and adults, and to protect their health. Emergency procedures of the work setting, including record keeping, must be adhered to. Every early years worker

has a responsibility to contribute to the protection of children from abuse, according to her/his work role.

3　*Working in partnership with parents/families*

Parents and families occupy a central position in their children's lives, and early years workers must never try to take over that role inappropriately. Parents and families should be listened to as expert on their own child. Information about children's development and progress should be shared openly with parents. Respect must be shown for families' traditions and child care practices, and every effort made to comply with parents' wishes for their children.

4　*Children's learning and development*

Children learn more and faster in their earliest years than at any other time in life. Development and learning in these earliest years lay the foundations for abilities, characteristics and skills later in life. Learning begins at birth. The care and education of children are interwoven.

Children should be offered a range of experiences and activities which support all aspects of their development: social, physical, intellectual, communication, emotional. The choice of experiences and activities (the 'curriculum') should depend on accurate assessment of the stage of development reached by a child, following observation and discussion with families. Early years workers have varying responsibilities concerning the planning and implementation of the curriculum, according to their work role, but all contributions to such planning and implementation should set high expectations for children and build on their achievements and interests. Child-initiated play and activities should be valued and recognised, as well as the adult planned curriculum. Written records should be kept of children's progress, and these records should be shared with parents.

5　*Equality of opportunity*

Each child should be offered equality of access to opportunities to learn and develop, and so work towards her/his potential. Each child is a unique individual; early years workers must respect this individuality; children should not be treated 'all the same'. In order to meet a child's needs, it is necessary to treat each child 'with equal concern': some children need more and/or different support in order to have equality of opportunity. It is essential to avoid stereotyping children on the basis of gender, racial origins, cultural or social background (including religion, language, class and family pattern), or disability: such stereotypes may act as barriers to equality of access to opportunity. Early years workers should demonstrate their valuing of children's racial and other personal characteristics in order to help them develop self-esteem.

These principles of equality of access to opportunity and avoidance of stereotyping must also be applied to interactions with adult family members, colleagues and other professionals.

6 *Anti-discrimination*
Early years workers must not discriminate against any child, family or group in society on the grounds of gender, racial origins, cultural or social background (including religion, language, class and family pattern), disability or sexuality. They must acknowledge and address any personal beliefs or opinions which prevent them respecting the value systems of other people, and comply with legislation and the policies of their work setting relating to discrimination. Children learn prejudice from their earliest years, and must be provided with accurate information to help them avoid prejudice. Expressions of prejudice by children or adults should be challenged, and support offered to those children or adults who are the objects of prejudice and discrimination. Early years workers have a powerful role to play in nurturing greater harmony amongst various groups in our society for future generations.

7 *Celebrating diversity*
Britain is a multi-racial, multi-cultural society. The contributions made to this society by a variety of cultural groups should be viewed in a positive light, and information about varying traditions, customs and festivals should be presented as a source of pleasure and enjoyment to all children including those in areas where there are few members of minority ethnic groups. Children should be helped to develop a sense of their identity within their racial, cultural and social groups, as well as having the opportunity to learn about cultures different from their own. No one culture should be represented as superior to any another: pride in one's own cultural and social background does not require condemnation of that of other people.

8 *Confidentiality*
Information about children and families must never be shared with others, without the permission of the family, except in the interests of protecting children. Early years workers must adhere to the policy of their work setting concerning confidential information, including passing information to colleagues.
    Information about other workers must also be handled in a confidential manner.

9 *Working with other professionals*
Advice and support should be sought from other professionals in the best interests of children and families, and information shared with them, subject to the principle of confidentiality. Respect should be shown for the roles of other professionals.

10 *The reflective practitioner*
Early years workers should use any opportunity they are offered or which arises to reflect on their practice and principles, and make use of the conclusions from such reflection in developing and extending their

practice. Seeking advice and support to help resolve queries or problems should be seen as a form of strength and professionalism. Opportunities for in-service training/continuous professional development should be used to the maximum.

(Reproduced with permission of the Care Sector Consortium)

Principles and values are an important basis of practice, but will only have impact on children and families if they are interpreted in the reality of everyday practice and expressed in specific context and aspects of practice. Broad statements of good intentions only have meaning if they are an intrinsic part of the minutiae of interaction with children and families. Values are not an 'add on'. Candidates must consistently demonstrate that their practice derives from the underlying principles and make them operational in work practice.

This approach to values further strengthens our assertion that S/NVQs have a major, positive contribution to make to the provision of quality early years services.

Rigour and consistency of assessment

The initial operation of S/NVQs from 1992 has thrown up several problems, notably of insufficient rigour and consistency in some assessment. This has threatened the integrity of the achievement of candidates who have been taken through rigorous and consistent assessment. The Review of 1996–7 and the subsequent plans of the awarding bodies have sought to address these issues. One key change is to specify the collection of certain evidence through direct observation in real work settings.

The lynchpin of assessment of S/NVQs lies with the assessor and the internal verifier. Assessors must have recent relevant occupational experience and a level of underpinning knowledge and understanding greater than the level required by the candidate they are assessing. As early years care and education is carried out in mostly small-scale settings there are more peripatetic assessors than work-based assessors. This results in a higher level of objectivity on the part of the assessor as they are able to see a number of different work settings and therefore are more able to acquire an overview of good practice. However, peripatetic assessors can only spend limited periods of time observing in candidates' workplaces so such candidates may have to produce a larger amount of diverse evidence in order to demonstrate competence. The Beaumont Report (*Review of 100 NVQs and SVQs*, 1996) mentions the introduction of a greater level of externality into the assessment of S/NVQs. What is meant by 'externality' is not entirely clear but it seems to refer to objective forms of assessment verified from outside the candidate's workplace. The use of peripatetic assessors certainly fulfils this requirement.

In order to gain a greater level of consistency between assessors and internal verifiers, centres are expected to have regular standardization meetings. These meetings should be attended by all the assessors and internal verifiers and assessment judgements can be verified, decisions made on interpretation of the standards and other problems of consistency discussed. It is important that assessors and verifiers from a centre all use the same recording documentation, the same sampling frame and have absolute understanding of the processes required by them. In the past, differences between requirements of awarding bodies have been another area which has contributed to inconsistency. The awarding bodies are working together in the present review of the standards in order to eradicate these anomalies.

It takes time for all new qualifications to become accepted by employers and S/NVQs have not been an exception to this. However, it will greatly help the credibility of the qualification for employers if it can be clearly shown that the assessment is rigorous and consistent.

Funding issues

S/NVQs were developed as employment-led qualifications and in a field such as early years care and education where there are very few large employers this has led to repercussions in terms of funding and access. In the S/NVQ model, there is an expectation that large employers will use the NVQ system in order to develop the competence of their staff, the expense for this being borne by the employer. In a situation where there are few large employers the candidate is left in the position of having to find his/her own funding. There is no doubt that the lack of funds is one of the greatest barriers to access of S/NVQs. The lack of a properly resourced strategy for ensuring that sufficient funds are available to meet the costs of assessment, training and other guidance (or mentoring) is a great deficiency of the S/NVQ system. Young people entering the early years area of work have had access to some resources via Training and Enterprise Councils (TECs), but little has been forthcoming for experienced, mature workers. There are many early years practitioners who come into the work when they have reared or are rearing their own children and it is only later that they consider gaining qualifications.

There are thousands of potential candidates, held back only by their inability to find the money. For instance, a survey of some 50,000 members of the National Childminding Association in 1996 revealed from an 80 per cent return that almost 50 per cent of respondents were considering embarking on an NVQ. The Preschool Learning Alliance has 20,000 preschools in membership who employ in total over 90,000 staff (paid and unpaid). Most of these childminders and preschool staff are women who are poorly paid and do not fit any of the funding schemes for S/NVQs, that is, they are too old (over 24 years) and already in work.

Training and Enterprise Councils hold government-allocated funds for NVQs along with the Further Education Funding Council (FEFC) who fund NVQs via colleges. There is a great disparity between TECs in the way they draw up their criteria for funding and in many cases funding is allocated to employers or private training providers rather than to individuals who wish to gain an NVQ. Some TECs have been proactive in supplying funding to centres to enable the assessors and internal verifiers to gain the appropriate Training and Development units. For the individual playgroup or preschool worker or childminder who wishes to be assessed for an S/NVQ there is often no alternative but to finance themselves. As we have already stated, early years care and education is viewed as low status work and this is reflected in the very low pay of the workers. Being low paid workers and having to finance themselves through the NVQ requires a tremendous commitment to the qualification. It is to be hoped that the new Labour Government's strategies concerning early years work will include addressing the issue of funding and breaking down this barrier to access.

Recognition of the qualifications

Another disappointing aspect of implementation of the qualifications has been the failure of some local authorities to recognise S/NVQs for employment and registration purposes. It is difficult to ascertain the underlying reasons for the qualifications not being accepted but there have been questions raised about the credibility and relevance of the qualifications. In some areas the non-recognition, when investigated, has been due to lack of information about the qualifications on the part of personnel and registration officers. Bad publicity about S/NVQs in other industry areas (only some of it well founded) has led to a blanket suspicion of all S/NVQs. Even where S/NVQs are recognised, there is not always understanding that different level qualifications are appropriate for work roles requiring different levels of skill and carrying different levels of responsibility. Greater clarity is needed that level 2 is appropriate for workers who work under supervision, covering a limited range of functions, whilst level 3 is suitable for those who plan and organize their own work (and perhaps that of others), without supervision.

The Beaumont Report (1996), whose researchers consulted widely with employers, made a number of recommendations which would make S/NVQs more acceptable and therefore lead to them becoming more widely recognized. The main areas which Beaumont said needed to be addressed:

- greater externality in the assessment of the knowledge aspects, i.e. multiple-choice question papers, short tests, non-work-based assessors;
- less bureaucracy in the administration of the qualifications;
- the language of the standards made more 'user friendly'.

At present, aspects of Beaumont are being refined and implemented and it is hoped that once this is completed employers will show a greater faith in the product.

There is also doubt about the recognition of S/NVQs by higher education. Very few higher education establishments will as yet accept S/NVQs as entry qualifications for degrees in related subjects. This means that in addition to the credibility problem with employers there is also a credibility problem with the academic world.

In 1996, Sir Ron Dearing published his report *Review of Qualifications for 16–19 Year Olds* (the Dearing Report). In this document there is a framework for all qualifications, level 3 S/NVQs appearing on an horizontal axis with 'A' levels. Moves are now being made towards implementing the recommendations in the Dearing Report and part of this is the construction of the framework. The merging of the National Council for Vocational Qualifications with the Schools Curriculum and Assessment Authority in October 1997 to produce a new organization, the Qualifications and Curriculum Authority, will be significant in the production of a comprehensive framework. Perhaps it will only be at this point that higher education will become more open to accepting S/NVQs for entry to their establishments.

Links with other training and qualifications

While extolling the virtues of the S/NVQs, we must not forget that there is also a place for other training and qualifications. There are a number of existing courses which are able to offer the underpinning knowledge and understanding for S/NVQs, for example, the Kirklees project Pathways to Professionalism, described in Chapter 10. Appendix 2 in *Education and Training for Work in the Early Years* (Pugh 1996b) gives information about the wide range of training provided by many early years organizations, most of which have links to S/NVQs. The Preschool Learning Alliance's Diploma in Preschool Practice is one of the courses listed in Part X of the Children Act Guidance as an appropriate qualification for the leader, deputy and half the staff in a playgroup (preschool). The Diploma provides candidates with the underpinning knowledge and understanding for NVQ level 3. The organization also awards certificates for a range of shorter courses many of which provide knowledge and understanding for S/NVQs at levels 2 and 3.

In 1998, the National Childminding Association is launching its Developing Childminding Practice courses which will provide a stepped approach of training courses for childminders, designed to build their knowledge and skills ready for assessment at level 3.

There is a body of opinion which believes that 16–19-year olds are best accommodated on courses which offer them help, advice, support and the opportunity to grow and develop, rather than attempting to undertake S/NVQs. CACHE has a Certificate in Child Care and Education which is aligned with level 2 S/NVQ and a Diploma in Nursery Nursing which is aligned with S/NVQ level 3. A candidate, having gained one of these CACHE qualifications, is then able to be assessed once they are working in employment or as a volunteer for the S/NVQ. The work which they did on the CACHE course and any assignments or projects may be brought forward into their portfolios as evidence from the past. In some colleges, candidates will be registered for the CACHE course and the S/NVQ, the competencies for the S/NVQ being assessed when they are in their placement. It is often not possible for the candidate to gain both qualifications, but the S/NVQ can be completed when they are in employment. The units which candidates who are also college students have most difficulty in completing are those relating to Child Protection and Working with Parents, as these are areas with which a student would not be involved.

At present there is no S/NVQ at level 4 in Child Care and Education. A recent feasibility study (Wildeboer 1997) showed that there is clear evidence that there are sufficient numbers of workers in the area to justify the development of a level 4 qualification. This work has now begun. Managers, field-workers and registration officers play a pivotal role in sustaining the quality of practice within the workforce. Therefore there is a need for a qualification and career progression for experienced able workers. The long-awaited emergence of a National Training Organisation (NTO) should go some way towards meeting this need.

At present, there is a dearth of post-qualifying courses which would be able to offer the underpinning knowledge for level 4. CACHE has an Advanced Diploma in Child Care and Education (ADCE) and is also one of the awarding bodies for the Specialist Teacher Assistant Certificate. The Preschool Learning Alliance's Diploma could also contribute to underpinning knowledge for S/NVQ level 4. In the early years training sector there are a number of courses that would immediately or with some development, enable candidates to gain entry to Early Childhood Studies degrees (see Chapter 8).

CACHE Advanced Diploma in Child Care and Education modules carry Credit Accumulation and Transfer (CATS) points from the Open University which enables a student who has successfully completed six modules to negotiate dispensation from the first year of a related degree course. Whatever is developed at level 4 will need to be credible to both employers and higher education.

The introduction of S/NVQs has encouraged many people to seek a qualification and progress to higher education when they might not have previously had the confidence to do this. Awarding bodies continue to make links with universities in order to forge a progression route for those candidates who wish to study for a degree or other higher education award. It is important that NVQs are not undervalued because they are not the perceived conventional route to degree courses. It is expected that the implementation of the Dearing Report and framework will bring academic qualifications closer to vocational qualifications thus removing arguments about parity of esteem.

Some indicators of desirable future developments

We write at a time when a new Labour Government has set out its strategic principles for early years services. The authors are optimistic about the future and the development of a comprehensive progression route for all early years care and education workers. We hope that the Government will consult with and listen to early years practitioners. There is a common agreement in the early years sector about the importance of a well-trained high-quality work-force. We look forward to policymakers sharing this view and joining the commitment of the sector to ensure the availability of knowledgeable, skilled and reflective practitioners in all settings which serve young children and their families. The continued development and strengthening of the S/NVQ system has a key role to play in building effective early years services.

Praxis NVQ early years assessment centre – a case study: putting the candidate at the heart of the process

Sue Owen and Gill Thorpe

'It was difficult at first, but I'm glad I managed to do it. I have more confidence now. I know why I'm doing things instead of just doing them. It's made me think about what level of development the children are at, and to put things in the programme to help them achieve. I am now working temporarily full-time with a child with special needs – I wouldn't have got that without the NVQ. I would advise people to do it – it's worth it.'

This quotation is from one of the latest candidates who achieved her level 3 NVQ Child Care and Education – Special Needs, through Praxis NVQ, formerly known as the Humberside Early Years Assessment Centre. In this chapter, we will show how the centre was set up, how we tackled access, quality, and funding issues, and why we believe that NVQs are a vitally important development within childcare and education.

Introduction

National Vocational Qualifications are described in Chapter 6. The awards are delivered locally by assessment centres which are expected to maintain high and uniform standards of assessment for candidates, and to undertake all the administration of the system. These centres are accredited by one of the national awarding bodies for childcare and education NVQs.

The Humberside Early Years Assessment Centre chose the Council for Awards in Child Care and Education (CACHE) as its awarding body because it is a consortium of all the major organizations in childcare and education and has very high expectations of its assessment centres, particularly in terms of assessment standards and equal opportunities practice. These aspects mirror what we feel is important about our own centre, and about developments in childcare and education generally in this country. There is:

- a challenging of traditional barriers between 'care' and 'education' and a commitment from all childcare sectors to work in partnership;
- a commitment to the importance and distinctiveness of early years skills and a recognition that the awards must be controlled by early years specialists;
- a commitment to equal opportunities and antidiscriminatory practice as integral to every aspect of the required skills and knowledge and to the process of assessment.

NVQs have been hailed by many early years specialists as a revolutionary way of addressing the needs of existing workers, the recruitment of new workers, and the raising of overall standards of service, and the last is perhaps the most important aspect of the whole process. While status and qualifications will boost the personal development of workers and *indirectly* improve standards, we need a training and qualification process which will show a direct and immediate effect on the care and education offered to children and their families. Because NVQ assessment is work based it can do this, by showing candidates the direct application of elements of skill and knowledge to the work they are doing. The process of gaining an NVQ is one of acquiring the habit of continual reflection on one's everyday practice.

The aim of our assessment process is for the candidates, rather than the assessors, to decide if they are not competent in any of the elements. Obviously the assessor, backed by verifiers, is the final arbiter but the relationship with the candidate should be one in which decisions are mutual: the candidate learns what is standard good practice and recognises whether or not she or he meets those standards. This means that assessment is not a passive act of judgement, but a dynamic learning process of discussion, reflection and negotiation – a shared process where the candidate gradually assumes ownership and control and her work practice develops and changes as a result.

How the Centre was set up

The Humberside Early Years Assessment Centre was officially launched in May 1993 after 18 months of discussion, preparation and anxiety. It began as a consortium of 21 organizations which was relatively easy to pull together because we already had a good early years infrastructure on which to draw, including an Early Years Training Forum consisting of early years trainers in the county. It was the forum who decided to take the plunge and investigate the possibility of becoming a county coordinated assessment centre.

The Centre was successful in obtaining significant grant aid from the Humberside Training and Enterprise Council and the Rural Development Commission towards the cost of setting up the centre in its pilot year. The partnership arrangements made with consortium members were crucial at this first stage in terms of paving the way to implementing the Centre's initial activities. Members' networks were used to promote the NVQs and to create a pool from which to draw assessors and candidates. Members were able to donate resources, both human and physical to the Centre: a group of members formed a management committee, and all attended annual partnership meetings. The Centre coordinator and office space came from one of the partners in the consortium, Save the Children, via a specific consultancy agreement.

A further major contribution from some partners was 36 hours per year donated assessment time. This was a considerable asset in view of the fact that childcare and education NVQs require peripatetic assessors and are labour intensive. Most workers are in one-person settings or very small workplaces, and most are unpaid or low waged. This is a very different situation from that of most NVQs which can be delivered by in-house assessors in large, localized workplaces.

In our first year, we were able to offer resources to partners in return for their commitment and support. These included:

- free assessor training;
- free publicity and materials;
- reduced fees for their candidates;
- career progression;
- a ready source of demand for their training.

There were difficulties, especially in terms of coordination and communication, with such a large body of organizations – and, as with so many aspects of early years work, the forces which impelled us into partnership and cooperation were counterbalanced by other imperatives. Early years specialists in further education colleges, for example, had to fight hard to maintain a role in the consortium at a time when their colleges were becoming financially independent and were encouraged to set up their own centres to assess only their own students. NVQs were unfamiliar and underrated by employers and workers and the cost, in terms of time and money to achieve a qualification, was an unknown factor.

We began to tackle these problems by setting clear aims for the centre, to unify the partnership, communicate our value base, and to implement our policies and practice:

- increase NVQ access for paid and unpaid childcare and education workers;
- provide quality assessment, verification and training services;
- improve early years status and standards.

Development of the Centre – access and implementation 1993–7

The consortium-managed Centre gave us the structure; we then had to develop policies, create systems and carry out activities to reach the position of actually registering and assessing candidates. Equal opportunities is central to our work; as well as being accessible to low-paid or unwaged workers, we also wish to provide qualifications for disabled candidates and candidates from minority ethnic groups. We established an equal opportunities policy and strategy, adopted the antidiscriminatory performance criteria for assessors and internal verifiers and set up an appeals procedure for candidates.

We established targets for the pilot year and followed this pattern of development in roughly three stages:

1 Set up structures and administrative systems.
2 Train a pool of assessors and internal verifiers.
3 Promote and publicize the qualifications and register 50 candidates.

Affordability and funding

Initially, we trained over 30 assessors from all areas of child care and education (details of how we developed the assessor training programme are discussed later in this chapter), some of whom donated time as workplace assessors as part of their job role; others acted as peripatetic assessors and were paid an hourly rate of £10 plus travel costs. We plumped for 6 hours assessor time per unit, having no idea at that stage whether this was a realistic estimate or not – it was a starting point and allowed the development of the assessment process to our current target of around 35 hours assessor time for level 3, plus 6–8 hours group induction time.

The qualification needs to be affordable in order to be accessible to candidates and this posed real problems for us. The initial funding allowed us to offer the qualifications minus the assessor cost; this meant that candidates were only paying for the awarding body registration fees, and a percentage towards the Centre's administrative costs. For example, at level 2, the cost to candidates was £175, as opposed to an estimated full cost of about £800. However, even £175 is still way beyond the reach of most of our candidates who are low waged and without a large employer to support their training. We tackled this problem by fund-raising. Funders who know about childcare and education and believe in its importance will recognise that a centre such as ours, which insists on high standards, equality and accessibility, finds it very hard to become self-financing. We hoped to be able to forge deals with those large employers which do exist, for example, the local educational authority, social services and some private nursery groups. They were already members of the consortium, and it was hoped they might be interested in purchasing assessment packages for workers. One employer scheme was initiated in the Centre's first year when the LEA provided grant aid over two years for school-based early years workers (including parents, volunteers and meal-time supervisors) to access the awards. However, we fell foul of local government reorganization when Humberside County Council was abolished in April 1996, and the four new authorities did not all find it possible to continue to support their workers in this way. Additionally, we made it as easy as possible for individuals to pay. We developed our own computer database which tracked candidates administratively making it possible for us to organize a range of payment schemes, including payment by instalments.

Funding remains an issue. After the pilot year, we successfully applied to the European Social Fund (ESF) for a grant to support 100 candidates, which was matched funded by a three-year Joint Finance grant and through 'in kind' resources from the consortium. We were not prepared however for the interminable delay before receiving firm confirmation from the ESF. It was September 1994 before we heard and the deadline for achieving goals was December 1994. The inevitable shortfall in our targets meant that our bid for 1995 was not successful and we relied extensively on the support of Save the Children Fund to keep the Centre viable. We try hard to diversify our funding sources to support the annual target of 100 candidates. ESF funding supports 25; the remaining receive financial support through our fund-raising efforts from a variety of sources.

In April 1996, the centre was re-named Praxis NVQ Early Years Assessment Centre. It is now a limited company with charitable status managed by a group of trustees. This change came about for several reasons, including the impact of local government re-organization and the planned withdrawal of Save the Children Fund. Praxis NVQ is still committed to the same aims, as the choice of name, the blending of theory and practice, highlights. All the trustees are ex-members of the original consortium except for one who was brought in to provide financial advice. We employ a Centre coordinator and part-time administrator, and contract with a pool of about 20 to 25 assessors and five internal verifiers at a time.

Since September 1993, 44 candidates have completed level 2 and 40 have completed level 3. We have 101 candidates currently working on their NVQ and 29 waiting candidates. We have trained 60 assessors, some of whom are ex-candidates themselves, and 10 internal verifiers – 25 of these have achieved their TDLB qualifications.

We struggle constantly, however, to keep funding flowing so that candidates are able to access the qualifications. Recognition of independent centres such as ours by the Further Education Funding Council would make an enormous difference. Although some Training and Enterprise Councils offer financial help to experienced candidates, this support is patchy and inconsistent across the country and is frankly not sufficient, and not easily accessible; indeed it is sometimes non-existent. NVQs are designed to open up access to learning and assessment in ways which differ from traditional routes. We now need some creative financial packages to complement and recognize this radical change in learning patterns, otherwise there will be no change taking place.

Publicity and promotion

As we prepared to promote the NVQs in our pilot year, we recognized that most people had never heard of them, and those that had were unimpressed by their status.

Our starting point is the candidate. We produced a user-friendly leaflet called 'Making Sense of NVQ' (Figure 7.1) which explained the process in straight forward language and we created an open learning pack called 'NVQ

Making Sense of .... NVQ

National Vocational Qualifications in Child Care and Education

THE HUMBERSIDE EARLY YEARS ASSESSMENT CENTRE

" What are NVQ's ? "

▲ National Vocational Qualifications are new qualifications for people who work with young children and their families.

▲ They are awarded for the ability to do the job to a national standard in real work situations.

▲ They reflect the knowledge and under-standing of the work.

▲ They are designed to give people credit for the experience, skills and knowledge they already have.

" Why are NVQs so important? "

▲ They define the complex skills needed to work with young children and their families and so enhance the status of such work.

▲ They offer opportunities to a wide range of people working in child care and education to have their skills valued and accredited.

▲ They will be recognised throughout England, Wales & Ireland by employers and others.

(Scotland already have SVQ's - Scottish Vocational Qualifications)

" Can I take this qualification? "

▲ Yes, if you have the skills and knowledge needed to meet the specified standards and be assessed as competent. Otherwise, there are no entry requirements.

" Do I have to go on a course? "

▲ Not necessarily, if you already have sufficient skills & knowledge you may be ready for assessment at least for some units.

▲ Less experienced people or those who identify gaps in their knowledge may need to prepare for assessment through some training.

▲ This can be formal training or informal learning in a group or individually.

▲ NVQ's are not tied to any specific course, and no course leads automatically to an NVQ.

Courses cannot be NVQ accredited.

Making sense of the NVQ language

ASSESSMENT	the process of judging a demonstration of competence.
ACCREDITATION	the formal act of approval from the awarding body.
CANDIDATE	You! the person who is acquiring an NVQ.
COMPETENCE	the ability to perform work activities to the standards.
ELEMENT OF COMPETENCE	the function or activity a worker should be able to do.
PERFORMANCE CRITERIA	the outcomes by which an assessor can judge that a candidate can perform to a level acceptable in employment.
UNIT OF COMPETENCE	units are the smallest part of a qualification which will receive separate accreditation.

For further information contact
Gill Thorpe or Jackie Burnett
Humberside Early Years Assessment Centre
373 Anlaby Road, HULL HU3 6AB
Telephone: (0482) 569457

The centre is:-
Co-ordinated by **Save the Children**

Accredited by Council for Early Years Awards
Supported by Humberside County Council
Funded by Humberside Training and Enterprise Council,
& The Rural Development Commission.

"How are NVQ's assessed?"

▲ Candidates are expected to provide evidence that they are competent to the national standard on which the NVQ's are based.

▲ An assessor will observe you at work either where you regularly work as an employee or volunteer - or on a work placement if you are a student.

▲ Together with your assessor you will work out other evidence of your competence which you can gather in a portfolio or file.

▲ You will also have to satisfy your assessor that you have the knowledge to be able to sustain competent performance in a variety of situations.

▲ When you have gathered sufficient evidence to convince your assessor that you are competent to the standards, the assessment centre will credit you with a unit towards your qualification.

"How much will it cost?"

▲ The Humberside Early Years Assessment Centre is funded this first year by Humberside Training and Enterprise Council.

▲ For this year (March 93-94) the registration fee (which lasts 5 years) is £25 and each unit costs £15.

▲ There are possible sources of help towards costs. Currently you are entitled to a 25% reduction of fees in the form of tax relief even if you do not pay tax.

"Will the qualifications I already have contribute to an NVQ?"

▲ It is not possible to 'trade in' previous qualifications for NVQ's.

▲ But the knowledge acquired for such a qualification can make a contribution to assessment for NVQ.

▲ It is possible to make some use of evidence of competence reflected in previous qualifications.

"What is the pass mark for NVQ's?"

▲ There is no pass or fail. You are either assessed as being competent or not yet competent in which case you can be directed to training or learning. It is not an exam.

"How long will it take?"

▲ There is no time limit.

▲ You can acquire units at a pace which suits you.

▲ You can take units in any order.

Start-Up'. The pack guides the candidate through the process of gaining an NVQ, explains the terms involved, the role of assessors, how to identify evidence, how to organize a portfolio, and puts them firmly in control of the decision-making process: which qualification for me? Do I have enough evidence? What extra learning do I need? Can I fill knowledge gaps? Where shall I start?

All registered candidates are given an NVQ 'Start-Up' pack, and those who are unable to have an assessor allocated immediately are offered group 'Start-Up' sessions so that they are able to begin the process of identifying and gathering evidence. The candidate is given the information, techniques and support to understand the NVQ process so that she or he can ultimately assume control of it. Centre assessors too, receive copies of the pack and their training programme mirrors the information it contains. In this way we develop consistency in assessor practice.

Raising the status of early years work

There is an argument that because National Vocational Qualifications measure competent performance against standards they are about 'doing', rather than 'knowing', the implication being that they mainly reflect skills in practice rather than a person's knowledge and understanding of why they perform those skills. Consequently the NVQ has been labelled as merely an exercise in making sure that certain tasks are carried out according to clear standards, giving rise to the 'tick-list' approach to assessment, and casting the NVQ as a low status qualification.

We take the opposite viewpoint and agree with Alison Wolf (1989) that competence is a construct, and not something we can observe directly. She argues that in measuring performance or 'behaviour' we are also measuring knowledge and understanding, and that a person carrying out a task, or performing a skill, implicitly knows and understands why. This is particularly apparent in childcare and education and the NVQ process reflects this. For example:

• The childcare and education standards are explicit about the required knowledge and understanding.
• The awarding body, CACHE, is rigorous about the recording of knowledge and understanding.
• Our assessor training programme has an emphasis on enabling candidates to become explicit in their evidence of knowledge and understanding.

Candidates who are 'not yet' competent and find they require further knowledge to meet the standards can select an appropriate method of filling their knowledge gap. For example, they could attend a training programme or day course, research and write about a particular topic, complete projects, assignments or case studies, answer questions verbally or written and so on.

Candidates who are already experienced but unqualified, emerge from the NVQ process more confident in their work and worth. Their day-to-day practice changes and develops as a result of their self-assessment which has a direct impact on children and families.

Quality assessment

Assessors are key people in determining effective, quality assessment. Working for the centre their practice reflects our standards as well as national assessor standards. The phrase 'all singing from the same hymn sheet' sums up the emphasis on communication systems to create consistency. The Centre has a number of key indicators of quality assessment.

For candidates

- Subsidized fees – payment plan to take the stress out of payment.
- User-friendly explanations/materials about the NVQ framework and process.
- Induction programme to identify and gather evidence for one unit, complete the unit – then allocated an assessor.
- Protected by Centre's equal opportunities policy, antidiscriminatory practice standards and the appeals procedure.
- One assessor throughout aimed for.
- Encouraged to self-assess, plan, meet self-imposed deadlines.
- Coached in a variety of evidence-gathering methods.
- Gradually assume responsibility for the process.
- Receive holistic observations of natural performance.
- Receive speedy feedback, copies of all plans, observations, feedback.
- Can contact assessor/Centre coordinator by telephone by arrangement.
- Can be put in touch with other candidates for mutual support groups.
- Receive congratulations when completing units and qualification.

For assessors and internal verifiers

- Recruited in line with the Centre's criteria.
- Participate in the Centre's training programme – even if qualified – before acting on its behalf.
- Carry out assessment and verification according to Centre guidelines and national standards.
- Attend three assessor team/standardization meetings per year.
- Assessors visited/observed by internal verifier once a year.
- Verification per portfolio = one full unit, all unit summary sheets and relevant documentation.
- Paid a reasonable fee for work on the Centre's behalf.
- Qualify within two years of acting for the Centre.
- Required to re-apply annually to continue to act for the Centre.
- Receive copies of the quarterly Centre Bulletin.
- Encouraged to contact each other for mutual support.
- Offered at least one annual 'get-together' support and training day.

For trustees, Centre coordinator, Centre administrator
• Plan and review work to achieve the goals and aims of the Centre.
• Agree a business plan and work to it.
• Fund-raise, explore and follow up new funding opportunities.
• Monitor the progress of candidates, coordinate the work of assessors and verifiers.
• Work to the requirements of the awarding body.
• Promote the Centre and ensure effective administrative and communication systems.
• Manage the Centre according to required legislation and the constitution.
• Develop the Centre's activities.

Assessor training programme

The aim of the assessor training programme is to: 'Equip participants to provide consistent quality assessment to NVQ candidates in childcare and education on behalf of the Centre.'

The training programme has evolved since we began training assessors in 1993, before we actually had any candidates registered with us. The first programme was contracted in from a consultant recommended by the awarding body, and at that stage we all needed to understand the NVQ process first, before we could incorporate our principles and candidate-centred approaches. 'Guinea pig' candidates were persuaded to submit to assessment as part of the trainee assessors' practice – and we learned from their experience.

Apart from actually contacting a candidate for the first time to begin the assessment process the main difficulties trainees have are (a) deciding how much evidence is enough for judging competence, (b) coping with the time-consuming recording systems and (c) working in isolation.

The training programmes reveal the real commitment and enthusiasm of trainee assessors who represent all sections of childcare and education; some trainees are now ex-NVQ candidates which is a tremendous advantage. There is a mutual bond which ensures that the time spent together is enjoyable – the atmosphere is relaxed and we use a range of learning methods. This all combines to demystify and humanize the NVQ system: we are convinced that it is people who matter – not paper!

We use the three 'P' model as a basic structure for the programme: Principles, Processes, Practice.

Principles
• share and consolidate values and beliefs and experiences about childcare and education;
• compare these with the principles underpinning the national standards;
• explore the value and establish the principle of a candidate-centred approach to the NVQ process;
• appreciate the significance of the NVQs to the child, family, employer and the status of the work;
• know the policies adopted by the Centre.

Processes
- understand the structure and framework of NVQs;
- understand the Centre's quality assurance processes;
- become familiar with the standards both of childcare and education and the Training and Development Lead Body standards for assessors;
- define quality assessment and the role of assessors;
- understand the Centre's systems and processes for candidates from registration to qualification;
- examine how to assist candidates to identify a range of evidence gathering methods;
- examine how to judge competence;
- identify the range of evidence gathering methods;
- be clear about advising candidates on organizing their portfolios, and the quality not quantity of evidence guidance.

Practice
- introduce the plan–do–review model of practice;
- practise implementing the candidate-centred approach with assessment planning, identifying and gathering evidence, observations and feedback, portfolio advice;
- participate in standardization exercises;
- practise recording and become familiar with the documentation;
- practise self-assessment of performance;
- practise development of communication skills;
- carry out a practice assessment and receive constructive critical feedback;
- raise and resolve practice issues;
- evaluate the programme.

The programme is usually a three-day course and we also offer a further day if required to assist trainee assessors to build and organize evidence for portfolios for their own assessor/verifier awards (TDLB D32, D33 and D34) which the Centre is also accredited to assess. We have a similarly structured but shorter programme to train our internal verifiers and we produce guidance booklets which are adapted as new developments emerge for all our assessors and verifiers.

Assessment: maintaining quality, reducing cost

Mike Heron from the National Council for Vocational Qualifications made this remark about quality in an article in the *Further Education* magazine:

> If I tell you to produce a glass and insist that it costs five pence, you will come up with a bloody awful glass. But if I say produce a glass then we'll see how to cut the cost, you will have a good product. Quality is in the design.
>
> (Heron 1994)

What we did initially at the Centre was to design a candidate-centred approach to our principles, processes and practice. It did indeed cost a lot of money, especially in terms of assessment time. We no longer have the luxury of development funding and we have learned a great deal since 1993, not least from the candidates themselves, about how to improve the quality of the assessment process, while reducing assessment costs.

We have recently developed strategies and techniques which put assessors in the position of a 'coach first–assess later' approach. We noted that most candidates were taking three or four months initially to become familiar with the NVQ process, and then after that, once one unit was completed and organized in their portfolio, they became more confident and took more control of the process. Most of our candidates are mature and experienced workers who already have paid or unpaid positions in childcare and education settings.

What most candidates need, they tell us, is more techniques about how to identify and gather evidence, how to organize it in a portfolio, and how to cross-reference it to other elements/units, where appropriate. They do not want to wait for an assessor to visit them and tell them what to do; they want the support and resources to be able to get on and do it themselves. They also want deadlines – realistic targets which are achievable for them.

The induction sessions we offer candidates are part of the coaching process which is carried out by our Centre coordinator – these include exercises to become familiar with the standards as well as the NVQ process. Once an assessor is allocated, the coaching process continues combined with assessment/action planning sessions.

The candidate learns how to become a reflective practitioner by making self-assessment against the standards part of their daily routine at work. They are helped to identify and carry out techniques to gather evidence, for example the following:

- Candidates are encouraged to identify a person(s) at work who can testify that their evidence is valid. (This person completes a 'witness' criteria form for the Centre and is visited by the assessor.)
- Work diary. The candidate targets a work diary to record activity which reflects performance criteria. The candidate cross-references the record to the relevant performance criteria and has it signed by the witness.
- 'Tell a story' method. This can be done by talking to another person, by making a recording, or by writing. Again, the candidate targets an element or elements and recalls a recent incident or situation which demonstrates the direct involvement of the candidate. This is best done in the first person. The candidate then records it, cross-references, has it witnessed.
- Use of photographs. The candidate asks work colleagues to take photos of them at work; candidates mount them, give a description of what they were doing, what was happening and the witness signs it. (All witnessed evidence is verified by the candidate's assessor.)
- Projects, assignments and case studies are useful tools to produce evidence for situations, at a candidate's workplace, which are not routine.

- Self-questioning. Candidates are encouraged to create their own knowledge questions from the written knowledge requirements. Their responses can either be written or recorded and cross-referenced.
- Use of video. Candidates are helped to plan a focus for a video recording which a colleague helps them make at work to record performance. Twenty minutes is long enough at a time. The candidate should cross-reference the video to the performance criteria. The assessor assesses.

Witnessed evidence involves others in changing and developing practice in the workplace. Childminders, who do not have co-workers, could make reciprocal arrangements with other childminders, ask colleagues with childcare and education experience, or parents. A criterion for witnesses, verified by the assessor, assures quality. Observation and questioning time by the assessor can be reduced through using these methods, which extend the 'shopping basket' of evidence available to the candidate. These include the usual work products, child observations, analogue evidence and prior achievement. Knowledge and/or performance gaps are identified and candidates are helped to find ways of filling them. This may include reading and research, joining a training programme, shadowing another practitioner or carrying out a project.

Candidates are also encouraged to complete an Element Summary Sheet which summarizes what type of evidence they have, which part of the standards it relates to and where it is in their portfolio. This sheet also has space to cross-reference evidence to other elements/units. It helps assessors to quickly check and assess evidence in portfolios which they summarize and record on evidence log sheets in the usual way. There is flexibility in our systems to allow for candidates' individual learning differences even though we have to try keep to our target assessment times of 25 hours + 6 hours induction for level 2 and 35 hours + 6 hours induction for level 3. These are achievable targets, and several candidates have now completed their qualification using the methods and techniques described here.

Case study of a candidate

The most rewarding moments for all of us involved with the Centre has been the candidates' achievements. Their excitement, sense of satisfaction and sheer delight when they realized they had completed their NVQ has been, and still is the fundamental purpose for the continuation of the Centre. One candidate, whom we will call 'Jenny', made the remarks quoted at the beginning of this chapter. She said: 'The best bit was when I got the phone call to say I'd done it. That was the best bit. Brilliant.' 'Jenny' was determined to achieve level 3 and she did it in a remarkably short space of time, seven months. You can see some detail of her work and progress in Box 7.1. Other candidates have taken almost two years – but there is no hard-or-fast rule in terms of completing – except, of course, if there is financial pressure to finish. Candidates find support from family, friends and other candidates. The NVQ route can be very isolating, and often candidates drop out because this

Box 7.1

Case study of a candidate

This is an example of one candidate's pattern and progression to achieve her level 3 Special Needs Child Care and Education Qualification.

Jenny – Meals Supervisor at an Infant School, and sometimes helps with Early Admissions Class. Beaver Scout Leader, working with 6–8-year-old boys for the past $6^1/_2$ years.
Works $6^1/_4$ hours per week, paid work.
Previous training – City & Guilds 7321/0 Learning Support Certificate, Scout Training.

- Funded through the 1996 ESF Grant with 25 others.

- **8 July start date.** Late start due to late notification of ESF funding.

- Attended 3 group induction sessions between July and September 1996 allocated an assessor.

- Decided on level 3 after induction.

Record of Assessment plans

- **8 July 96** Units E1 and E2 were chosen – portfolio-building discussed – evidence identified.

- **16 July** Jenny had produced evidence for E1 for assessor to 'look at'. Evidence identification reinforced Agreement to work on E2, P2 and C2.

- **29 July** Written feedback on E1 from assessor – guidance especially about cross-referencing – encouragement about evidence. Invitation to phone.

- **18 September** Observation and Feedback. Assessment Planning. Jenny produced evidence for C2/E1/E2 and some of P2 – advised about types of evidence and cross-referencing again. Arranged observation with focus on C11 – agreed to a case study for C15.

- **10 October** Jenny produced portfolio with evidence for C2/E2/P2. Talked through C10 – assignment handed over. Looked at C15 – resource identified so Jenny could see the 'depth' required.

- **15 October** A review. Jenny had gathered some or most evidence for all units except C7/C11/C16 and the endorsement unit. Talked about how to sort it. Comment made that evidence was excellent.

- **13 November** Observation and Feedback.

- **11 December** Units completed and waiting assessment – C2/E2/P2/ C5/C3/C10/C11. Jenny congratulated on her progress.

- **27 January** Special Needs endorsement decided. C2/C3/C10/E1/E2/ C5 assessed and unit sheets signed. Discussed Special Needs evidence. Portfolio with remaining evidence handed over. Jenny aiming to complete by 28 February.

- **10 February** Jenny congratulated on the quality of her work – unit summary sheets signed. Discussed few points Special Needs.

Jenny completed her Qualification on *28 February 97 – 7 months from the start date.*
It was assessed by the beginning of March 1997. Jenny was immediately telephoned with the news.
It was verified by the end of March 1997.

Evidence gathering methods
- Witnessed work diary entries
- Witnessed 'telling a story' method
- Examples of her work/other products
- Photos – Projects – Assignments – Case study
- 2 Assessor Observations
- Questioning

Candidate time
About 8 hours a week – more towards the end – Approx 250 hours.

Assessor time
34 hours + 6 hours group work.

---

method of learning does not suit them – even with support. Our candidates have given us sound advice about assessment and support processes which has shaped the Centre's development. We know that many have gained in confidence; one told us with pride how the teachers in her school were amazed at the breadth and depth of her work in her portfolio. We are aware that many have successfully applied for employment or gone into further education.

There has been a sense of adventure about this new route to a qualification, enhanced by candidates' reported effect on their work with families and children. The phrase, 'It's made me think, about what I do' has been repeated many times. They have told us about actual changes in their settings brought about by their search for evidence to meet the standards, small, but significant changes, such as the repositioning of an oven, to attitude change such as encouraging children to select and work with activities for themselves.

Comments from ten candidates

Ten Centre candidates were asked to give some comments and tips about their NVQ in Child Care and Education. They speak for themselves!

'A lot of people are capable of doing it but they can't because they don't understand it – they think it's something different and not what they know.'

'The assessor is really crucial – they can make it easy or hard.'

'More contact with the Centre needed, perhaps a newsletter or something.'

'First impression – HELP.'

'National Standards – it's just like doing a crossword really – you just have to "suss" out the writer and then you can complete it.'

'Why did they write that book [the standards] like that? It really put me off at first, I just couldn't understand it – those words! My assessor helped me understand and it's not too bad now but I really think it could be written better than that.'

'I was very nervous before my first assessment, but when I got busy working with the children I almost forgot my assessor sitting in the corner.'

'Be positive!'

'I nearly gave up. But I thought I am doing this to prove I can do it. I can hardly believe I have actually done it. I am so pleased.'

'I was so upset when my assessment didn't work out as I expected but my assessor pointed out all my performance against the criteria and I soon realised I had done better than I thought.'

The way forward?

Soon after this chapter was written, the financial position of the Centre worsened and the trustees had to make some serious decisions about its future. The plan to diversify our funding sources had not worked as successfully as we had hoped, for a variety of reasons. It was clear that the Centre could not continue to manage the European funding grant system of retrospective payment, and we were still running a county centre in what had become four unitary authorities through government restructuring.

In order to survive, the Centre has also begun a period of restructure. Sadly, this has meant the loss of the two members of staff. The Centre has reduced the intake of candidates and moved to Lincolnshire where it will continue to strive to achieve the aims of access, quality and raising standards through these NVQs.

The question for us, and other centres in the country which were set up independently from existing educational infrastructures, is why, when we are successfully facilitating access to national qualifications to experienced people, is it so very difficult to find the financial resources to support this work?

The 'radical reform' of this country's training system, mentioned in the 1989 Government White Paper, is simply not radical enough yet for childcare and education NVQs. The basic principle of overcoming traditional provision by allowing learners to have real choice and responsibility for what they learn means that non-traditional provision needs to be encouraged, not discouraged.

The way ahead for centres such as ours is to promote the continuing demand from experienced childcare and education workers for NVQs to fundholders; to demonstrate how to provide accessible and quality assessment; and to continue to offer learners an effective alternative to traditional routes to qualifications.

It was suggested earlier in this chapter that NVQs offer a revolutionary way forward for early years workers. Revolutions usually make quite a lot of noise: perhaps that is just what is needed now.

⑧ Early Childhood Studies degrees

Mary Fawcett and Pamela Calder

Origins

From the early 1990s, a number of people, drawing on their own experience and different circumstances, began to think seriously about establishing degree programmes in Early Childhood Studies. There were several driving forces, which are evident in other chapters of this book. Perhaps above all was the need for an interdisciplinary preparation that would bridge the divide between education and care and in the longer term bring about coordinated services for young children and their families. Concern about the continuing poor status of such work and its low-level, inadequate training was also an important factor. Research from USA (Whitebook *et al.* 1990), with its rather similar uncoordinated erratic range of services, indicated the link between quality of provision and the level of education of the staff. Finally, European colleagues were moving towards graduate level qualifications for most pre-school staff.

A group of early years trainers, advisors and educators began meeting in 1992 at the National Children's Bureau to examine the mismatch between training needs of staff and what was actually available in terms of training. The background to these discussions was one of considerable uncertainty in two relevant areas: changes in teacher training and the developing National Vocational Qualifications in childcare and education. However, by the time the group concluded with the publication of its first discussion paper (NCB 1993) degrees in Early Childhood Studies at Suffolk College (validated by the University of East Anglia) and the University of Bristol were already underway. By autumn 1997, there were 15 degree programmes. The picture is as outlined in Table 8.1. In addition, University College Cork in the Republic of Ireland also has a degree in Early Childhood Studies. There is also a Main Subject pathway in Early Childhood Studies in the BEd programme of Rolle College, the University of Plymouth, an important development in the bid to raise the status of Early Childhood Studies within teacher education.

Table 8.1 Early Childhood Studies degree programmes

Birmingham College of Food
Bristol University
Canterbury Christchurch College
University of Hertfordshire
Leeds Metropolitan University
Liverpool John Moore's University
Manchester Metropolitan University
Norfolk College
University of North London
St Helen's College, Stockport College of Further Education
Stranmillis College, Belfast (Northern Ireland)
Suffolk College
University of Sunderland
Swansea University
Worcester College of Higher Education

The context

The degree developments have taken place in the context of the existing qualifications and training opportunities of the early childhood workforce. A chart setting these out is given in the early years training group's second discussion paper (Pugh 1996) and other chapters in this book examine some of the variety of forms of education and training.

Historically, the two systems of care and education, both tending to have a compensatory focus, have led to different arguments contending the need for change. Though these two debates have led to pressure for expansion and development, higher education has not been seen as a necessity (Calder 1997). First, there were those who focused on expanding nursery education, for children between 3 and 5 years, believing it was good for every child and should be universally available. Second, there were those who focused on developing provision that benefited children between birth and 5 years, which encompassed care and education, and which would also allow mothers to take paid employment and participate in education and civic life.

Members of the National Children's Bureau early years training group argued for setting up Early Childhood Studies degrees and were aware of these different emphases. But they shared the view that the quality of any service depends on the education and training of those working in it. While there was agreement that Early Childhood Studies degrees could lead to enhanced multi-professional work (better collaboration between teachers, health visitors, social workers and nursery nurses), some also hoped for a more radical transformation whereby the current division between nursery teachers and nursery nurses would disappear and be replaced by a degree-level qualification for multifunctional/educare work in multifunctional/educare centres, on a model similar to the training of social educators in Denmark (Friese *et al.* 1995). All agreed the development of new degrees was important. The arguments for the necessity for graduate-level training depended on two key premises:

1 Training was necessary for looking after, bringing up and educating other people's children.
2 Graduate-level training had advantages over academically lower-level training.

These premises rest on certain assumptions. Are these assumptions warranted? The following points can be made:

- Our society judges worth and status by qualifications. High-level status is associated with qualifications. By not offering status to those who rear, care for and educate children, not only do we devalue them and their work but we also indicate the low regard society gives to children.
- The absence of degree level training suggests the work itself does not need high levels of skill since we assume that professions where we believe high levels of skill are needed, for example, medicine and the law, expect graduate entry.
- Degree-level education is expected to bring a critical edge and an enquiring attitude to those undertaking it. The absence of a requirement for degree-level education suggests such attributes are not thought necessary. Indeed, with reference to childcare and early education, Chris Woodhead (HMI and Chief Inspector of Schools) speaking in 1996 on the radio programme 'Today', has said: 'One does not need a PhD to teach four-year-olds.'
- Research, mostly from the USA, has made links between level of training and qualifications of staff, and child outcomes (Whitebook *et al.* 1990; Kontos *et al.* 1995). Most of the measured outcomes have either been concerned with trying to establish some concurrent link with the personality or behaviour, language or cognitive development of the child or with effects on later schooling. Evidence from the UK has come from Jowett and Sylva (1986) and Shorrocks *et al.* (1992). Little research has looked at wider ecological effects, on the wider family, or society. There have been few specific attempts to measure the effects of levels of staff training, and the level and kind of staff qualifications have often been incidental to studies which have indicated the positive effects on children of being in nurseries (Andersson 1992, 1989; Schweinhart *et al.* 1993a). However, Rodger *et al.* (1994) in their research project aimed at the identification of factors influencing the quality of educative provision for children under five, found that the level and type of staff training was a significant factor.
- Practitioners themselves often believe that having specialist early years training leads to a more appropriate curriculum for children. Blenkin *et al.* (1996: 12) report that, of the 'factors considered by heads of institutions to be most significant to constraining the development of an appropriate curriculum for young children' the one most often mentioned (by 53 per cent) of respondents was 'staff not trained for early years specialism'.

We would argue that not only is existing training insufficient, and is at the wrong level, but that even where specialist graduate level education does exist (for nursery teachers), it is not currently appropriate for all the jobs that are required in early childhood services and excludes services for under-threes. The estimate (Moss and Penn 1996) that only 5 per cent of the workforce in early childhood services currently have a degree is an extremely low percentage compared with figures from the *Labour Force Survey* (OPCS 1996) which show that among 25–44-year-olds in the workforce, 23 per cent have higher education qualifications.

We want to argue that the introduction of Early Childhood Studies degrees will lead to improvements that cannot be matched by NVQs alone (Calder 1995, 1996c) and that the introduction of degrees provides a large step forward in laying the foundation for a coherent, integrated, childcare and education service, with a highly qualified workforce.

The nature of Early Childhood Studies degrees

Each degree has its own history. In some institutions, the course was initially in response to local needs, but for most the early years training group's first discussion paper (National Children's Bureau 1993) has been a stimulus. Some courses have evolved from certificate and diploma courses which were aimed at offering nursery nurses opportunities for more advanced study.

The move to modularity by most universities has probably facilitated the rapid expansion. It has allowed modules/units from different departments and disciplines, for example, social work, nursing, health, management, sociology, psychology and education, to be combined together into a new degree. Modularity brings practical advantages in that it may offer the possibility of access at different levels for people who already have some qualifications. However, it can lead to a 'pick-and-mix' approach which may have consequences for the integrity of students' learning and a lack of balance. In an attempt to overcome this, a number of courses are designed to achieve some linearity, that is, all Early Childhood Studies students are obliged to attend a proportion of core modules/units as well as having access to a range of elective/optional modules/units.

In terms of organization, Early Childhood Studies degrees may be offered as a full-time or part-time course. Some universities, Manchester Metropolitan University (MMU) is an example, run both routes and they have found that the experience and backgrounds of the students on these two routes to be very different. Full-time students tend to be school-leavers with perhaps some voluntary work or baby-sitting experience with young children. On the other hand, those enrolled on MMU's part-time route included: manager (family support centre), social services registration and inspection officers, play coordinator/facilitator (voluntary agency), social services under-eights' officer, nursery officers (combined centres), nursery teachers, nursery proprietors (private day nursery), nursery nurses (reception and nursery classes), principal officer (from the National Childminding Association), lecturer in child development and child studies (further education college), hospital play specialists, sister (from an intensive care unit), health tutor, team manager (children and families division), paediatric nurse, parents, teachers in mainstream and special schools. The implications for teaching, research projects and placements, (the part-time students undertake research in their own work place) are clearly far-reaching.

A serious issue for mature students must be the cost of study. Until now, full-time study has attracted a mandatory grant, while part-time has had to be self-funded. Evidence from about half of the Early Childhood Studies degree courses is given below.

Costs to students

The price (at 1997) per module/unit varies from £50.00 to £100.00, with some programmes having eight modules per year and others twelve. The course programme will last at least three years, making the financial outlay a considerable item.

Access

Entry requirements are similar across the various degree programmes, thus typical undergraduate A levels are expected for school-leavers. Mature entrants can benefit from flexible access, with systems of APEL (Accreditation of Prior Experience and Learning) being developed in some courses. Given the diverse education, training and work experience of potential students, this must be an eventual aim for all.

An institution's location is an important issue for mature students, making distance-learning methods a likely development in the future, though indeed they are already employed by North London University. Stranmillis College in Northern Ireland is currently using video-conferencing for students living some distance away, another technique with potential for future development.

Numbers enrolled on Early Childhood Studies programmes

From a survey of the current programmes it appears that there are currently (1997) between 1500 and 2000 undergraduates. The number expected to graduate in 1998 will be around 300.

The aims and content of Early Childhood Studies degrees

All the courses aim to have a multi-professional approach, with some, as we have seen, providing a rich forum for the sharing of concerns across sectors, departments, establishments and authorities. Whether an Early Childhood Studies degree will become a foundation for a particular kind of professional (such as a teacher or a social worker) who will be better able to work as a team member, or whether it will develop as a degree level qualification for multi-functional work, remains to be seen.

Aims

A summary of the aims from a sample of courses includes:

- In-depth understanding of learning and development in years 0–8;
- Critical awareness of early years issues, theories and research;
- Recognition of the ecological, social and diverse contexts of family life;
- 'Educare' philosophy of practice underpinned by sound and valid principles and values;
- Commitment to equal opportunities and to promoting the holistic development of all children;
- Enthusiasm for interprofessional collaboration and the management of change;
- Acknowledgement of the experience, knowledge and skills of practitioners.

Core curriculum areas

In attempting to achieve these aims (and most of the sample universities were rather similar) the core curriculum areas were variously organized. These have been summarized below and are not in a particular order:

- personal learning/professional development;
- research methodology (including observation);
- child development, including play, language and learning (psychology);
- health issues;
- policies, legislation and services for young children and their families (social policy);
- working with parents:
- interprofessional approaches;
- family support and child protection;
- international perspectives and comparative studies (sociology and history);
- dissertation.

In addition, some courses give more time to special educational needs, others to historical studies, while the practical early years curriculum, such as learning through music, drama, movement, art and science, is also included in another. Counselling and management issues are part of one programme.

Practical work

The sampled courses have a variety of arrangements. Those studying on an in-service basis continue in their workplace and may have research tasks to be carried out there. Mentor-supervised practice placements are a feature at MMU, as well as job exchanges on the part-time course. Suffolk College has two 15-week modules involving supervised practice in different types of services as well as direct work with children. Students also work with a family, observing and making videos. In contrast, the University of Bristol has no practical work. All courses, however, have visits, some including the shadowing of professional workers. A dissertation which incorporates some research work (interviews, observations) in early childhood services is a feature of all courses.

Early Childhood Studies students' motivation, career expectations and paths, and graduate perspectives

We have some evidence from the few degrees which have so far produced graduates. A questionnaire survey of students at Bristol (Fawcett 1997) provides an example of some the reasons behind this group's selection of university and course. A high proportion of the respondents lived in the locality, and were restricted geographically, a typical issue for women, but they had chosen Early Childhood Studies (ECS) because it linked with their interests in children, family support work and because the mix of subjects on offer looked interesting and attractive.

The psychology component was frequently mentioned as a strong interest, but the concept of studying across a broad range of topics relating to children seems to have been even more important. A typical response, indicating an aspiration for a broad foundation, but not a vocational course, was evident: 'I am very interested in working with children, but I don't necessarily want to become a teacher. Doing ECS teaches [sic] me on the subject I love, without forcing me into a career at this stage.' Among students from each year, the value and stimulus of the interdisciplinary study was reiterated and its usefulness as a holistic and ecological basis for a future career mentioned.

Students felt the degree programme was living up to their expectations, but was more challenging and complex than they had anticipated; those in the final year believed that from the end of the second year the different aspects began to come together. The University of Bristol course programme lacks practical work and students in all years regretted this. Very few had plans to enter the teaching profession, but a career in some aspect of psychology was planned by a sizeable number of those replying to the questionnaire. Others were expecting to do a Diploma in Social Work, several mentioned therapeutic work and others expressed interest in working in family centres. There was not much difference between the various years with regard to career aspirations though one-third of students in the final year are planning to proceed to higher degree study.

We look forward to surveys from other courses.

Career paths

So far, the numbers who have graduated are limited. A large proportion of Suffolk College's 1996 cohort proceeded to a Postgraduate Certificate in Education, though not all intend to teach children, and several are preparing to work in adult education. From all those universities who have had graduates the destinations are varied: educational welfare officer, the Diploma in Social Work, advisory roles, early years tutors, community support workers, voluntary sector workers and family centre workers.

Many of these early graduates have been mature, experienced people; it will be interesting to see how the younger students, entering university as school leavers, decide to proceed with their ECS degrees. Among the mature graduates from the Manchester Metropolitan University one has become a mentor for new students while another has been instrumental in establishing a joint nursery centre (with the LEA and social services departments in collaboration) instead of the two separate services (a nursery class and a family centre) as originally planned. Research is underway to track the careers of graduates.

The currency of the new Early Childhood Studies degree is still an issue. Entry to the Postgraduate Certificate of Education generally requires a National Curriculum subject, though some courses are accepting students without this. In other career settings, there is a lack of familiarity with the new degree and potential employers do not seem yet to accept the degree as they would any other, bearing in mind that it is very common for graduates to work in fields which are unrelated to their degree subject.

In addition to the careers already mentioned, recent developments are creating new roles for which Early Childhood Studies graduates are well suited. As a result of the Utting Report *Children in the Public Care* (DoH 1991), Children's Services Plans are now statutorily required from every local authority. Informed by the collaborative principles of the Children Act, a range of services, including provision for children under eight and their families, are to be planned across the services. Under the leadership of the social services department, all the various departments concerned with the welfare of children are expected to be involved, including education, health, the probation service, housing, legal departments and the range of voluntary agencies which provide support services for children and families. Workers for the task of researching and assisting in drawing up the plan will require skills of quite a different order from those needed in direct work with children.

The early years development plans required from local authorities will be creating new roles too. Inspectorial tasks have also increased in the last few years.

Some perspectives of Early Childhood Studies graduates from the University of Bristol

Two new graduates were interviewed about their views of the degree course programme in relation to their roles as family centre workers. Their family centre, jointly funded by education and social services, works with children who have been excluded from school for 'emotional and behavioural difficulties' and their families. Daily work entails regular collaboration with other professionals: head teachers, teachers, social workers, educational psychologists, special educational needs coordinators (SENCOs), health professionals such as senior clinical medical officers, GPs and health visitors. They assist in the classroom supporting the class teacher and act as key workers for individual children. This can involve individual therapeutic sessions with children and/or their families, supporting them in their re-integration into mainstream schooling and liaising between all professionals involved. Neither of these graduates have a vocational qualification, but they have had considerable experience in a voluntary capacity. In particular, they both acted as leaders in a Pyramid Trust project working with children who were causing concern in school; one has worked for many years with AIDS patients and the other on a helpline for women in situations of violence.

Do BSc Early Childhood Studies enable students to meet the demands of their roles in a family centre?
In terms of interprofessional understanding, students believe their course to have been very beneficial. From their first day, they understood something of the different aims and values of the various professionals with whom they are now working. An open-minded, broad perspective has been developed as a result of their studies. They are working with children and families with a range of difficulties and feel that their way of thinking means that they can take account of the various aims of other professionals but 'still keep the child and their family in focus'. Both of these graduates separately mentioned their course as a broad, solid base on which they could build and gradually specialize at a later stage. They know they have an ecological grasp of the children's circumstances; at the centre, the word 'systemic' is used, implying the importance of taking the whole context of a child's life. Their course had enabled them to see the value of working in partnership with parents and other professionals, treating all with respect.

A strong sense of children's rights was mentioned. This concept had often been debated on the course. They found that the course had been useful in giving them a broad knowledge of basic terminology and theoretical principles and this had been particularly useful in meetings and case conferences. This has given them confidence: they have felt able 'to argue and to know why you are doing it'. Clearly, report writing presented no problems. A university education had taught them 'how to research, how to find out' and how to write it up. They appreciated having been taught 'to be more sceptical'.

The students' only negative comment was that the course lacks practical work, which in fact they had remedied by seeking this experience in their own time.

Conclusion

The importance of increasing the number of graduates in the UK is clear. The EC Network on Childcare (1996b) has set a target for ten years hence, of a minimum of 60 per cent of staff working directly with children in group settings to have at least three years at post-18 level of higher education.

Among other targets set by the Network is the employment of men, at least 20 per cent, among staff in group settings.

In providing a comprehensive foundation for people to work either directly with, or on behalf of children, the degrees enable further developments. They can offer a better education and training for those working in advocacy, in inspectorial roles, and in managing services. They can provide a better foundation for existing careers in early childhood such as nursery teaching and social work and for those working in a multi-professional team. With the addition of further supervised practical experience, the degrees have the potential to provide the basis for a new integrated professional training for educare.

The unexpected, and in some cases spontaneous, evolution of Early Childhood Studies degrees in the 1990s has been without any formal requirements or legislation at national or local level. Though perhaps a manifestation of 'private enterprise', similar to the unplanned growth of the commercial pre-school sector, they are nevertheless a positive and potentially powerful new resource. Early Childhood Studies degrees in the UK are already demonstrating the challenging breadth of the interdisciplinary study of children and childhood. The significance of early experiences and their impact, not simply on day care arrangements, but on health, education, children's rights and lives in general, is now reaching a far wider group of people.

This chapter has described the way in which Early Childhood Studies degrees have emerged in the UK and their present characteristics; it has not looked in detail at how these degrees might develop should they become a mainstream professional requirement. If the degree is to become a preparation for a new type of integrated service incorporating health, education, care and family support, the aims, purposes and underlying philosophy of that service, as well as the curriculum content and skills of the degree programme, will need to be defined. Some progress in this direction might now be expected and will be aided by such discussions as those presented in Peter Moss and Pat Petrie's (1997: 11–12) *Children's Services: Time for a New Approach*. We now look forward to the developments forecast in the Labour Party's (1996: 14) paper, *Early Excellence*: 'We will encourage the emergence of new courses which offer integrated training, like those at Manchester Metropolitan University and Suffolk College.'

The pathways to professionalism project – a case study: making an Early Childhood Studies degree accessible

John Powell

This chapter describes the progress and current development of the innovative partnership project, Pathways to Professionalism, between Kirklees Early Years Service (KEYS) and the Manchester Metropolitan University (MMU). The chapter will raise a number of questions relating to issues specific to a new and innovative course development.

My own professional background has provided me with important experiences which have influenced the course, but its development would not have been possible without the involvement of Lesley Abbott and Brenda Griffin from MMU and Laura Ramsey and Ruth Beazley from KEYS who have energetically contributed to the course and its success. My role has been to work closely with the project coordinator, helping to overcome any institutional barriers and participate in delivering course modules.

As a social worker working with families with young children from birth to 11 years, I had access to the multi-professional context of child protection and an introduction to the idea of negotiating across agency boundaries, as well as assessing problems and their attendant risks. As a lecturer in further education I taught both NVQ and GNVQ courses. Later as a manager of a team delivering the care curriculum for a large inner-city further education college, I became concerned with issues of access and the difficulty that students often found in negotiating their progress into higher education. My interest in the Advanced Diploma in Child Care and Education (ADCE) for which I was responsible as a manager, led to me becoming one of the moderators for CACHE. I am now the course leader for the BA(Hons) in Early Childhood Studies for both part- and full-time routes as well as being the manager for the Multiprofessional Centre for Early Childhood Studies. This story of the Pathways to Professionalism project is a personal one which recalls my development in an exciting, innovative programme.

The Pathways to Professionalism, Early Childhood Studies course developed against the background of a number of influential developments that took place in the early 1990s. The Rumbold Report *Starting with Quality* (DES 1990) considered the quality of 'educational experience which should be offered to 3- and 4-year-old children, with particular reference to content, continuity and progression in learning having regard to the requirements of the national curriculum' (DES 1990: 1). The Rumbold Report was also concerned with what it considered an

> essential need: a closer linkage between the three strands of health, care and education in initial and in-service training; a pattern of qualifications for child care workers which will bridge the gap between vocational and academic qualifications; safeguarding both the rigour and relevance of initial training for teachers of the under-fives, and affording improved opportunities of in-service training for child care workers in educational settings.
>
> (DES 1990: 27)

There were, in addition, important recommendations regarding training which the report emphasized should 'reflect changes and developments in the nature and aspirations of provision for the under fives'. These recommendations also included a concern about 'easing access' to training while maintaining the 'quality' of entrants (DES 1990: 32). Some difficulties were raised by Rumbold and 'easing access' was one of them. Such an expression implied that quality would be dependent on the extent to which the doors to higher education would be opened and to whom. At the time of publication, most higher education establishments would have found it difficult to justify an easing of access regulations while at the same time claiming that their courses reached the standards necessary to maintain their academic reputations. It is heartening that much has been done to address this issue since 1990.

The challenge of the Rumbold Report was for institutions of higher education to develop a new style of degree which emphasized the importance of a multi-professional focus and was available to early years practitioners who wished to further develop professionally. A small group of universities began to develop such degree courses (see Chapter 8).

The Manchester Metropolitan University introduced two innovative additions to its provision in response to Rumbold. The first of these was the setting up of the BA(Hons) in Early Childhood Studies part-time degree route for practitioners already working in the field of early childhood. The degree emphasizes the importance of a multi-professional curriculum. The course is structured in three phases each of which has a particular focus: 'The child and the context of Educare'; 'Young children learning'; and 'The multi-professional context'. The degree is concerned with the world of the practitioner, and with academic rigour and the way that practice is represented through text.

The students represent a wide range of early years disciplines and backgrounds including teaching, childcare, social work, play work, nursery management, inspection services and nursing. All have been mature students and in many ways initially 'unconfident' about academic institutions and their ability to succeed in their studies, although some were already well qualified, and wished to spend more time refining early years interests at a higher educational level. There has always been a strong sense of comradeship among the students who have established social and academic support networks. Many are already expert and highly skilled in their own professional areas and have entered the degree to access a process of critical challenge which would help them to continue their professional development as well as developing their awareness of their own practices and how they might better influence institutional practice.

The tutors are mainly established lecturers from within the Faculty of Community Studies, Law and Education at Didsbury. Most of their professional backgrounds are in working with young children, teacher education, social work and management. The range and breadth of experience of the tutor group helped to establish a 'multi-professional ethos' with which the degree was centrally concerned. The range of departments and disciplines make the course significantly different from other courses in the university. The multi-professional curriculum supported by the tutors gives the course a richness and diversity. There is a strong sense of sharing different academic, vocational and professional perspectives which makes the degree an interesting and challenging area of study. All the tutors, along with the students, are chiefly interested in the early years as an area of academic and vocational development.

The other major innovation which the university introduced was the setting up of a Multiprofessional Centre for Early Childhood Studies. The Centre's aims were to develop links that crossed professional and organizational boundaries and provided an opportunity to explore early years issues and concerns and practices through a developing discourse. The Centre has been involved in developing and supporting multi-professional networks and in responding to the professional needs of early years workers. The importance of the Centre is also to be seen in the links that it encourages between the further and higher education sectors through the active partnerships that have been developed with further education providers.

The Multiprofessional Centre initiated an early years network with seminars which have a strong professional focus and offer early years practitioners the opportunity to share their experiences and their concerns. These meetings are useful in many ways but primarily in establishing an agenda for training and identifying ways in which practice may be improved. David (1993: 47) argues

> the perceptions held by colleagues from other professions will be formed as a result of many factors, but the likelihood of their being positive will, at present, depend upon their knowledge of that profession, its status within society and personal interactions based on personalities, rather than any carefully structured mechanisms for those liaisons to occur.

The Centre offers a forum for multi-professional discussion as a means of exploring different professional insights, perceptions and languages.

It is part of my role as the manager of the Centre to encourage relationships with both training and service providers. This includes developing bids that may lead to the development of work between the Centre and potential partners.

A developing partnership

In April 1995, Kirklees Early Years Service (KEYS) approached the Multiprofessional Centre in Early Childhood Studies to discuss the development of a partnership project to support students funded through the European Social Fund to access the first stage of the BA(Hons) in Early Childhood Studies part-time route. Students would also be able to complete the National Vocational Qualification level 3. Later, after negotiations with the Council for Awards in Children's Care and Education (CACHE), the Advanced Diploma in Child Care and Education was included as a qualification which could be achieved at the completion of the course.

The whole of the course was to be run outside the MMU campus at the Deighton Training Centre in Kirklees in order to be accessible for local people and to be clearly identified as a local initiative. Many students had never previously been into a university and felt intimidated by the prospect. There were a number of concerns linked to questions of access, including: the distance that students would have to travel if the course was to be run in Manchester; the need to provide students with local work placements; the importance of providing child care to those who needed it; and the need to have someone accessible from KEYS as project coordinator, who would be available to support students.

The project: the Pathways to Professionalism early childhood course

The Pathways to Professionalism course recruited 26 mainly unemployed women who were all highly committed and enthusiastic, as well as nervous about developing their skills and abilities in educare to the first stage of the BA degree. An assessment of competence relating to various areas of practice took place while students were at their placements and related to units of study for National Vocational Qualification programmes at level 3. The development of NVQ level 4 will be particularly important in the future expansion of innovative training and as a provision in the climbing frame of early years career opportunities.

The course is delivered by two tutors from the BA(Hons) Early Childhood Studies Team at the MMU. A third member of the team is involved in a longitudinal qualitative research exercise in which the experiences of students, tutors and project coordinators are monitored, analysed and later disseminated to an audience made up of transnational partners from Denmark and Ireland.

The course includes a requirement that students attend work placements with a variety of professional agencies. These placements are essential for student development because they offer variety and opportunity for assessment relating to the different modules in the programme.

The overall management of the Pathways to Professionalism course is the responsibility of a project coordinator who looks after the day-to-day running of the course, ensuring that it remains focused and within budgetary constraints, while offering support to students in response to a variety of academic, vocational and personal difficulties. The MMU School of Education manage the day-to-day resourcing and staffing of the teaching of the course and support the KEYS project coordinator in developing the course. National and local steering groups, which met regularly, have been set up to overlook the project and to support it in reaching its aims.

A challenge has been to write an early years course which offers the same number of modules as the first stage of the BA(Hons) Early Childhood Studies at the MMU. In addition, assessments needed to be adjusted to reflect the character of both the Advanced Diploma in Child Care and Education (ADCE) and stage 1 of the degree. This has meant that the curriculum has to reflect the modules of the ADCE and the modules of the first stage of the BA. The major innovation at this point has been to count the child development assessment as the ADCE dissertation. While students were to some extent limited in their choice of the dissertation, it was weighted to reflect the importance placed on it by the university. To compensate for the difficulty of writing a long piece of 6000–7000 words, the students were offered the writing in two parts to coincide with two modules in the subject.

The chief concern was to ensure that students' writing went towards ADCE assessment which would give them a recognized higher level qualification. In this instance, the ADCE modules closely resembled the first stage of the BA(Hons) in Early Childhood Studies which meant that for students wishing to continue their studies at MMU, they would have no difficulty in having their work recognized for Accreditation as Prior Experiential Learning (APEL). The ADCE is a qualification usually offered in the further education sector but in this context it was modified to meet the requirements of higher education, and as such can be shown as overlapping sector boundaries, to the benefit of the students.

Accessing degree-level work

The question of access was always at the forefront of course planning. Recruitment for the course followed an open day which was very well attended. Interviews were offered to many more women than the course could offer places to and the process of deciding who should be offered places was determined through a series of group interviews. The agreed criteria, in addition to the employment status of applicants, was their ability to articulate ideas about childcare practice relating to a video they had all watched together.

The access issue here is very difficult to resolve. It became apparent that the view that good communicators should make good students was not necessarily an accurate or fair way of determining access to the course since it could exclude those candidates who seemed less confident in talking with a group of strangers. However, the ability of applicants to discuss the issues in the video indicated to the interviewers those people who seemed aware and interested in early childhood issues and could express their views in a thoughtful manner and interviewers actively included applicants who were not being given the chance to participate. This form of interviewing was probably less threatening than an interview panel and allowed us to emphasize the process of active participation. This was a critical key ingredient to the success of students in developing and sharing ideas and interests.

The result of the interviewing process was that the new student group comprised people with varying experience and qualifications. Importantly, all the students appeared to be enthusiastic and committed to working in early years contexts. There was a range of academic achievements present amongst the selected students: some had GCSEs and A levels and a few had the Diploma in Nursery Nursing. The majority stated that they would have found access onto a degree-level course a problematic and probably negative experience but had found the Pathways to Professionalism course a more positive experience than they had expected.

The course started with a double induction module which was meant to put the new students into a more relaxed state of mind. Many found the idea of being involved in a higher educational course a very threatening prospect and were quite convinced they would not succeed. Tutors were able to empathize with the students. Having also been mature students, they recognized the daunting experience and negative feelings that surrounded returning to education as a mature learner. However, after the induction module the students were introduced to written assignment work where they were expected to develop analyses as well as to offer descriptions in their writing. Most students found the first piece of writing to be a real hurdle. Many had not undertaken a substantial piece of writing for several years and were naturally nervous of having to do so. Most of the students probably did not feel in those early days that they were going to be able to do the work that was required of them and the tutors also had moments of doubt. It was important for students to feel that they could believe themselves able to do the work and for tutors to introduce and develop ways in which the students' confidence could improve.

The tutor style

The significance of tutors having had experience of studying as mature students was important to the success of the course since there was common ground immediately established that reflected an awareness of feelings and values. It became clearer as time went on that the manner in which tutors communicated to students was extremely important. As a tutor on the course and as the manager of the assessment procedures, I was concerned to develop a more sensitive communication style which emphasized the 'voice' of the student as important in its own right. I believe that heeding what students say and recognizing the importance of providing direct and positive responses in reply, helps to develop self-confidence while pragmatically making links between personal culture and the culture of the course. By emphasizing the need for students' involvement in discussions and debate, I assumed that they would begin to feel more confident and included within the dominant educational discourse by developing a sense of ownership of their ideas and recognizing that they connected to academic and theoretical ideas.

As one of the tutors (and the only male), I encouraged the students to voice their interest: 'speaking becomes a way to engage in active self-transformation and a rite of passage where one moves from being object to being subject' (bell hooks 1989: 12) as well as listening to my own 'inner voice' (Fiumara 1990: 128) and by acknowledging that I was learning from the students. I attempted to give status to students' voice(s) by emphasizing their importance as central to a questioning ethos in developing understanding. However, it was also important to recognize the status of the course with its content, structure and regulations. This resulted in situations where the structure and content of the course were the focus of discussion but the students used their own words and were encouraged to relate to their own experiences. These were teaching techniques which usually differed from initial expectations and took the students some time to become accustomed.

Women's voices as 'unique experiences' are 'often muted'. Anderson and Jack (1991) argue that 'a woman's discussion of her life may combine two separate, often conflicting, perspectives: one framed in concepts and values that reflect men's dominant position in the culture and one informed by the more immediate realities of a woman's personal experience'. Anderson and Jack remind those interested in hearing women sharing their experience that they 'need to pay more attention to the narrator than to our own agendas' (Anderson and Jack 1991: 12). The tutor as a representative of a dominant educational culture can (coupled with being male) silence the personal voice(s) of (female) students.

The increase in student participation improved as students accessed their learning more from an increased sense of being valued for their contribution to the learning discourse. As Barone (1995: 64) indicates 'Just as discourse partaking of a critical science format and patois can promote emancipatory moments, so can story genres (biography, autobiography, literary journalism and the novel) that are derived from literary forms and that honour the norms of everyday speech'. Relevance was established between life stories and course content initially through verbal interaction and later through written text which had resulted from talk.

A comment from a reflective journal I kept during the course read: 'I am beginning to learn that trust is a major concern. I need to be reminded that learning is a socially constructed experience which requires students speaking out as bell hooks (1989: 5) describes "speaking as an equal to an authority figure".' What I was beginning to recognize is the need for trust to be established if students and their tutors were to feel comfortable about treating each other more equally. The sense that anyone makes of their experiences depends on the kind of constructions that can be made in an accessible language. The impact of the course on the lives of the students was difficult to appreciate though there were often moments when information was shared by students with tutors which indicated that they were experiencing major changes in their social, personal and professional lives as a result of attending the course.

The student experience

As a tutor, I know that the students have progressed a great deal down the road of self-confidence and self-questioning. They have become more at home with their student role as they have developed their 'voice' which I believe can be represented as them taking risks by asking questions and engaging in research. This does not mean that all the students find the work to be easy and unproblematic. They often find it difficult and complex, but they are now more familiar with learning as a developing experience and more accepting of themselves as students with their particular self-expectations. They have had to negotiate with family and friends and develop effective support systems able to deal with issues such as providing care for their own children while on the course and being part of support groups for dealing with assignment work to maintain their progress on the course.

The course has had a powerful effect on the lives of students. I now include the brief writing of two students who have developed their thinking about themselves from a life history perspective.

Kristina

Kristina recalls that her early memories of school were not happy ones and that her feeling at junior school was that it was to be endured. She recalls sitting quietly and becoming known as a 'bright' child. When she moved to secondary high school her reputation of being bright made her unpopular with her friends, but despite this, she was always highly placed in tests and exams. After the third year in high school she began to socialize more and her position in class deteriorated. Her parents were not British and did not know much about the education system. Kristina then left school and chose to study science but later went to work and had a succession of jobs. Just before entering the Pathways to Professionalism project, she had her first child. She was attracted to the project amongst other things because it offered support with childcare. She writes about the project as follows:

> 'The first two days on the course were exciting and frightening – the one factor which made me feel secure was that the tutors were there to support us and help us make it work.'

Kristina recounts how she was concerned to find good childcare for her child and how she was being woken three or four times a night and therefore getting little sleep. She recalls that developing friendships on the course helped her as they shared their experiences and problems. She writes about work on the project as follows:

'I was learning to write to a certain style and criteria. I was reading, researching, typing and making notes and having to cook, shop, clean and wash.

'I realized that I was coping and was using my mentors, tutors, colleagues and they were all there even when I was ill or miserable. It is through realizing that everyone has a difficult time learning later in life and talking about it with other students that I am still here and wanting more. I would like to point out that without childcare and support I would not be here. Also the fact that the course offers several levels of study and an opportunity to be successful on whichever level feels comfortable is an incentive to continue. I am now achieving high grades. I can meet deadlines, use libraries, understand academic literature, engage in and open discussion and debate. My confidence has escalated and I feel powerful enough to voice my concerns and thoughts without fear of seeming stupid. I am an accepted student – I remember telling my tutor I felt like a fraud in the beginning. I now believe I am not a fraud and that this is the most real experience alongside motherhood in my life.'

Sajda

Sajda left school with seven CSEs and went to sixth-form college to study Science O levels. However, her marriage was arranged in Pakistan and this affected her studies. She was married at 18 and spent all her time raising her four children. Sajda recalled that she lost contact with all her friends and that she had no social life and was trapped in a life cycle in the four walls of her house. She recalled how she lost her confidence and had low self-esteem and that she felt that her feelings and happiness were no longer important. Later Sajda recalled how she joined a basic childcare course where she was encouraged and supported by the tutors. Writing about the project she states:

'I applied for the course knowing that there were childcare facilities for my 1-year-old daughter. I went through the interview process and was taken on the project. Then you could say a different struggle to life began. Not a struggle with domestic responsibility, but a struggle for freedom. A struggle for my needs and a struggle to be valued and respected. My family could not understand the value or need for me to go into education and reminded my that my children should be my priority. However my mother supported me and talked my husband into it. Despite anxiety about the academic side of the project because I find difficulty in writing, especially since English is my second language, I was overjoyed by the decision that I could attend the project.'

Sajda experienced concern because her son was not settling at school and she felt powerless to intervene. The coursework, which had a direct linked practice, was a helpful source of examining how she could improve the situation with her son, and after confronting the local education authority, she managed to transfer her son to a local educational establishment. Sajda comments that her husband was overjoyed as he knew that it was the Early Childhood Studies course that had made change happen. Another first for Sajda was being chosen to visit one of the transnational partners in Denmark. Sajda recalls that there is a cultural barrier in the Asian community with women not being encouraged to travel alone. Sajda's comment on the course is as follows:

> 'The Early Childhood course has made me look at myself, my attitude and beliefs which have influenced my thinking. I now feel it is important that childcare workers need to understand children and how they learn and to value and respect them.'

She remarks that she receives support and encouragement from her husband and family and has developed academically and vocationally, becoming more assertive and confident.

These life history extracts indicate a personal and academic progression from being accepted onto the course through to working in different modules. The importance of support from both family and friends was significant though the way in which the course was able to provide childcare support as well as day-to-day contact was also a key to their success. The extracts show the complexity and balancing act that students are involved in between domestic, vocational and academic responsibilities. There are also phases of loneliness as students take the step of committing themselves to new and forbidding studies often without the full support of families or friends. The course had to establish itself as being helpful in private and domestic contexts outside of academic objectives to earn the support of students' families. During their time on the course, students have developed a wide range of skills and abilities and have grown confident about researching and writing. The importance of the developing voice(s) of students as having something to say that is relevant to academic study has been an empowering experience as they have negotiated a variety of difficulties.

Conclusion

There have been some interesting and probably unique features developed as part of the Pathways to Professionalism Early Childhood Course, such as the multiple outcomes which include the ADCE, NVQ level 3 and work equivalent to the first level of the BA(Hons) in Early Childhood Studies. There is a real sense of difference in the experience that students could expect to have if they were mainstream university students. For instance, the admissions policy applied to the Early Childhood Course was linked to European Social Fund criteria of offering places to unemployed people which meant that academic requirements for admission were not applied in the usual way. Because of this difference, the tutors had to be far more sensitive to developing confidence and self-esteem, especially during the early days when students were unfamiliar with the requirements of the course. What was positive as an experience for tutors and students was to be involved with so many highly motivated students who put everything into the programme and were not completing their education for its own sake but were concerned to 'learn'. The outcome for the students is far more woven into their lives as a 'lived in' experience. This experience of committing themselves so fully has happened despite the range of results gained by them, with some students having performed adequately while others have reached high academic levels.

Finally, the life history narratives of the two students Kristina and Sajda allow educators like me to access the liberated feelings that students can experience, especially students like these who once believed that they were failures and have now come to believe that they are successful.

There are a number of questions that need to be addressed in the future if other courses like this are to be developed. For example, would universities be willing to extend their work into the community with people who wish to continue their education to university level but who are unlikely to feel confident enough to directly access such a world? Where would courses such as these run and where would the funding come from? Will universities invest in this new era with cooperative partnerships with further education providers as well as local authority early years departments? Will tutors need to be trained in the application of communication skills to further the confidence and self-esteem of students? Will degree courses that are developed in and for the community be treated as having the same status as the ones located in the academic environs of the universities?

I believe that all of these questions pose serious challenges for the academic world but 'access' sums up the central concern with which higher education has to learn to live. There is the concern that students may be able to access the first stage of degree-level courses in the community as they have done in Kirklees but may not be able to continue with their studies to further their careers. The question of access remains a complex one and is dependent upon sensitive and responsive government policies as well as creative and progressive university partnerships with community providers.

It is essential that projects such as the one described in this chapter should be expanded to match the increasing responsibilities and status of early years practice and the need for quality educational opportunities to be developed to train early years practitioners to the highest skills and abilities. Finally, I wonder whether society will get the quality services for the early years that it aspires to with a strong infrastructure and corresponding career structures to match and staffed by highly qualified, skilled professionals.

Painting the cabbages red . . . ! Differentially trained adults working together in early years settings to promote children's learning

Janet Moyles and Wendy Suschitzky

Introduction

The findings from our recent nursery and Key Stage 1 research, briefly outlined in this chapter, suggest that significantly larger numbers of classroom assistants are being employed by nursery/infant and primary schools to compensate for escalating class sizes and increased numbers of children identified as having special educational needs. In addition, many classroom assistants are being 'trained up' through the Specialist Teacher Assistant (STA) programmes sponsored by the Government. This is creating a dilemma for schools as to how these partially-trained people are deployed and where their role fits into existing employment and pay structures in relation to the longer established role of two-year, further education trained, nursery nurses.

It is clear that many classroom assistants have little or no training and are employed (as many headteachers insisted during interviews) because they have shown their willingness as volunteer helpers. A few local education authorities, colleges and universities – the number is gradually increasing given the rise in numbers of classroom assistants – are offering short courses with either no formal qualification attached or some level of 'foundation' (pre-first-year degree) award. However, as any training is often discretionary upon heads and particularly on classroom assistants themselves, only a small proportion ever undertake any form of training. It was with this background in mind that the Government originally contributed £3.6m to the training of Specialist Training Assistants, sponsoring those courses which offered training in English, Maths and general basic skills teaching mainly to support the achievements of KS1 children. The scheme was extended from the original 22 providers in 1994 to 46 in 1995–6 and, since that time, money has continued to be provided for non-teaching staff training through GEST funding, a change which has meant that now classroom assistants must 'compete' with teachers (and nursery nurses) for their share of funding for in-service training.

As we shall see, heads and governors vary in their perceptions of what the role actually entails or what they really want from their classroom assistants and, therefore, what form of training is needed for non-teaching personnel. There appears to be a general belief that teachers can and do 'train-up' classroom assistants 'on the job' and, indeed, many assistants have learned their skills in this way. This is, however, dependent upon the relationship and understanding built up in time between the partners and many KS1 classroom assistants do not have this continued contact with individual teachers either because of the part-time, sessional nature of their role or because their working week is spent in supporting many different teachers rather than receiving any form of training.

The questions underpinning our extensive national study were as follows:

1 Is this practice of employing non-teaching staff in early years schooling, as the Government seems to believe, necessarily a 'good' thing or is it a way of actually reducing the professionalism (and impact?) of nursery and infant practitioners generally and a back-door way of introducing a 'mum's army' through a misguided belief that anyone can teach young children?
2 What implications does this practice have for the day-to-day roles each practitioner fulfils and how supportive are the established frameworks within which they work?
3 What is the impact of these on-going classroom practices on the quality of children's learning experiences when working with differentially trained adults?
4 What training opportunities need to be available for all those who operate in these 'classroom teams' if they are to work together most effectively and efficiently, with each using the strengths they are able to bring to their particular role?

To a certain extent, the findings which we will outline gave some answers. It also became evident, however, that much deeper issues lie at the heart of working as a differentially trained team, just a few of which will be taken up in the concluding paragraphs.

To begin, the research methodology is outlined briefly in the next section, after which we move to a discussion of different practitioners' perceptions of their own role and that of their classroom partners, the nature of those roles as evidenced by the research findings and the quality of children's learning experiences. We conclude by outlining some of the findings, implications and issues for discussion.

Theoretical basis of research

The theoretical basis for the research came from work undertaken by Dunkin and Precians (1991), Berliner (1992) and Bennett and Carré (1993). All these researchers note that there is a difference in the way that teachers think about teaching and these cognitive differences explain teachers' decision-making, thereby influencing the moment by moment interactions that take place in classrooms between teachers and children. Hence, by categorizing these behaviours and actions, it is possible to distinguish between, for example, expert and novice (inexpert) practitioners as well as the intermediate stages which it is postulated exist between the two extremes. It was anticipated, for example, that whereas classroom assistants were frequently found to be operating within the 'inexpert' domain, nursery nurses – because of their more extensive two-year training – may well operate at the intermediary stage. The various categories of behaviour identified by these researchers as representing different levels of operation between expert and novice, are mainly related to:

- motivational activity – how far the practitioner is able to motivate children during learning activities through improvised, spontaneous actions rather than reliance on a set plan;
- the structural/instructional level of the activity – the underpinning conceptual knowledge of the practitioner versus a limited knowledge of procedures;
- encouraging independence in children – the practitioners' ability to emphasize learning process as opposed to task outcomes;
- establishing relationships – whether tasks are undertaken through negotiated learning opportunities or the systematic use of rules and maxims.

These elements were included during each phase of the research to give an emerging picture of practice, both perceived and actual.

The practical basis of the research was drawn from the Ofsted inspection criteria, Schedule 5.2 on the quality of teaching (Ofsted 1995a). (For more details of the research theory/practice bases, see Moyles 1997a, b.)

Perceptions of roles

Responses from both groups of practitioners revealed few significant differences on questionnaire returns in relation to their perceptions of the roles of non-teaching personnel. Following interviews, we concluded that this was because several of the partnerships had shared their responses prior to returning individual forms and had, essentially, written similar answers (despite being asked to complete the return as an individual)! This latter probably says something about the fact that classroom assistants and nursery nurses have rarely, in the past, been asked for their individual opinions, a statement confirmed during interviews.

Responses to questionnaires and semi-structured interview questions gave some useful insights and many variations in regard to practitioners' perceptions of their own, and their partner's, role and the views of head teachers, as shown in the following comments (CA = classroom assistant; HT = head teacher; T = teacher).

Roles of classroom assistants/specialist teacher assistants in KS1 classrooms

'I'm forever moving on to the next thing or the next class.' (CA)

'Very deep curriculum stuff is not really relevant to CAs' (HT)

'She has more time to pick up on emotional problems.' (T)

'They are not here to wash the paint pots. These people are professional but untrained.' (HT)

'The STAs are now involved in special group work, giving additional support to those children who need to enhance their skills. There used to be a time when they did the jobs around the school.' (HT)

Roles in the nursery

'The nursery staff are clear on their role dimensions.' (HT)

Descriptions of day-to-day actions by nursery nurses (NN) and nursery teachers (NT):

'We swap, alternate, rotate, interchange, take turns.' (NTs and NNs)

'The buck stops here.' (NT)

'It is my final responsibility but I want the NN to have as much say as myself.' (NT)

'If something goes wrong it is my responsibility . . . but I suppose that is also true if it goes right.' (NT)

'I think that it is important that parents know who is the NT and who is the NN and who is making the decisions.' (HT)

It became clear that while the overall verbal expression of practitioners was that they are doing similar things in the classroom context, differences were perceived in relation to levels and types of responsibility, for example, for curriculum, planning, social welfare and resources. Heads seem generally clearer than the staff themselves of the differences in the roles (though this is not always reflected in policies). At nursery level, the role of nursery nurse is much more clearly defined than for the classroom assistant at KS1 level, where there is uncertainty as to what is the present role, given the shift in emphasis from teacher support to supporting children's learning. In fact, in several schools, concern was expressed over just who is to do the more mundane tasks if classroom assistants are increasingly adopting a teaching role!

Children's perceptions

Children were prompted in giving their interview responses by the use of photographs, taken with a Polaroid camera during the observed session. Generally at KS1, whilst emphasizing that everyone was there as 'helpers', children clearly perceived some aspects of the teachers' roles as being prominent. At nursery level, children's comments revealed that there are more similarities between the relationships of the nursery nurse and nursery teacher but analysis of the data suggests a definite similarity between the KS1 teachers and the nursery teachers, with the two groups gaining more responsibility and control over children in the children's eyes. The classroom assistant and nursery nurse play a similar role to one another, as more of a carer and helper (for a longer discussion see Moyles and Suschitzky, in press).

Children's comments included the following.

KS1 children of teachers

'The teacher is the boss.'

'Mrs. M [teacher] has to stay in this classroom – the classroom belongs to her.'

'The teacher does the register.'

'The teacher sits in the teacher's chair.'

'She [the teacher] gives us maths tasks.'

'She says "Very good"!'

'She helps us with our work.'

KS1 children of classroom assistants

'She is sometimes a teacher.'

'She does things with us/for us.'

'She has to watch us.'

'She helps us if we get stuck.'

'She helps us with jobs.'

Nursery children of teachers

'The teacher is a grown up.'

'She talks to children what are naughty.'

'Miss M – she talks to mummies.'

Nursery children of nursery nurses

'Mrs C gets toys out for us.'

'Mrs W [NN] helps Miss B [NT] as well.'

'Well, you see, Miss G helps us if we hurt ourselves.'

Sadly, from our point of view, few of the children at either phase (slightly more in the nursery) perceived the practitioners' roles as being involved with *play*. Most children felt that the adults did not play because 'They are grown-ups' or that they are 'Too busy to play!' (Moyles in press). This, and other findings, were mainly supported during interviews when all practitioners (although less so classroom assistants) felt that play was a vital feature of classroom practice but that there was frequently insufficient time for adults to be involved. (Incidentally, our view was also that training in how to meet curriculum intentions through play was vitally needed for all practitioners.)

Those areas of significant difference in perceptions of role included planning and curriculum involvement as well as training opportunities.

Planning for children's activities

The most significant difference emerging from both age phases was the greater part played by teachers in the planning of activities. Whereas much planning in the nursery was said to be 'joint' or 'team', this often in reality meant that there was an overall discussion about the topic or areas to be covered, the teacher then developed the overall plan and individuals within the team were responsible for generating one or more activities to meet the curriculum intentions. At KS1 teachers did most of the planning, to the extent that classroom assistants had little idea of the learning intentions behind activities (see Table 10.1). Planning is another area in which there is training potential for all personnel.

Table 10.1 Involvement in planning for children's activities

Involvement in planning	T(%)	NT(%)	NN(%)	CA(%)
I do all the planning	82.4	48	1	0.0
I do no planning	0.0	0.0	7	27.8
I plan for certain groups only	0.0	3	9	31.6
I plan for certain individuals only	1.5	0.0	0.0	17.7
Other (team planning)	16.2	49	83	22.8

* T = teacher; NT = nursery teacher; NN = nursery nurse; CA = classroom assistant.

Curriculum involvement

In relation to curriculum involvement of practitioners at KS1 and Nursery, some small differences were revealed as shown in Figure 10.1. Essentially, this shows that:

• teachers at both phases have greater involvement in all aspects of the curriculum, with nursery teachers having greater involvement than KS1 teachers except history and geography;

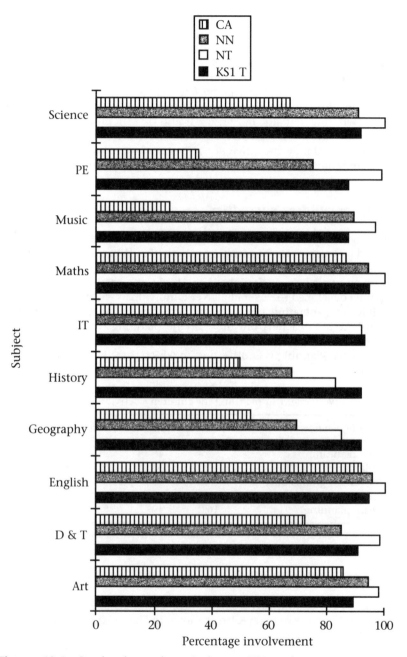

Figure 10.1 Graph of stated curriculum – KS1 and nursery practitioners. CA = classroom assistant; NN = nursery nurse; NT = nursery teacher; KS1 T = Key Stage 1 teacher

- classroom assistants have less involvement in all aspects of the curriculum than other practitioners, especially music and PE and spend the highest proportions of their time in art, maths and English activities;
- nursery nurses spend more time on curriculum aspects generally than classroom assistants but equally spend least time on music and PE and a greater part of their time on maths, English and art.

Overall, the graph makes it clear, as might be expected, that teachers at both phases have greater involvement (and responsibility) for the curriculum than their non-teaching partners. This appeared to be related not only to this emphasis in their initial training but was also related to the status this conferred upon teachers. It could also be conjectured that much of teachers' in-service training over the last decade has been focused upon curriculum delivery. This has not been so, on the whole, for either of the other groups.

Nature of roles during observations

Certain categories were identified from the theoretical and practical underpinnings of the study against which we tracked practitioners' roles during observations to establish similarities and differences. Tracking and frequency data (of behaviours/actions) was collected directly in the classroom. In addition, video clips were taken and later analysed. The overall criteria are shown in Table 10.2.

Table 10.2 Criteria for role categorization used during tracking

Criterion	Explanation/justification
Management	Adult organizing the children, resources or other adults in order to ensure the smooth running of the learning environment (Moyles 1992)
Monitoring learning	Adult supervising children to ensure concentration on task, encouragement and assistance with understanding task demands
Monitoring behaviour	Adult supervising children to ensure safety and appropriate social behaviour
Supporting learning	Adult interacting with child/children to extend knowledge and develop concepts and skills
Direct instruction	Adult providing information or explanation including story-telling
Social/physical needs	Adult involved in meeting a child's social or physical needs
Assessment	Assessment of children by formal (explicit) means
Recording	Making a record of outcomes or assessments
Resource provision	Preparation, maintenance or organization of resources
Control	Adult behaviour primarily concerned with controlling the behaviour of children

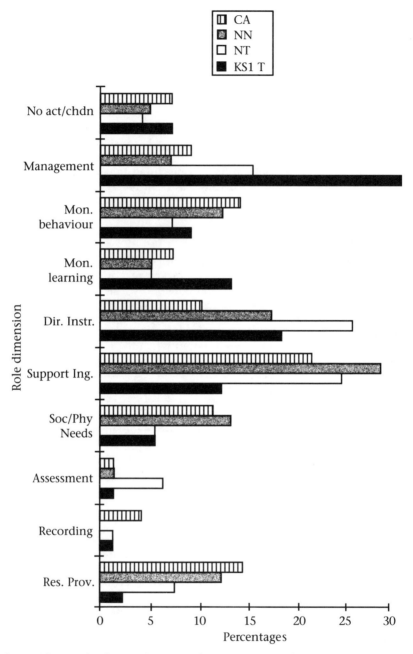

Figure 10.2 Roles during classroom observation. CA = classroom assistant; NN = nursery nurse; NT = nursery teacher; KS1 T = Key Stage 1 teacher

Figure 10.2 shows the roles as undertaken during this observational tracking by the various practitioners.

This gives evidence, amongst other things, that in relation to other practitioners:

- KS1 teachers occupy a far greater managerial role;
- nursery nurses spend more time supporting children's learning and dealing with social/physical needs than others;
- classroom assistants spend more time in monitoring behaviour and in resource provision;
- nursery teachers spend more time in direct instruction, that is, in directly *teaching* (usually groups of) children and on assessment.

Is it interesting to conjecture how far these roles relate to individual's training, be it formal or informal.

Perhaps surprisingly, few practitioners during the observations spent any time on *explicit* assessment and recording, despite much focus in teacher, nursery nurse and STA training courses, though they may have felt that this tied them down too specifically when an observer was in the classroom. Interviews revealed that some assessment was happening but this was implicit within the activity being undertaken.

Quality of children's learning experiences

Of greatest concern to us as early years teachers ourselves are the implications for the quality of children's learning experiences at the hands of differentially trained practitioners. This was the hardest aspect of the research and required greater subjective interpretation of data than other phases, not least because separating out teaching and learning is almost impossible! As we had no way of knowing the capabilities of individual children involved in research occupying such a short time-scale and with small numbers of participants, it was impossible to evaluate quality learning *per se*. Instead, we tried to establish through the field observations and video whether certain attributes were more frequently shown by one practitioner than another in relation to the quality of their teaching and, by implication, children's learning. Eventually this led to a definition entitled 'mainly exhibit' which meant that for at least a quarter of the time, the specific practitioner was providing evidence of fulfilling the criteria on Ofsted's Inspection Schedule 5.2 in relation to the quality of teaching. Some aspects, of course (marked with * on Table 10.3), were not shown on the video analysis because of the limited duration of the classroom observation, i.e. about 6–7 minutes of video per person.

As can be seen, teachers in both phases exhibited more of the characteristics identified by Ofsted than either of the other two groups. The implication of this is that they would be in a better position to provide quality learning experiences for children.

Table 10.3   Ofsted Inspection Schedule 5.2

Criteria for quality teaching	KS1 Ts' mainly exhibit	NTs' mainly exhibit	NNs' mainly exhibit	CAs mainly exhibit
Have secure knowledge/understanding of subjects/areas	√	√		
Set high expectations/clear objectives		√	√	
Challenge pupils	√			
Deepen children's knowledge and understanding	√	√		
Match methods to curriculum objectives	√	√		
Match methods to needs of children	√	√	√	
Manage children well	√	√	√	√
Use resources effectively	√	√	√	√
Assess children's work thoroughly and constructively		√		
Use assessment to inform teaching	√			
Ask relevant questions	√			
Gather resources children will need	√	√	√	√
Differentiate	√	√	√	√
Use exposition/explanation that is lively and well structured	√			√
Probe children's knowledge and understanding	√			
Offer purposeful practical activity (e.g. play)		√	√	√
Allow children to think about what they have learned				
Meet special education needs (SEN) code of practice requirements	*	*	*	√
Plan effectively	√	*	*	
Provide continuity/progression	√	*	*	
Create effective systems for assessing children which are used to inform curriculum planning	*	*	*	*
Ensure sound record-keeping systems	*	*	*	*

* Not shown on video analysis.

Some findings, implications and issues

General

Both this research and previous research into nursery practitioners' roles (Moyles and Suschitzky 1994) revealed that they *feel* strongly that both are doing the same job and bend over backwards to be seen by the outside world to be 'equal'. This is not always the case when the reality of the situation is analysed or, indeed, in the underlying perceptions of both groups. Neither does this match the content of their initial training.

This same sense of equality is increasingly the case with classroom assistants, including those trained to specialist teacher assistant level, who showed evidence of modelling themselves on the teacher with whom they mainly worked. Our research revealed that, in reality, non-teaching staff are only doing the same job at a basic day-to-day *operational* or functional level even, to a certain extent, in the nursery. Children appeared to understand from the general overt behaviours of the two groups that there was a differential in the underlying roles related to status.

Relationships between differentially trained practitioners are generally good but are based on implicit rather than explicit expectations in both KS1 and nurseries. This to a certain extent has happened because of the teacher 'modelling' feature identified above in that when someone else's style and practice appears to match their own, it is easy for teachers to believe that these other people have the same underlying knowledge and understanding.

From a traditional role of 'doing the chores' and supporting teachers' work directly, classroom assistants have inexorably moved towards a teaching role and a greater involvement in children's learning. Nursery nurses' traditional role as 'carers' with concern for children's social and emotional needs as well as support for the 'chores' has changed little, though there is a slight increase in their own and teachers' expectations that they can and do fulfil teaching roles which include expectations for curriculum implementation, both *Desirable Outcomes* (SCAA 1996) and the lead-in to the KS1 curriculum, an expectation rarely fulfilled through training.

Clearly, with research of this scale, it is impossible to develop every aspect touched on above. From the overall findings and recommendations, we have picked out a few specific findings under headings related to the questions identified at the start. The evidence for making these decisions is, in some cases, given above: in others, readers must refer to the full research reports for greater support as well as to other chapters in this book.

1   Is employing non-teaching staff necessarily a 'good' thing – can anyone teach young children?
All practitioners showed themselves to be keen on their roles and determined to do their best for the children in their care. The best specialist teacher assistants and nursery nurses recognized that their training had given them some additional knowledge to that of untrained personnel but also recognized the greater level of conceptual knowledge acquired in teacher training.

Some classroom assistants and nursery nurses indicated that they felt their role to be similar to that of a teacher but, in each case, when analysed, this usually meant at a practical and procedural rather than at a theoretical or conceptual level, confirming, to some extent, the expert/novice dimensions indicated by the researchers whose work formed the theoretical basis of our study.

Many classroom assistants showed evidence of operating at a procedural level in that they were intent on children following through an activity to a successful outcome – hence the title of this chapter – even to the extent of doing the work for them, showing their difficulties in understanding young children's need for independence and the need for training in this aspect. Several teachers actually got frustrated by classroom assistants' insistence on doing things for the children but it was rare that they attempted to redress this situation through on-the-spot training. STA-trained personnel were better than untrained classroom assistants at motivating children but were still not as good as teachers in dealing spontaneously and building upon children's responses.

On the whole, then, we found teachers to be better at meeting the overall curriculum needs of children because of their greater emphasis on the processes of children's learning. Nursery nurses give greater focus to the child as a whole and classroom assistants concentrate on products.

2   What implications do employment practices have for the day-to-day roles each practitioner fulfils and how supportive are the established frameworks within which they work?

At the level of responsibility and status, teachers in both phases have a more extensive role in schools. In day-to-day actions, all practitioners are involved in many of the same jobs, particularly in working with children. Teachers tend to operate more in working with the whole class; the trend is for nursery nurses and classroom assistants to spend a greater portion of their time with groups and individuals. Teachers in both phases carry a greater management or 'overseeing' role and, it could be argued, might consider focusing their greater curriculum and learning processes knowledge in group and individual teaching whilst the more routine jobs of monitoring children's activities could be undertaken in KS1 classes by classroom assistants given the 'common-sense' nature of this task.

At KS1, there is little time in which teachers can involve classroom assistants in planning. The employment of classroom assistants only in school time has significant implications for the time available for teachers to convey to them the learning intentions behind planning curriculum activities or training them in general classroom skills. Hence, a common experience for the researchers was to find that the classroom assistant arrived at 9 o'clock in the morning and was asked by the teacher to achieve something with the children, in one example, 'Can you please do number bonds to ten with the Red Group?' This classroom assistant later confessed that she had no idea what the teacher meant and the children spent the morning grouping Unifix cubes into columns of ten in a range of various colours. On another occasion, the classroom assistant was asked to do some weighing and, quite inappropriately, sent the children off to find fir cones and other small items against which to balance a shoe in a 'bucket-and-chain' scale.

At nursery level, the time implications are different with nursery nurses spending time outside school hours in planning meetings, usually lunchtimes. However, in this situation, because the teams work together day-in and day-out they assume an underlying knowledge exists between the two groups of adults which, it was revealed in interviews and observations, is not always the case. As an example, there was an implicit assumption among some teachers that the nursery nurse, because of her initial training, was dealing with the 'social' side of things more frequently than, in fact, they were in our analysis of their activities.

Head teachers and governors need to establish policies for the employment, deployment and training of non-teaching personnel. In most schools, this was fairly ad hoc for classroom assistants and the management of nursery nurses' roles in nurseries was often left very much to the discretion of the teacher, most of whom had received no training in team management and support.

3   Is there a difference in the quality of children's learning experiences when working with differentially trained adults?
Given that the Ofsted criteria (used in determining the quality of teaching and, by implication, the quality of the children's learning experiences) is about the quality of teaching and is equally applied to other classroom adults during the inspection process, the findings (shown in Table 10.3) are interesting from the point of view of 'expert' and 'novice' practitioners, on which were based the theoretical aspects of our research. It raises a further question as to whether different criteria should be used for differentially trained personnel or whether there should be some kind of sliding scale operating from novice-to-expert characteristics. In fact, it also begs the question of what are the different competencies one would expect to find in differentially trained personnel and how should these be applied in a training context.

The vast range of subjects and contents which now makes up the KS1 curriculum (and by implication the *Desirable Learning Outcomes* 'curriculum' which leads into it), is difficult enough for teachers to handle. Classroom assistants, in particular, are often employed to support this aspect of teachers' work yet get little, if any, training themselves in deepening and extending their own curriculum knowledge. This is similarly the case for nursery nurses whose original training has a greater child development and observational focus than one based in subject curriculum. Few nursery nurses, and even fewer classroom assistants, attend curriculum staff meetings and, when they do, they are not always able to understand the ideas presented. Yet these people are expected to undertake a curriculum teaching role alongside teachers and, mainly, under the direction of the teachers. However, as teachers have little time in which to explain the learning processes involved for children in different aspects of the curriculum, the experience then given to the children by nursery nurses and classroom assistants is often not at the same conceptual level as that which is undertaken with the teacher – and we cannot expect it to be! As a consequence, we found that classroom assistants concentrate almost wholly on the products of learning and nursery nurses in reality focus on social aspects sometimes to the exclusion of curriculum content, though their perception of involvement is different as we saw earlier.

*4   What training opportunities need to be available for all those who
operate in 'classroom teams' of differentially trained personnel?*
Clearly, the implications for training in relation to the research are huge. They
are also dependent upon a clear job description being given to all non-teaching staff (only about one-quarter of nursery nurses in the original sample had
a job description, many of these supplied as pro-formas by the LEA, and less
than 20 per cent of classroom assistants had job descriptions). Without this, it
is difficult to know what skills and competencies are required of non-teaching
personnel. Having to identify (and audit) their role would be a useful strategy
for most schools to apply as it would be the beginning of identifying strengths
and needs and, by implication, competencies and training needs. Alongside
an audit of school requirements for non-teaching personnel and a matching
of people to jobs, this could also add immeasurably to overall school effective-
ness.

The big issue is . . . *IF* both classroom assistants and nursery nurses are
expected and required to undertake greater teaching roles – and we feel that
this may be debatable – then further in-service professional development and
training is vital to upgrade their knowledge and skills to a greater conceptual
level particularly in relation to the implementation of required curriculum
areas.

Alternatively, practitioners, especially nursery nurses, could be acknowledged for the skills and knowledge they already possess through training and
experience, and utilized in a way which matches their strengths and initial
training. Nursery nurses require in-service training which builds on the fact
that they have successfully completed two years of full-time further education
and most would appreciate, for example, enhancing and extend their well-
developed skills of child observation and assessment or deepening their
understanding of learning through play in the contexts of the under-fives,
and national curricula. This represents a very different form of training than
that required by many classroom assistants, particularly those who have
received no form of training to undertake their increasingly diverse role.

Many non-teaching staff have little opportunity for training other than the
specialist teacher assistant courses open to some classroom assistants dependent mainly upon geographical location and school priorities. Yet we found
that they need support in changing their roles from the traditional support of
teachers to understanding the complexities of children's learning and the
kind of planning and assessment needed to support quality experiences.
Given that their own education ranges from leaving school with no qualifications whatsoever (8 out of 81 questionnaire respondents) to those already
holding degrees and diplomas (13 out of 81), the whole question of accreditation of prior learning is likely to become a real issue if training for classroom
assistants is to be developed appropriately.

If the number of multidisciplinary centres increases, as seems likely, present
forms of training will need to be reviewed. STA training, with its heavy
emphasis on the National Curriculum and 3Rs is unlikely to be appropriate
for those teaching under-fives. All those involved will need a better understanding of the individual roles different team members fulfil and how each

person's skills can be identified, acknowledged, documented and, as a consequence, valued in order to set this alongside the dimensions of the roles needing to be fulfilled by each team member. All those in multdisiciplinary setting may well, for example, need training in understanding the child in the family and citizenship contexts.

Teachers generally like having other adults around in the classroom and *feel* that children get a 'better deal' though no systematic monitoring of this appeared to be undertaken in schools. Teachers need training in how to manage teams of teaching and non-teaching personnel who now regularly share the classroom activities and evaluate the impact of that role upon the children's experiences. If the current content on teacher training courses was not so overloaded one might hazard the opinion that more should be included in such courses for intending teachers. In similar vein, as the classroom assistants' and nursery nurses' roles move towards a more teaching-based dimension, one could also argue that teacher training should include a greater emphasis on child development to give extended knowledge of 'whole-child' issues to teachers. Or is this yet another of those role issues which in itself requires acknowledgement, i.e. that teachers should be valued for their main contribution to curriculum aspects? If all personnel, especially nursery teachers and nurses, continue with their intention of 'being the same' in all day-to-day matters, surely neither is being fair to themselves or to the role they could most usefully fulfil on the basis of their initial training and continued professional development?

Finale

Many questions remain from this research not least of which is what do we mean by 'teacher' and 'professional' in terms of those not actually qualified as teachers. These terms have been used extensively and interchangeably by practitioners in the research and appear to us to be at the heart of deciding on a continuum of competencies which it may be possible to determine on the scale of novice to expert (see Eraut 1994; and Chapter 7). Such competencies would allow roles within classroom teams to be clearly defined and appropriate remuneration and training given to those operating at various different levels within the framework. If roles were clearly defined and acknowledged, it is possible that the whole issue of 'status' amongst differentially trained staff could at last be laid to rest and everyone valued for their contribution to the whole. This would undoubtedly be to the ultimate benefit of the quality of the learning experiences of the children with whom they work.

(11) | A European perspective on early years training

Pamela Oberhuemer

In recent years a number of cross-national case studies and reviews have helped to extend our knowledge of early childhood education and care in different cultural, economic, historical and ideological contexts. This strand of research, conducted both across continents (e.g. Olmsted and Weikart 1989; Cochran 1993; Lubeck 1993) and at a European level (e.g. European Commission Network on Childcare 1996b; Penn 1997b) reflects a growing interest internationally not only in learning more about policy and practice in different societies, but also in developing conceptual frameworks for comparing different systems of early childhood education and care.

This interest is not, of course, confined to researchers. Amid a generally growing awareness of the importance of transnational perspectives, policy-makers, employers and training institutions are increasingly referring to cross-country studies and reports. Not least, early childhood practitioners are also showing interest in a comparative perspective, both as a form of 'taking stock' professionally, and as a necessary knowledge base for considering the possibility of job mobility.

The aim of a recent study carried out by a team of researchers at the State Institute of Early Childhood Education and Research in Munich[1] was to help elaborate that knowledge base by collating data on early childhood provision and staff training in the 15 European Union countries (Oberhuemer and Ulich 1997). What, we asked, is the situation facing early childhood educators if they wish to work in another European country? Will the level of training expected be the same? Will the approach to work with children and with parents be similar? Will they meet with similar concepts of professionalism in their workfield? In order to highlight the complexity of these questions, I shall start with two possible scenarios.

Scenarios

Jens: from Denmark to France

Jens is contemplating a move from his home town Århus in Denmark to Paris, where his French girlfriend is studying history. Jens is a qualified *paedagog* and has recently completed a 3½-year course of training at a higher education vocational college. He now works in an early childhood centre for 0- to 6-year-olds. Jens' training (a new amalgamated scheme introduced in 1992) has prepared him for work not only in early childhood settings – which in Denmark may be a day nursery for under-threes, a kindergarten for 3- to 6-year-olds or an 'age-integrated' centre for a wider age range – but also for work with older children and adults in a variety of settings outside the compulsory education system.

During a visit to Paris, Jens informs himself about the possibility of employment in a similar institution in France, and is surprised to find himself confronted with a very different system. For example, staff in the dominant early childhood institution, the *école maternelle*, attended by nearly all children aged 3 to 6 years and by a large number of 2-year-olds, are also qualified to work within the compulsory education system as primary school teachers, and this is a central aspect of their professional preparation. Their two-year postgraduate training follows a successfully completed three-year university degree course. Preschool teachers in France (*professeurs des écoles*) work within a centralized, state-regulated curricular and administrative framework. This contrasts with Denmark, where there is no prescribed curriculum and the administration of early childhood centres is decentralized, each centre having considerable autonomy. Through a system of parent boards in early childhood centres, parents in Denmark are entitled to participate in decision-making processes concerning the programme and budget allocation of each centre. Again, this differs considerably from the situation in France, where parental involvement in the *écoles maternelles* is rare, and does not appear to be part of the prevailing 'professional culture'. This professional culture has evolved over a long period of time, reaching back to 1881, when institutions for young children were officially integrated into the public education system. In Denmark, early childhood provision is not part of the education administration, and the professional self-image of *paedagoger* is very different from that of school teachers.

Maria: from Germany to Greece

Maria's parents are Greek. They came to West Germany during the early 1970s, a time when many migrant workers left their homes in southern European countries to seek employment in northern Europe. Maria, born in Germany, is bilingual. She has successfully completed a three-year course of training as an educator (*Erzieherin*) and has worked for two years in a kindergarten. In recent years she has returned to Greece at regular intervals, keen to strengthen her links with her family origins. Maria now wishes to work in Thessaloniki for a while and sets about finding a job there. First of all she discovers that there are two main types of institution for young children: half-day kindergartens for 3- to 6-year-olds under the responsibility of the Ministry of Education, and full-day centres for 0- to 6-year-olds under the Ministry of Social Affairs. For each kind of institution there is a different kind of training. Kindergarten pedagogues in Greece have a four-year, university-level training specializing in the age range 3 to 6 years. Staff trained for work in the full-day centres complete a 3½-year course at a polytechnic-type institution, with three years based at college and six months in a workplace setting. Both these schemes focus on the early years, whereas in Germany, *Erzieherinnen* have an intermediate-level, broad-base training for work in a variety of facilities with children and adolescents of different ages, for example, kindergartens, day nurseries, afternoon provision for school-age children, open-door youth centres. Maria is surprised to learn that kindergarten educators in Greece often have to wait up to nine years before finding a job in a kindergarten. Unemployment is high, and permanent posts in the state-maintained kindergartens (*nipiagogia*), where staff have civil servant status, are much sought after. Because of the employment situation, they often initially seek a job in one of the full-time centres. In some cases, then, it may be that two sets of professionals are competing for the same job. What does this mean for Maria? Quite apart from the lower formal level of Maria's training, which may also be a hindrance, it would seem that the only realistic option open to her is to seek work in a private day-care centre – a form of provision which is not common in Greece.

These two vignettes illustrate that – despite the common link of a workplace in and training for the early childhood field – there may be a number of initial obstacles to overcome when professionals trained in one country seek work in another. One of the immediate challenges for administrators in all countries is to try and ease these transitions as much as possible. Training goals, status, and content focus – and the resulting self-image of the professionals – are closely linked to cultural notions, historical traditions and administrative practices in the field of early childhood education and care. I should now like to consider the link between different systems of administration of centre-based provision and training in a more systematic way.

Training in the context of different administrative systems

There are three basic models of administration of publicly-funded, centre-based provision for young children. In Belgium, France, Italy, Luxembourg and The Netherlands, childcare and education services are split administratively between 'welfare' and 'education', with different forms of provision catering for different age-groups, and different forms of training for work in institutions in each sector (see Table 11.1). Staff working in institutions under the welfare administration are more likely to have a health or social care qualification and are on the whole trained at a lower level and for a shorter

Table 11.1 'Split' systems of provision and training

Country	Welfare: publicly-funded, centre-based provision for age group/years	Education: publicly-funded, centre-based provision for age group/years
Belgium	0–2½	2½–6
France	0–2½	2½–6
Italy	0–3	3–6
Luxembourg	0–4	4–6
The Netherlands	0–4	4–5

Training schemes for work in provision under welfare administration: mainly paramedical or social care orientation.
Training schemes for work in provision under education administration: educational orientation.

period of time than their colleagues in the education system. While France is exceptional among these countries in requiring a three-year, post-18 training for work in all centre-based provision for children under 3 years, including parent cooperatives, there is nevertheless a divide between the staff who work in the two sectors. Children in a *crèche collective* will be supervised by a *puéricultrice* with a three-year nursing qualification followed by a one-year specialist training for work with children, or an *éducatrice* with a 3-year vocational college training in education and social care. Children over the age of 3 years who attend an *école maternelle* will, as pointed out earlier, be supervised by staff trained at postgraduate level both as primary and nursery school teachers.

Countries with parallel systems – Greece, Ireland, Portugal and the UK – have institutions both under welfare and education which overlap for certain age-groups, mostly for the two or three years preceding compulsory school

Table 11.2 'Parallel' systems of provision and training

Country	Welfare: publicly-funded, centre-based provision for age group/years	Education: publicly-funded, centre-based provision for age group/years
Greece	0–6	2–6
Ireland	0–6½	4–6
Portugal	0–3–6	3–6
UK (England, Wales, Scotland, Northern Ireland)	0–4/5	3–4/5

Different training schemes for work in different kinds of provision in Greece, Ireland and the UK.
Same training scheme for work in different forms of provision in Portugal.

entry age (see Table 11. 2). In Greece, Ireland and the UK, training schemes for work in the different kinds of provision differ, with a higher formal level of training for work in the education system (in all three countries at university).

Four countries have chosen to coordinate all forms of provision either under welfare or under education. These countries – Denmark, Finland, Spain and Sweden – and to a lesser and less coherent extent Germany and Austria – have systems of training which generally cover a wider age-range than the countries with split or overlapping systems (see Table 11.3). These are either training schemes with a focus on early childhood settings prior to compulsory education, as in Finland, Spain and Sweden, or they offer a broad-base training for work both in early childhood and in other forms of provision for children and young people (Germany) or, additionally, for work with adults with special needs (Denmark). An important link between these countries, in particular between Finland, Spain, Sweden and Denmark, is that in terms of official policy they consider the very early years – before the age of 3 years – to be an important phase in the young child's education, and not just a matter of providing care facilities for working parents. This was one of the main ideas behind the 1990 reform of the education system in Spain, where all provision for children from 0 to 6 years now comes under the Ministry of Education.

Having looked at different administrative systems of early childhood provision and the place of training within these, I shall now turn to some selected aspects of training and consider these in a comparative light (for a more comprehensive account, see Oberhuemer and Ulich 1997).

Table 11.3 'Coordination' systems of provision (i.e. under the responsibility of one administrative system)

Country	Welfare/youth authorities: publicly-funded, centre-based provision for age group/years	Education: publicly-funded, centre-based provision for age group/years
Denmark	0–3–7	
Finland	0–7	
Spain		0–3–6
Sweden		0–7
Austria	0–3–6	
Germany	0–3–6*	

Training just for age group indicated: in Finland, Spain and Sweden.
Training beyond the age group indicated (broad-base training): in Denmark, Germany (to a certain extent in Austria).
* In two of the 16 federal states (*Länder*), kindergartens come under the education ministry; in some federal states (in particular Northrhein–Westfalia) there are age-integrated institutions for 0–6-year-olds.

Entry requirements

In most European Union countries, the majority of children attending provision during the two years prior to compulsory schooling – and in some
countries also younger children – are in groups led by staff educated and
trained at a formally high level. In all countries excepting Germany, Austria
and Italy, the usual requirement is a minimum of 12 years' schooling and the
grades or examinations considered appropriate either for entry to university
or tertiary level vocational education. In two of the countries with 'parallel'
systems (see Table 11.2) – the UK and Ireland – this applies only to the staff
working in early childhood institutions under the education system. Staff in
publicly-funded provision under the welfare system (in both countries the
level of provision is very low) are trained either at a lower level (UK) or for a
shorter period of time (Ireland). In addition, parent-managed playgroups are
a widespread form of provision for 3- and 4-year-olds in both countries. In
the UK for example, official guidelines to the Children Act 1989 (Department
of Health 1991: 33, 43) state that local authorities 'should encourage' independent providers to develop training policies, and that at least half of the
staff in sessional day care such as playgroups 'should' hold a 'relevant' qualification or have completed a training course specified by the Pre-School Playgroups Association (now Pre-School Learning Alliance) or other voluntary
body. However, no binding standards concerning the level and quality of the
qualifications are stipulated.

A recent trend in several countries is the increased introduction of flexible
entry routes for mature students with prior learning experience. One example
is the training scheme for *paedagoger* in Denmark. Course requirements are
either a university entrance qualification or a differentiated point system for
'other' candidates which is used to evaluate prior education, training, employment and life experiences. Such candidates make up 80 per cent of the intake,
and consequently the average age among students is considerably higher
(approximately 28 years) than in courses attended predominantly by school-
leavers. The recently introduced interdisciplinary degrees in Early Childhood
Studies at some UK universities are proceeding along similar lines. For example, at North London University, a part-time, modular degree course
accepts candidates who have work experience with young children without
the usual formal academic entry requirements (Smidt 1993: 24). As yet, these
courses do not lead to a professional qualification with recognized status, but
many experts in the field see this approach as the way forward (National
Children's Bureau 1993: 6), rather than the competence-based National
Vocational Qualifications scheme (Calder 1995: 49ff.). These courses have
now developed further (see Chapter 8). Most degree courses do not, of course,
in themselves lead to a professional qualification.

The field of early education and care has traditionally been a women's
domain. The involvement of men in, and for, this work remains an issue, one
that it is not possible to elaborate on here. However, with regard to training it
is important to note that, while most schemes do not attract men in significant numbers, the Danish scheme for *paedagoger* does. This could well have

something to do with the generally high status accorded to professional educare in Denmark, or with the fact that job prospects are currently favourable. A further explanation is perhaps the broadly defined framework of the profession, one which not only allows for mobility and side-stepping within the profession, but also provides a basis for developing a professional culture which is appealing to both women and men.

Age-related specialization and/or generalization?

Countries differ in approach when it comes to questions of age-related generalization and/or specialization in the preparation for work with young children. In Finland, Sweden and Spain, for example, staff with group responsibility in the main form of publicly-funded early childhood provision are trained for the age group 0–6 or 0–7 years, depending on compulsory school entry age. A number of schemes focus more specifically on the years immediately preceding school entry, e.g. in Greece (*nipiagogos*) on the 3- to 6-year-olds, in Belgium (*institutrice de maternelle/kleuterleid(st)er/Kindergärtnerin*) on the 2½- to 6-year-olds, in Luxembourg (*instituteur de l'éducation préscolaire*) on the 4- to 6-year-olds, in Austria (*Kindergärtnerin*) on the 3- to 6-year-olds. By contrast, Denmark's *paedagoger*, as previously noted, are qualified to work not only in all forms of early childhood services but also with school-age children in out-of-school provision and in various services for children and adults with special needs. A similar kind of broad-based training is that of the *éducateur* and the *éducateur gradué* in Luxembourg, two recently upgraded professional qualifications for working in services for children and adults (but not with children in the state-run preschool institutions which since 1992 have been compulsory for 4- and 5-year-olds). Another case is Germany: although the majority of educators (*Erzieherinnen*) work in kindergartens, they are trained to work with a much wider age range (theoretically from birth to the age of 27).

Courses training for a broader age range obviously offer candidates more flexibility in terms of job market options. Proponents also argue that the knowledge base (such as educational theory, human development, childhood as a social phenomenon, family studies, policy developments), skills (for example, cultural awareness, group management, observation and planning) and understanding needed for work with children of different ages and in different settings are similar, and that true specialization can start only in the concrete workplace setting. Others argue for the need to focus more specifically on the early years. As the need for flexible social and educational institutions grows, these lines of argument will need to be discussed more widely.

Course content

Comparing course content is a difficult task. First, most higher education institutions have considerable autonomy in the development of curricula, although this is not the case in the UK, as is clear from Chapter 5. Second, our data base (Oberhuemer and Ulich 1997) does not allow us to make very explicit comments, since to do this, a detailed analysis of reading lists, seminar topics, lectures, etc. would be necessary, and this was not possible within the wide remit of our study. A further difficulty is that commonly used terms for areas of study (for example, 'education', 'developmental psychology', 'professional studies') may in fact reflect quite different approaches and contents. We noted differences of emphasis on general education subjects, such as the extent of foreign language instruction in the training curriculum. We also noted in the countries with differences of content emphasis in the training required to work with children under 3 years of age (paramedical, healthcare orientation) and with those from 3 or 4 up to compulsory school entry (educational orientation) that this dichotomy has been a focus of critique for some years now, with experts in the field stressing the need for a more educational emphasis in the work with very young children. However, these demands have not as yet been transformed into significant policy reform.

A challenge to be met by all course compilers concerns recent critiques on both implicit and explicit assumptions concerning the 'universal' nature of theories of child development. In this connection, Sally Lubeck (1996) – reflecting on the situation in the USA – has suggested that some of the prevailing tenets of early education need to be seen in a new light.

Training and the role of research

In the few countries where the main form of training for work in early childhood provision is not integrated into tertiary education (Austria, Germany, Italy), applied research and development work in the early childhood field are not systematically interlinked with initial training. However, the fact that in many countries courses are now offered at university level, and consequently require research commitment on the part of course tutors, means that the early years are becoming a more sustained focus of practice-related research.

As students are encouraged to participate in fieldwork, to observe children closely, to learn about different kinds of research methodology, to question varying aims and practices in early childhood education, so the potentially positive effects on innovation, critical reflection and professional self-image within the field will grow. Generally, however, this field is still under-researched, and a wider debate on different research paradigms and methodologies is necessary (David 1996b). For example, calls to develop more expertise in qualitative and interpretive research methods, in collaborative work, and generally in studies that locate children's experience in specific cultural and historical contexts (Graue and Walsh 1995: 150) need to be taken seriously if early childhood research and practice are to effectively improve their own field-specific techniques of self-appraisal and quality development.

The training of support staff

If we look at the main forms of provision in each country, three patterns of ancillary staffing emerge (Oberhuemer and Ulich 1997: 23):

- professionals with group responsibility are supported by a qualified worker who has completed a (mostly two-year) post-16 full-time training scheme, such as the *Kinderpflegerin* in German kindergartens, the *barnskötare* in Swedish early childhood centres, or nursery nurses in British nursery schools;
- staff with group responsibility are assisted by paid, non-qualified auxiliaries who are expected or obliged to attend courses offered by the local authorities, such as the assistants in the French *écoles maternelles* or in the Danish day-care centres;
- professionals with group responsibility are not assisted by paid or voluntary helpers, such as the teachers in junior infant and senior infant classes in Irish primary schools or the kindergarten pedagogues in Greece.

A recent development in some countries is the trend towards replacing training schemes focusing on childcare alone (and, it is argued, on a limited choice of workfields) with broad-based schemes for work in a variety of social care and socio-pedagogic settings. Examples are to be found in Finland and the Netherlands, and in some regions (Länder) in Germany.

In parent-run groups, cooperation between professionals and parents both in the management and programme development of services is matter of fact. In Germany a number of pilot projects have pointed towards the need for closer collaboration between professionals, parents, self-help groups, and freelance workers in mainstream centres. This is a general direction which in future years will inevitably call for a new understanding and essentially a redefinition of professional roles.

Training and professionalism: some concluding remarks and questions

Within the constraints of a single chapter, I have attempted to illustrate just some of the differences between countries in terms of training for the early years. These differences give rise to a number of questions concerning the concepts of professional role and professionalism which guide training. Who defines these concepts and how clear are they? How do they relate to the specific national, regional and local cultural and socio-political context? What does it mean to be a 'reflective practitioner' in early childhood institutions in France, in Denmark, in the UK, or in Germany?

In a number of countries (e.g. Sweden, Denmark, Germany) policies of decentralization and devolution are influencing the role of institutions and thus the role of practitioners in the local community infrastructure. How do educators in Denmark view the inclusion of parents in the regular planning of programme content? What effects is this having on their concept of professionalism? Where do they see the advantages, where the problems of this new form of close collaboration? Or in Sweden: how are practitioners making the transition from a highly professionalized welfare state system of centrally regulated early childhood centres (with high-quality standards in terms of staffing and resources) and a weak tradition of parental involvement to a decentralized system where experts stress the need to utilize locally based forums or 'plazas' to discuss the aims of early childhood education in a wider democratic context (Dahlberg and Åsén 1994: 167)? Or in Germany: how are practitioners – not least in the eastern federal states – adapting to their changing role within an increasingly decentralized system of local government and a legislative framework (Child and Youth Services Act 1990) which expects kindergartens and other day-care establishments to orient their programmes 'educationally and organizationally towards the needs of the children and their families' and to network with other organizations and services in the community?

Concepts of professional roles are, of course, strongly linked to long-standing institutional traditions. In some countries, the emphasis is on preparing practitioners to become teachers or early childhood specialists – experts in working with children, transmitting knowledge and cultural traditions in accordance with a well-defined curriculum framework. In others, the goal is to prepare for a broader role, one which alongside education includes aspects of care, social and community work. It seems that countries need to continually review their systems of training for the early years in terms of the kind of services considered necessary to meet both the multifarious needs of young children and their families and the diverse needs of trainees. In both cases current developments – not least the rapid changes in employment patterns in Western societies – point towards the need for a move away from static institutionalized forms to flexible, dynamic systems open to change.

My view is that it will be necessary for early childhood institutions to adapt more to an integrated and multipurpose role for all children under school age and their families. Split systems of provision, or the training of different kinds of professionals for different institutions, hinder a holistic view of children based on continuity and stability. And these are crucial factors in the lives of young children.

In his latest work on pedagogy and symbolic control, Basil Bernstein (1996: 6ff.) refers to the democratic necessity of ensuring three interrelated pedagogic rights in educational institutions: (1) the right to individual enhancement; (2) the right to be included, socially, intellectually, culturally and personally; (3) the right to participate in procedures 'whereby order is constructed, maintained and changed'. If we take these demands to be a necessary foundation for work with children and parents, then early childhood practitioners are faced with considerable challenges. Consensus building, civic discourse, advocacy: these are the broader parameters of early childhood education and care which are growing in importance. How prepared are professionals to question their role, aims and convictions, to enter into discursive debate with parents, other professionals in the field, administrators and politicians? The knowledge base that training institutions select, the skills they seek to develop, the attitudes they aim to foster will need to reflect a professional able to sensitively discuss pedagogical viewpoints against a background of increasing cultural, social and economic diversity, someone proficient in teamwork, in building empowering relations with parents, in leadership, in conflict management and in managing organizational change.

One of the challenges for training in the coming years will undoubtedly be to focus more on the wider social, economic and political context of educational settings for young children and on the transmission of knowledge and skills for working confidently and qualitatively not only with children from diverse backgrounds but also with adults in a variety of roles who may have widely differing views, expectations and perspectives on early childhood education and care.

Note

1 The IFP project was jointly funded by the German Federal Ministry for Family Affairs, Senior Citizens, Women and Young Citizens, the Bavarian Ministry of Education and Cultural Affairs, and the Bavarian Ministry for Labour and Social Affairs, Family, Women and Health. Research team: Pamela Oberhuemer, Michaela Ulich, Monika Soltendieck.

Training to work in the early years: the way ahead

Lesley Abbott and Gillian Pugh

The contributors to this book, coming as they do from a range of professional backgrounds and drawing on their different experiences as practitioners, trainers and academics, are united in their view on three key issues:

- that the early years of children's lives are critical in terms of all aspects of children's development;
- that the education and care of young children is a complex and demanding job requiring a highly skilled and well trained workforce;
- and that the current training opportunities for early years workers in the UK fall far short of what is required, both in terms of availability and content.

All three issues have been a common theme in all the major reports on the education of young children published over the last decade, not least by the Rumbold Committee (DES 1990), the National Commission on Education (1993) and the Royal Society of Arts (Ball 1994). They have also been central to the concerns of the Early Childhood Education Forum.

While this is predominantly a book about training, however, it has also become clear that the lack of commitment to the education and continuing professional development of early years workers is part of a wider and equally long-term confusion about what early years services should be provided, by whom and to whom and – perhaps most importantly of all – how we view childhood in this country and how this should affect our discussions on service provision. As Tricia David points out, the status of young children in the UK rests on outdated theories and beliefs, and on views which fail to recognize that young children have predispositions to learn different things. They are not simply bundles of biological urges slowly being transformed on the way to becoming fully formed as adults, and the childhood that our society has 'constructed' for them often underestimates their potential and capabilities.

This book reflects the confrontation between, on the one hand, a changing view of childhood – in which the dominant theories underpinning child development are challenged and greater attention is given to children's rights as citizens – and on the other an uncoordinated and low status profession in which little priority is given to a well-trained workforce. While contributors have argued for a more coherent approach to training and for a higher priority to be given to resources for this sector, this has to be seen as part of a wider debate about the future shape of children's services in general and early childhood services in particular.

Despite the new Labour Government's acknowledgement of the importance of high-quality early provision and the requirement that 'a qualified teacher should be involved in all settings providing early years education within an early years development plan' (DfEE 1997a) we still await a coherent national early years strategy with clear directives on how training is to be provided. Government circulars issued as these chapters were being written fail to address training issues, and while the announcement in the autumn of 1997 of early years as a priority for the new Standards Fund (formerly Grants for Education Support and Training, GEST) funding is to be welcomed, this will not fund the infrastructure required to provide training on a continuous basis. Where other countries in Europe are increasing the level of training and qualifications required of early years workers, there is no parallel direction in the UK. Even in the area in which there has been the greatest commitment to training – the training of teachers – there has been continuing neglect of the requirements of those working with children under 6 years.

Early education, 0–6 years

Our own view is that the current divisions between care and education and between services for the under-threes and over-threes would best be resolved by raising the age for the start of formal schooling to 6 years and establishing the age phase 0–6 years as an integrated and coherent first stage of education. As Pamela Oberhuemer points out, this is an approach that has now been adopted by Denmark, Finland, Spain and Sweden, and it is increasingly being recognized as the most appropriate way forward in this country (see for example Ball 1994; Moss and Penn 1996; Pugh 1996a). A move towards such an arrangement would begin to resolve a number of the concerns raised in this book: the rising numbers of 4-year-olds in reception classes, the inappropriateness of the curriculum for children going early into formal schooling, the lack of continuity between nurseries and schooling, the continuing neglect of services for children under 3 years, and the lack of coordination overall between the myriad of services providing care and education for young children. While these services could, in the short term at least, continue to operate separately within an overall national strategy for children from birth to 6 years, the integrated framework would build on the new early years development plans and the early years forums in creating a coordinated approach to planning, funding and managing services at local level. Over time the growth of centres and schools which themselves provide an integrated service – such as the existing combined nursery centres and the proposed early excellence centres – would begin to change the face of services nationwide.

Until there is clarity about how such an integrated early years service can be created and made operational, the other issues facing early years workers – uncoordinated systems of registration and inspection, lack of parity between workers on terms and conditions of service and lack of coherence and commitment to training and continuing professional development – cannot be satisfactorily resolved.

A climbing frame of qualifications

As the chapters of this book make clear, the early years workforce ranges from teachers with graduate and postgraduate qualification through to workers with no formal qualifications but often considerable practical experience. The continuing gap between vocational and academic qualifications and the often heated discussions about what knowledge, understanding and skills should provide the core of training, whether in the vocational or academic route, have been central to the early years training group and indeed to this book. The concept of a 'climbing frame' of opportunities for training and qualifications was one which we developed as a model to which those coming from different points of views on these issues could subscribe. In essence, this was an attempt to acknowledge the range of levels at which students would both gain access to and then exit from training opportunities. The 'climbing frame' reflects the growth in modular courses, and the development of integrated early childhood studies degrees which are specifically designed to draw on different disciplines in creating a more rounded training for work in early childhood centres. It also recognises the barriers that face many mature students who wish to access training courses and the importance of finding routes between the many existing training opportunities that currently exist; and the fact that while improving access is important so too is ensuring that overall standards remain rigorous and that courses are not 'watered down'. Figure 12.1 illustrates what such a climbing frame might look like for staff and parents in one early years centre (Pen Green Centre in Corby).

Encouraging developments

Despite the overall lack of strategy and commitment to training, this book does include examples of a number of encouraging developments and new training initiatives which, if adopted on a wider scale with government support and backing, could transform not only the training opportunities but also the career structure of early years workers. The development of National Vocational Qualifications has provided opportunities for those in work to be given recognition for the skills and knowledge they have already acquired while highlighting what additional training and experience is required.

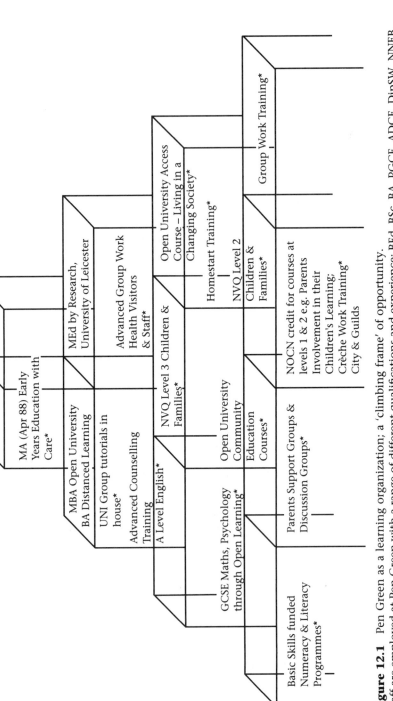

Figure 12.1 Pen Green as a learning organization; a 'climbing frame' of opportunity.
Staff are employed at Pen Green with a range of different qualifications and experience: BEd, BSc, BA, PGCE, ADCE, DipSW, NNEB, BTech Nursery Nursing, NVQ level 3, Health Visitor. These qualifications are seen as a starting point and all staff are committed to continue their training and personal development through in-service training, long and short courses. Currently staff and parents are undertaking training at all these levels and several are involved in action research projects. * Courses run from the Centre.

Maureen O'Hagan, Sue Griffin and Pat Dench argue in Chapter 6 that the advent of Scottish and National Vocational Qualifications has also brought the potential for practitioners to develop a more reflective approach to their work and to make more explicit the values and principles on which work in the early years field should be based.

The students whose voices are heard in Chapters 7 and 9 testify to the very positive benefits to be gained from workplace-centred, competence-based assessment. Sue Owen and Gill Thorpe's description of the development of an early years assessment centre and John Powell's account of an innovative training initiative arising from a partnership between a university and a local authority are both encouraging in their emphasis on increasing access to training and qualifications and providing for progression within a flexible framework that meets the needs of mature students.

The development and continuing health of multi-professional degrees in early childhood is an initiative of which all the contributors to this book are justly proud since most have been established by or developed from the ideas sown by members of the early years training group. In highlighting points of difference between courses in terms of emphasis, cost, organization and focus, Mary Fawcett and Pamela Calder show in Chapter 8 how, while adhering to common principles with regard to the needs of children in providing appropriately trained educators, each course is responding to the needs of the area and the student group which it serves.

It is encouraging that in *Early Excellence* (Labour Party 1996), the current Labour Government refers to the appropriateness of these multi-professional courses, citing some of those discussed in Chapter 8. As a degree which will service the needs of a multi-professional workforce required for 'early excellence' centres or the growing number of broad-based early years centres, and as a first degree on which an early years PGCE will build, this development must be celebrated and the currency of these degrees must be widely advertised. This is a role which the universities and colleges must take seriously, for until more of their graduates emerge in positions of responsibility, testifying to the value of the degree for a range of early years posts, publicity and information sharing must be a central role of the providers of such degrees.

Despite the lack of a training strategy there are, then, a number of interesting initiatives on which future developments can build. But there are still some critical issues which need to be addressed.

A curriculum for training

Over the past decade there has been extensive discussion about what is an appropriate early years curriculum (see for example Curtis 1986; Drummond *et al.* 1989; Anning 1991; Edwards and Knight 1994; Early Childhood Education Forum, in press; SCAA 1996) and central to this discussion has been the significant role played by adults in children's learning. Comparatively little has been written, however, about the content of training courses which prepare those adults on whom so much depends. The chapters in this book reflect some of the ongoing discussion about what is appropriate knowledge, understanding and skills and whether there is a core which, however short the course, should be covered. The curriculum framework given in the appendix draws on this book and on previous publications (including DES 1990; Hevey and Curtis 1996) in attempting to outline the underlying principles and the broad areas that we believe training should include. These underlying principles for training courses can be summarized as follows:

- promoting the rights, responsibilities and needs of children;
- offering all children equal access to opportunities to learn and develop;
- challenging oppressive behaviour and practice;
- working in partnership with parents;
- linking theory, experience and practice;
- activity-based experiential learning;
- encouraging multi-agency working.

The main areas of content included in the framework, drawing on broad-based training such as multidisciplinary degrees which we believe are best suited to prepare educators for work in early years centres, are:

- child and human development;
- young children's learning;
- curriculum;
- working as part of a team;
- childhood as a social construct;
- the child within the family;
- the child and family within society;
- equality of opportunity;
- policy, legislation and services;
- research;
- health care;
- family support and child protection;
- children with special educational needs;
- international perspectives and comparative studies.

The framework concludes with the personal attributes and dispositions which we believe should permeate the content and process of training of early years workers – for example, high expectations and respect for children, an enquiring mind, the ability to communicate, a willingness to work in partnership with parents, and so on.

But simple lists, while perhaps providing a starting point for course development, cannot ensure that courses are founded upon the process of 'becoming critical' about the nature and construction of knowledge and realizing the extent to which our views and values are embedded in our own culture, as Barbara Thompson and Pamela Calder argue in Chapter 4. Several chapters return to this theme. Tricia David in Chapter 2 stresses the importance of early childhood educators being able to explore their own thinking, to disembed their understandings from the cultural context in which they have grown into their professional roles, and to become reflective and reflexive in their practice. For her this means being able to 'stand in children's shoes' and to examine the ecological niche within which the family is living. The discussion about the deconstruction of child development in Chapters 2, 3 and 4 shows how important it is that training courses take account of new thinking and research findings.

Drawing on emerging practice across Europe, Pamela Oberhuemer talks of the need for early years practitioners to question their role, aims and convictions, and to enter into discursive debate with parents, other professionals and politicians. She argues for practitioners to be able to develop more expertise in qualitative and interpretative research methods, in collaborative work, in studies that locate children's experience in the specific cultural and historic context. And she points to the challenge for training in focusing increasingly on the wider social, economic and political context of families lives and of skills far beyond extending children's learning – managing conflict, working in teams, managing organizational change, empowering parents.

The theme of the 'reflective practitioner' is also picked up by Maureen O'Hagan, Sue Griffin and Pat Dench in Chapter 6 who argue that the introduction of competence-based qualifications encourages the process of self-assessment, revealing skills and gaps in knowledge and understanding.

A further issue raised by both Helen Penn and Pamela Oberhuemer is the concept of social pedagogy, defined in Moss and Penn (1996: 104) as 'all the processes of nurturing and upbringing of children outside the family'. It encompasses therapeutic, caring and educational work with a wide range of ages, not just young children, and is not specific to a particular situation or institution. Moss and Penn suggest that it has gained currency as an early childhood qualification particularly in countries with little or no tradition of providing services for young children within the education system – countries such as Germany, Scandinavia and France. In Denmark, where social pedagogues work in out of school settings and with children with special needs as well as preschools, Oberhuemer points out that many more men are involved in work with young children. As a model this approach does not seem to us to fit well into the UK context, particularly given our support for 0–6 years as the first stage of the education system as argued above, but we should consider carefully what it has to offer.

The issue of a training curriculum poses a particular challenge for teacher training, as Lesley Abbott and Ian Kane acknowledge in Chapter 5. The strength of our current system, as the comparative analysis of training across Europe in Chapter 11 points out, is that the UK is the only country where the training of early years teachers is of equal status to that of all other teachers. The other side of this coin is that the continuing emphasis within teacher training on the subjects of the National Curriculum and the very limited time given within primary courses to a specialist focus on early years in general and child development in particular, means that the current teacher-training curriculum is far from ideal as a preparation for work with young children. They suggest a 'wrap-around' model of continuing professional development as one way of providing support for early years teachers and ensuring that early years specific issues are addressed in order to meet the needs of our youngest children.

Continuing professional development

A further theme throughout this book is the critical importance of continuing professional training and development. Training should not be a one-off injection that sets students up for life and yet the research evidence we cite shows that the vast majority of early years workers are not involved in ongoing training. Linked to this is the lack of a tradition within the private and voluntary sector, as there now is in schools, for training days which give the whole staff an opportunity to work together on issues of common interest. Drawing on the experience of the nurseries of Reggio Emilia in northern Italy (Edwards *et al.* 1993) and the evidence from UK projects such as the Effective Early Learning project (Pascal *et al.* 1994b), a key element in the effective development of early years staff is the support of an advisory teacher or mentor or 'pedagogical coordinator' who can act as facilitator to the staff team as they plan and then review their development plan.

An effective national system of ongoing training and professional development would need to: incorporate an expectation that all staff were involved; the opportunity to visit other early years settings; a requirement that all early years settings close for perhaps five days a year for in-service training; adequate budgets that would include supply cover; and a national network of advisors.

Funding

Continuing lack of funding for students on part-time courses, both those leading to NVQ accreditation, and early childhood studies degrees is a major barrier to increased take up of training. Some support is available from some TECs, but there is disparity between TECs in the extent to which they support childcare students. The precarious nature of NVQs and their related assessment procedures is well illustrated by the experience of Praxis in Chapter 7.

Constant reference by the Teacher Training Agency (TTA) to the eligibility of 'school teachers' only, to funding for continuing professional development does little to reinforce teamwork and support the collaborative in-service activity which developed in the post-Rumbold era. The increase in the number of higher degrees in multi-professional and early years studies is to be applauded, but there is little encouragement for graduates of the new multi-disciplinary degrees to pursue such a qualification when teachers are funded but they are required to fund themselves.

There is an urgent need for ring-fenced money for early years training and increased opportunities for all staff to pursue further study. It is hoped that the new Standards initiative will, to some extent, provide for this but this is likely to be only a short term solution. What is needed is a coordinated policy ensuring equality of opportunity to appropriate training for all those working with young children and their families.

Access

As noted above, the main barrier to training, apart from the paucity of courses, is the cost, given that many students have no access to grants. A further barrier is students' lack of confidence in their ability to cope with training, particularly when they are returning to study many years after they left school, and fear failure. This suggests the need for more courses like the one in Kirklees which specifically bridges the gap between vocational and academic routes, forging a partnership between local authority trainers and higher education and enabling students to experience the reality of the 'climbing frame' in relation to their training.

The lack of students from ethnic minority groups particularly in teacher training is a cause for concern. While there has been an increase in access courses and support for school leavers considering teaching as a career, there remains the need to encourage and facilitate the recruitment of workers from black and ethnic minority groups to training for work with young children in a variety of roles.

There are a number of developments which are helping to improve access. One is the increase in the number of modular courses, although if students are allowed total freedom in the modules that they select, there is the danger that the overall course could become somewhat unbalanced and fragmented. Core modules when shared, whether by students in initial training or practitioners adding to their qualifications, provide opportunities for shared experiences and perspectives and offer the kinds of support and encouragement required by students returning to studying or whose confidence often requires a boost.

Another development is the gradual growth in distance learning, both through the Open University but also linked into mainstream universities such as the University of North London, the Manchester Metropolitan University and Stranmillis College in Northern Ireland where, in the case of the latter, video conferencing allows students to participate in degree studies at a distance from the point of delivery. The continuing development of distance learning opportunities linked to a system of accreditation will meet the needs of those students for whom distance from a college makes training difficult.

A third is the growing acceptance of Accreditation of Prior Learning (APL) or Prior Experience and Learning (APEL) as entry to higher education as well as its central place within NVQ accreditation. While this development is to be welcomed, based as it is on a recognition that previous experience is an important part of any training process, it does present challenges to those responsible for the assessment of students' APL or APEL 'portfolios'. What criteria are to be used in judging whether a student has done more than simply attend a course or be loosely involved in a new development? How can tutors ensure that learning has taken place? How can standards be maintained? And what percentage of the requirements of any particular course should APL or APEL provide exemption for? There is a dilemma caused by the need to retain flexibility in responding to the needs and experience of individual students whilst ensuring that standards are upheld and that students, once accepted, are able to cope with the demands of a particular course. Whilst any form of standardization would conflict with the principles underpinning APEL and APL nevertheless nationally agreed guidelines for consideration by those involved in the process would prove extremely helpful.

Are some early years workers more professional than others?

One issue on which contributors to the early years training group and to this book continue to be divided is the comparative value of different forms of training and qualifications and the basic requirements that should be in place for all who work with young children. Should all workers be qualified teachers? Should every group include at least one teacher? Is a teaching qualification appropriate anyway? Are nursery nurses and teaching assistants who work alongside teachers doing the same thing as teachers? What level of training is appropriate for childminders and for playgroup leaders? Is a competence-based approach sufficiently rigorous?

The need for a balance between qualifications and experiences suggests that there is no easy answers to these questions, although we believe that a training and qualifications framework based upon our 'climbing frame' analogy would go some way to answering the questions. Janet Moyles and Wendy Suschitzky in Chapter 10 do however throw some interesting light on the comparative roles of teachers, nursery nurses and teaching assistants in nursery and infant schools, showing that while teachers operate at a theoretical or conceptual level, assistants operate at a practical and procedural level. They stress the importance of acknowledging the value of the different skills that different members of a team may bring to their work with children and of ensuring that initial training reflects this.

The ways in which early years workers become competent, knowledgeable and skilful will continue to be many and varied. What is important is that there is shared understanding amongst those responsible for training regarding the principles upon which is rests, irrespective of type or level, and agreement that knowledge about young children and their families and the way in which they learn, grow and develop should be central.

One of the criticisms levelled at vocational training is that there insufficient rigour and consistency in assessment of candidates for NVQs which has led to lack of acceptance of NVQs on the part of some employers. While there is a recognition that competence in the workplace is important, as evidenced by the move towards the inclusion of competence-based assessment in teacher training courses, there is also the acknowledgement that assessment of competence alone is insufficient. Sue Griffin and Maureen O'Hagan (1996: 18) respond to the myths which they claim 'seem to have developed around the NVQ/SVQ concept'. They claim that vocational qualifications enable progression to another level of qualification as a worker develops higher levels of skill and knowledge. What is needed is a more holistic view which brings vocational and academic training more closely together. Indeed their argument that, 'there are many routes of learning which enable an individual to acquire the competencies NVQs/SVQs demand, including formal training courses as well as experience', is further developed in Chapter 6.

There is an urgent need for the development of a level 4 qualification, both for those within centres who wish to improve their management potential, but also for others within the early years field for whom at present there are no appropriate qualifications, particularly inspectors and registration officers. Access to courses which provide the underpinning knowledge for level 4 is urgently required but whilst the insistence by the TTA on funding for many appropriate modules on in-service programmes only being available for teachers, this problem will remain.

The implementation of the Dearing Report (1997) and framework should do much to bring academic and vocational qualifications into closer proximity thus removing arguments about parity of esteem.

Childcare and early education as a gendered occupation

A continuing concern is the very small number of men who work with young children, variously estimated between 1 and 3 per cent. Helen Penn's research argues that the design of courses as well as the gendered nature of the profession ('it's women's work') are to blame, as well as low pay and lack of career opportunities. Should the recruitment of men into early years training become a higher priority for all providers? The European Commission Network on Childcare (1996c: 24) recognises that the issue is a sensitive one but nonetheless advocates efforts to increase the presence of men in all services. The Network views men working directly with young children as a means to challenge gender-stereotyped roles, as well as being beneficial for children and as a way of encouraging greater involvement of fathers in their children's early education. There are strategies that can be adopted, as other European countries have done, and targets can be set. Moss and Penn (1996) suggest a target of 20 per cent within ten years. Ways of attaining this target must feature high on the list of priorities for all providers of early years training.

Training the trainers

There has been little in this book about the training and ongoing support for early years trainers yet the need for trainers to be skilled and knowledgeable about current research, credible as practitioners and aware of the many changes taking place at local and national levels which affect the lives of young children and their educators, has never been greater. The increase over the past decade in early years research projects which involve practitioners and researchers has been heartening. Ways in which research findings can be disseminated have increased within the networks provided by the European

Early Childhood Research Association (EECERA), the International Early Years Conference held at Warwick University and their associated journals. The increase in number, although still relatively small, of early years journals provides opportunities for trainers to update and renew their knowledge which in turn will be woven into patterns of training.

Conference attendance is both costly and time consuming yet many trainers fund themselves in order to increase their knowledge and skill. Support both in terms of time for reading and updating and refreshment is not always forthcoming in training establishments where involvement in early years training and assessment is just one of many roles. Many trainers have additional responsibilities which involve management, administration, supervision and teaching on a range of courses for those working with other age groups.

Some trainers are themselves studying for further qualifications – for example, the BA Early Childhood Studies degree, Masters routes or PhDs. While this provides opportunities for sharing new knowledge with trainees, trainers often find little time to pursue their own interests. The renewal of school experience has been an important requirement of teacher trainers, thus ensuring that credibility is retained and familiarity with new requirements and curriculum changes lead to informed and appropriate training. Yet this initiative has suffered from an increase in teaching responsibilities brought about by over-full timetables and a lack of funding. The benefits of school or workplace based activity are also seen in an increase in applications for in-service training from staff alongside whom researchers are working. It is important that this opportunity is not only retained but is required if trainers are to keep abreast of current developments on the shop floor. Partnerships provide opportunities for new models of training and support to be developed in which there is mutual benefit for trainer and trainee. The need to safeguard the professional development of trainers at all levels must be a priority if the quality of early years training is to be assured.

Pay and conditions

The pay and conditions of early years educators has been beyond the remit of this book, but it is an issue that is clearly related both to the overall need for a comprehensive early years strategy as well as our specific focus on training. As with training, so with pay and conditions: there are very considerable variations between workers in different settings in relation to pay and a very distinct 'pecking order' in which teachers earn most and childminders earn least. But the pay, while related to the length of training and the level of qualification, is in inverse relation to the number of hours worked, with teachers having relatively short days and long holidays and childminders having long days and short holidays. While teachers undoubtedly work many hours beyond those during which the children are in school, the very considerable variations do add to the difficulties facing the development of integrated early years centres, most of which open from 8 a.m. to 5.30 p.m.

for 50 weeks of the year. The low levels of pay and poor conditions of non-teachers in the sector is also one of the factors which contributes to the difficult in encouraging men to 'enter the profession'. The European Commission Network on Childcare (1996c: 24) suggests that we should work towards the target in which all qualified staff employed in services should be paid at not less than a nationally or locally agreed wage rate, which for staff who are fully trained should be comparable to that of teachers. This raises questions regarding the definition of 'fully trained' but nevertheless reinforces the relationship between status and pay.

Recommendations

Our overall aim is to ensure that, as part of a national early years strategy in which the years from birth to six are seen as a distinct phase and in which care and education is combined, all early childhood workers are appropriately trained and qualified. More specifically, we make the following recommendations.

1   One national body should be established to take overall responsibility for standards, training and qualifications in the early years

Ultimately we believe there should be one national body for standards, training and qualifications. However, in the short-to-medium term we welcome the establishment of a National Training Organization as the 'lead body' for vocational training but will be concerned if it does not work in very close partnership with the Teacher Training Agency or any future body responsible for teacher training, the unions and the General Teaching Council on the one hand and the Central Council for Education and Training of Social Workers (CCETSW) and the proposed General Social Services Council on the other. We would also point to the need to provide adequate financial support for such a body, given the lack of well-resourced employers in the childcare and education field. Any moves to bring vocational and academic training into a closer relationship will be hampered unless the early years NTO and teacher training in particular work very closely together.

2   National targets should be set and adequate resources allocated for an appropriately trained early years workforce

This would include:

- All teachers working with children under 6 years to be early years specialists;
- All heads of centres, nurseries and playgroups to be qualified to graduate level or equivalent;
- All other early childhood workers to be qualified to NVQ level 3 or equivalent.

The training targets suggested by the European Commission Network on Childcare (1996a) are for 60 per cent of all staff working in centres to have three years training post-18 by the year 2005. While supporting this ambitious target, we recognize the paucity of research with regard to the number of workers this would involve and the resource allocations required.

3   *The NVQ framework for childcare and education should be completed with all urgency, and attention paid to issues of quality and rigour*

Levels 2 and 3 have recently been reviewed and revised but work on level 4 has not as yet got underway. In completing this work, attention should be paid to developing paths across vocational and academic routes allowing access to higher education from level 3, such as those described in Chapter 9 on the Kirklees Pathways to Professionalism initiative.

Concern has been expressed at the lack of rigour and quality in some assessment procedures for NVQs, sometimes due to pressure from external agencies to meet funding targets. The failure of some local authorities to recognize NVQs as an appropriate qualification reflects this concern. If the qualification is to retain its credibility, assessment procedures must be improved in line with the recommendations of the Beaumont Report (1996), i.e. greater externality in the assessment of knowledge aspects, less bureaucracy in the administration of the qualifications and the language of the standards made more 'user friendly'.

4   *All training should be adequately funded*

The priorities here are for:

- Grants for mature and part-time students (the majority of those taking courses other than the traditional undergraduate/PGCE teaching training route). Students taking full-time courses have in the past had access to grants. Those taking part-time courses, including integrated early childhood studies degrees, usually have not. The Government's recent decision with regard to students fees will hit early childhood students hard and will close doors for many.
- Funding should be made available for the replication in other areas of successful training initiatives such as Pathways to Professionalism outlined in Chapter 9. Projects such as this have to rely on external funding being sought, mostly from Europe. This approach is time consuming and fails to build on successful practice in ways which will benefit others.
- Funding should also cover the development of distance-learning materials to ensure that students unable to follow more conventional training routes are not disadvantaged. Availability of such materials would also go some way towards meeting the needs for NVQ candidates to gain relevant underpinning knowledge.
- A separate 'ring-fenced' fund set aside for early years training and flexibility in terms of access to training for all early years staff employed across sectors

and departments. The divisive recommendations from the Teacher Training Agency that *only* 'school teachers' are eligible for funding under the new Standards Fund is a retrograde step and will lead to a breakdown in the post-Rumbold collaborative activity in the provision of award bearing courses.

Estelle Morris (*Times Educational Supplement* 24 October 1997), outlining the Government's 'radical vision' for early years, said she wanted to see an end to 'fragmentation' and 'bureaucracy'. 'I want to see a uniform system with a common approach.' However, her confirmation that early years funding will continue to come from a variety of sources including DfEE New Deal for Schools, the new Standards Fund and administrative funds previously set aside for the nursery voucher scheme, did little to reassure anyone that fragmentation would disappear.

Unless heed is taken of the assertion made by Helen Penn in the same article that 'this isn't serious funding, it's just the scraps left over from other budgets', then the fragmented and uncoordinated system of early years training will continue.

Radical steps must be taken to properly fund high quality training if the Government's plans for *Early Excellence* are to be realized.

- Assessment of candidates seeking accreditation for NVQs. In other employment sectors employers fund training; in the early childhood field most employees work in small private or community based groups, or are self-employed and low paid. They are unable to afford the considerable costs of training assessments, and their establishments are often unable to cover the costs of replacement staff while they attend training.

5 The underpinning principles, content and approach of all early years courses should reflect the skills, knowledge and understanding outlined earlier in this chapter and summarized in the appendix (p. 166)

It is essential that study of the child is central in every course and that important early years issues such as leadership and management, working as a member of a team, play and learning, working with parents and carers, children's rights, legal issues, equality of opportunity, working with other professionals and requirements relating to assessment, the *Desirable Outcomes*, and continuity with the National Curriculum are fully addressed, alongside the other issues included in the appendix.

6 Early years should become a specialist area within teacher training, of equal value as subject specialisms

It will be important that this includes teacher training as well as specialist early years courses and Early Childhood Studies degrees and that course content includes all the areas outlined above. In initial teacher training, we welcome the development of some courses where child development has been accepted as equivalent to special subject study, or where early childhood studies is offered as the main subject. However, the growing emphasis on subject specialism and the overall neglect of child development is ill equipping most teachers to work with young children. The training of early years teachers should continue to be as rigorous as that of all teachers, but the knowledge base of early years as a specialism should be recognized as of equal value as a specialist subject area. There is a need to challenge the content of child development courses but also to celebrate the acceptance in at least one university of early childhood as a specialist area. There is also a need for the development of part-time early years teacher training opportunities to meet the needs of those students who, following a multidisciplinary degree, wish to take a postgraduate course whilst retaining their post in the workplace.

7   *Early years courses should continue to develop flexibly, incorporating both modular and linear structures*

Both NVQs and many degree level courses are adopting a modular approach which allows flexibility over access and often too over the length of time that students – many of whom combine training with employment – take to complete the course. We endorse this approach and would wish to see it develop further. It is also important that, particularly in part-time courses, the value of the student group in sharing experiences and perspectives and in offering peer support is recognized and incorporated into course planning. Degree courses which combine both a linear and a modular structure should continue to be developed.

8   *Early Childhood Studies degrees should be further developed as an appropriate underpinning for teachers working in all early years settings*

The development of integrated Early Childhood Studies degrees provides an exciting model for the future, but the currency of such courses in terms of their relationship with other courses and qualifications is still evolving, and the career paths open to their graduates is not yet clear. Further publicity on these courses for circulation to employers is urgently required if their value is to be formally recognized as a credible and more appropriate route to working with children than many current initial teacher training courses. The need for staff with multidisciplinary training is highlighted by the Government in *Early Excellence* (Labour Party 1996) yet the stress on a National Curriculum subject for entry to teacher training courses and the failure to recognize the appropriateness of Early Childhood Studies as a first degree will lead to the rejection of some of the best candidates. Clear endorsement by the Government through the Teacher Training Agency of the appropriateness of multidisciplinary degrees for postgraduate training is needed.

9   *Strenuous efforts should be made to increase the number of men working with young children*

The early childhood workforce is predominantly female. The European Childcare Network (1996c) has set targets for 20 per cent of the workforce to be men by the year 2005. If these targets are to have any chance of being met in the

UK, they will need to be linked in to the recommendations below on improved pay, conditions and career prospects; and specific campaigns such as those run in countries such as Denmark will have to be pursued.

10   Recruitment procedures and course content for all training courses are reviewed to ensure that more students from minority ethnic groups train to work with young children

Concern at the lack of students from minority ethnic groups on childcare courses in the 1980s and some potentially unlawful racially discriminatory admissions arrangements led the Nursery Nurse Trainers Anti-Racist Network NNTARN, now Early Years Trainers Anti-Racist Network (EYTARN), and the Commission for Racial Equality to review recruitment and interviewing procedures on NNEB courses in colleges of further education and to recommend changes which would lead to greater equality of opportunity (NNTARN 1987). Although there are no national statistics, anecdotal evidence from colleges and organizations working in the field do suggest some success in increasing the numbers of students from minority ethnic groups on these lower level courses.

The same cannot, however, be said for teacher training where, perhaps in part due to the lack of emphasis on equality issues in the content of courses, there continue to be very few minority ethnic students. The recent initiative on the part of the Teacher Training Agency to broaden the intake is to be welcomed. But as we have argued throughout this book, the teacher-training curriculum must also be broadened in line with other early years courses to reflect the underlying principles and content that we summarize in the appendix, and particularly those concerned with equality and anti-discriminatory practice. A major commitment of the Anti-Racist Teacher Education Network is to eliminate racism at all levels in education by political, institutional and individual action (ARTEN 1996).

11   Access to in-service training and continuous professional development should be the right of all early childhood workers; and all establishments should have at least five days closure a year for whole staff training

The 'reflective practitioner' discussed above cannot exist in a vacuum: all early years workers need the opportunity for time to reflect on and improve their own practice in the company of their colleagues, either within the centre or on multi-agency training in the locality. Opportunities for visiting other early years establishments should also be a part of this entitlement and specific time allocated to enable this to happen.

12   All early years workers should have access to the support of early years advisors

The development of in-service courses at local level is dependent upon the availability of additional resources and on a considerable increase in the number of early years advisors and training officers. The new early years partnerships are now required to take on responsibility for ensuring that all early years workers have access to training, but they will need resources if they are to fulfil this role adequately. There is evidence that in some areas local authorities are combining to appoint a training officer to identify and respond to training needs. Unless there is a national policy supported by adequate resources, funding will still be an issue. What is important in this kind of development is that training strategies are locally developed. Where these can be linked to early years development plans there will be an increased chance that training needs will be met.

13   As part of the national early years strategy, a working party should examine and resolve the current differentials in pay and conditions of early years workers

This recommendation has been a part of nearly all national reports in recent years but has not led to any action. Meanwhile, individual nursery centres and local authorities try to work out local solutions, with very little success. Moss and Penn (1996) argue that all early years workers, including teachers, should work a 35-hour week with six weeks holiday, and that all workers who have the graduate qualification should be paid at the same rate. While we support this view in principle, we would stress the importance of the relevance of the degree to work with young children and the need for assessed practice-placements either during the degree course (as in some early childhood studies courses) or as a postgraduate requirement (as in the PGCE teacher training course).

The Labour Government's commitment to maintain the professional status of early years teachers is an important one. While early years teacher training still leaves much to be desired it status must be preserved.

The opportunity which exists in the UK for early years teachers to work with other age groups, to take on roles and responsibilities across the educational sector and to apply for headship, is unique in Europe. In advocating a new standard qualification 'early childhood teacher' with specific responsibility for the 0–6 age group only, Moss and Penn (1996) seek to alleviate many of the problems raised earlier in this book with regard to specialist early years training. However, while the opportunity to undertake this kind of training should be available for those who wish to do so, the possible limitations on career progress must be recognised. Ability to influence practice by teaching across age groups and the potential loss of status which limiting training to 0–6-year-olds might bring are all issues which must be taken into account.

Finally, there is the question of whether we are seeking multi-professional teams or multi-professional workers. We have argued in this book, as have other contributors, for training opportunities which allow workers to increase their knowledge, skills and competence to work in a variety of contexts and with children of different age groups. As the Rumbold Committee recognizes:

The extent to which adults working with young children and their families possess different areas of knowledge and understanding, skills and attitudes will vary according to the role of the worker and the training they have received.

(DES 1990: para 16: 69)

It is our belief that it would be unrealistic to expect that all professionals would possess equal levels of skill or knowledge but that opportunities for progression must be available for all workers. While multi-professional training and practice opportunities are required for all those working with young children, they must be included in all existing training to a much greater degree. The framework proposed in the appendix is important in highlighting course content. The degree to which it is pursued will depend not only on the type and level of training but on the motivation, levels of understanding, skill and commitment of both trainer and student, for as Webb (1972) clearly recognizes:

It is not so much *where* we educate staff as *how* that will determine awareness, sensitivity and commitment in them for the future.

(p. 167, original italics)

Appendix
Curriculum framework for training to work with young children

Several of the chapters in this book have touched on the areas that training for early years workers should cover, while acknowledging the importance of understanding *process* as well as *content*. As both Barbara Thompson and Pamela Calder argue in their different views of the knowledge, skills and understanding required by early years workers (Chapter 4), the key for all workers, at whatever level of training, is a critical mind which challenges, questions and extends the student's thinking.

The postmodernist debate raises questions about the cultural relativity of values and of the universally agreed principles which underpin 'developmentally appropriate practice'. Nevertheless, the open-mindedness recommended by Bruner (see quotation in Chapter 4) requires us to recognize our own values as we explore and question those of others. It is in this spirit that we offer this framework, drawing on our own experience, on the contributors to this book and on Rumbold (DES 1990), Hevey and Curtis (in Pugh 1996) and Edwards and Knight (1994).

1 Underlying principles of courses in early childhood

Courses should equip early childhood workers to:

- promote the rights, responsibilities and needs of children;
- offer all children equal access to opportunities to learn;
- challenge oppressive behaviour and practice;
- work in partnership with parents;
- link theory, experience and practice;
- provide activity-based experiential learning;
- encourage professionals and agencies to work together.

2 Personal attributes/dispositions of early years workers

Early childhood workers should:

- have high expectations of children and self;
- have a genuine liking for, and sensitivity towards, children;
- respect and value children as autonomous young people in their own right;
- respect and appreciate the contribution of other adults – parents, colleagues and other professionals;
- be committed to work in partnership with parents;
- be non-judgemental in dealings with children, staff, parents and the wider community;
- be open-minded and eager to take on new challenges;
- be aware of and sensitive to the needs of others;
- be well adjusted with positive self-image;
- have an enquiring mind and be alert to the need for further personal professional development;
- be willing to support others personally and professionally;
- be willing to share knowledge and expertise in ways which promote professional development and team work;
- be able to communicate well with colleagues, parents and other agencies, and above all children, irrespective of their culture, religion and gender.

3 Curriculum framework

Child/human development

Knowledge
- A sound knowledge of theories of development for children from birth to 8 years.
- An understanding of the relationship between theory, experience and practice and of the ways in which adults' interactions with children support their development.

Skills
- In meeting children's needs in appropriate ways.
- In submitting bodies of knowledge to critical analysis.

Young children's learning

Knowledge
- An understanding of how children learn and of the role and value of play as central to this learning.

Skills
- In developing strategies to transmit knowledge to others.
- In organization and in strategies for effective learning.

- In observation and in effective recording, monitoring and assessment.
- In communication.

Curriculum

Knowledge
- A deep understanding of all subjects in the early years curriculum, with particular reference to the areas of experience/learning:
  personal and social and emotional development;
  language and literacy;
  mathematics;
  knowledge and understanding of the world;
  physical development;
  creative development.
- Knowledge and understanding of theories and research and the importance and relevance of play in the curriculum

Skills
- In responding to the prescribed curriculum in ways appropriate to the needs and developmental stage of the child/children.
- In developing particular skills, interest and expertise in a subject or curriculum area and awareness of appropriate strategies for work with young children.
- In planning the curriculum, learning environment and provision in order to ensure breadth and balance.
- In planning for transition and continuity between phases.

Working as part of a team

Knowledge
- Strategies for effective team work and management.

Skills
- In defining roles and tasks, for both staff and parents.
- In examining styles of leadership and appropriate organizational structures.
- In managing the process of organizational change.
- In professional development of staff and mentoring.

Childhood as a social construct

Knowledge
- The social and historical background to particular constructions of childhood and the consequences for children's lives.
- Citizenship – children's rights and responsibilities.

Skills
- In examining how different societies construct childhood.

The child within the family

Knowledge
- Recognition of parents as first educators of their children.
- Characteristics of working partnerships.
- Family patterns and lifestyles.
- Ecological, social and diverse contexts of family life.

Skills
- In working sensitively with parents (fathers and mothers), carers and the extended family.

The child and family within society

Knowledge
- Children's experiences within a wider cultural context.
- Societal pressures and expectations.

Skills
- In creating opportunities for parents and children to share their experiences and expectations of family life.
- In being non-judgemental.

Equality of opportunity

Knowledge
- Children's rights and entitlement as defined by UN Convention.
- Cultural and social similarities and differences.
- Antidiscrimination legislation.
- Inequalities – ways in which society and early years contexts promote inequality – knowledge of ways in which this can be redressed.

Skills
- In adopting appropriate means of communication with staff, children, parents and the wider community.
- In providing an environment and resources which reflect and value different cultures.
- In challenging stereotypes and inequality, promoting equality.

Policy, legislation and services

Knowledge
- Government policies, their underlying philosophy and their impact on early years settings.
- Different services, the contexts within which young children are educated and cared for, and the range of professionals who work with families and children.

Skills
- In applying policy and responding to legislative demands.
- In working collaboratively across services, sectors and departments and with differently trained adults.
- In sharing policies with parents and the wider community.
- In acting as an advocate for children.

Research

Knowledge
- Current research on young children's learning and development and understanding of its implications.
- Contribution of research to theories of child development.
- Research techniques and methodology, including those for observing children and methodology for reflecting on and improving practice. Epistemological basis of particular methodologies and the link between methodology and technique.

Skills
- In critical analysis and reflection on current research.
- In observation and the ability to assess and evaluate not only the programmes offered and the effects on children, but the adults' role.
- In practitioner enquiry.

Healthcare in the early years

Knowledge
- Of nutrition and diet, early childhood illnesses, mental health.
- The role of healthcare studies in promoting well-being.

Skills
- In supporting and responding to children and families in relation to healthcare and nutritional issues.

Family support and child protection

Knowledge
- Relevant legislation and the role of different agencies and departments.
- Case conferences, role of the particular setting.

Skills
- In dealing with parents and children and with different agencies and personnel.

Children with special educational needs

Knowledge
- Legislation, including the Code of Practice and relevant responsibilities.
- Range of special needs – physical, learning, emotional and behavioural.

Skills
- In responding appropriately to need.
- In providing an environment and curriculum which supports children with special educational needs, including observation and diagnostic skills.

International perspectives and comparative studies

Knowledge
- Different systems of early education and of how these reflect different cultures.
- Philosophical bases for practice.

Skills
- In evaluating and responding to alternative practices and provision.

Bibliography

Abbott, L. and Gillen, J. (eds) (1997) *Educare for the Under Threes – Identifying Need and Opportunity*. Report of the two year research projects funded by the Esmée Fairbairn Charitable Trust and the Manchester Metropolitan University.

Alexander, R. (1992) *Policy and Practice in Primary Education*. London: Cassell.

Alexander, R., Rose, J. and Woodhead, C. (1992) *Curriculum Organisation and Classroom Practice in Primary Schools: A discussion paper*. London: DES.

Anderson, K. and Jack, D. (1991) The feminist practice of oral history, in S.B. Gluck and D. Patai (eds) *Women's Words*. London and New York: Routledge Chapman and Hall.

Andersson, B.E. (1989) Effects of public day-care: a longitudinal study, *Child Development*, 60: 857–66.

Andersson, B.E. (1992) Effects of daycare on cognitive and socio-emotional competence of thirteen-year-old Swedish school children, *Child Development*, 63: 20–36.

Anning, A. (1991) *A National Curriculum for the Early Years*. Buckingham: Open University Press.

Aries, P. (1962) *Centuries of Childhood*. London: Jonathan Cape.

ARTEN (Anti-Racist Teacher Education Network) (1996) *Manifesto for Teacher Education*. London: ARTEN.

Assiter, A. (1996) *Enlightened Women: Modernist Feminism in a Postmodern Age*. London: Routledge.

Audit Commission (1996) *Counting to Five: Education of Children Under Five*. London: HMSO.

Ball, C. (1994) *Start Right: The Importance of Early Learning*. London: Royal Society for the Encouragement of Arts Manufacturers and Commerce.

Ball, C. (1995) Key stage zero, *The Guardian* (Education), 7 March.

Barnett, W.S. and Escobar, C.M. (1990) Economic costs and benefits of early intervention, in S.J. Meisels and J.P. Shonkoff (eds) *Handbook of Early Childhood Intervention*. Cambridge: Cambridge University Press.

Barone, T. (1995) Qualitative studies. Series 1, in J. Amos, Hatch and R. Wisniewski (eds) *Life History and Narrative*. London: Falmer.

Beaumont, G. (1996) *Review of 100 NVQs and SVQs*. London: Department for Education and Employment.

bell hooks (1989) *Talking Back. Thinking Feminist, Thinking Black*. London: Sheba Feminist Publishers.

Bennett, N. (1993) Knowledge bases for learning to teach, in N. Bennett and C. Carré (eds) *Learning to Teach*. London: Routledge.

Bennett, N. and Carré, C. (eds) (1993) *Learning to Teach*. London: Routledge.

Berger, P. and Luckman, T. (1997) *The Social Construction of Reality*. Harmondsworth: Penguin.

Berliner, D. (1992) Some characteristics of experts, in the Pedagogical Review, in F. Oser *et al.* (eds) *Effective and Responsible Teaching*. San Francisco: Jossey Bass Press.

Bernstein, B. (1996) *Pedagogy, Symbolic Control and Identity. Theory, Research, Critique*. London: Taylor and Francis.

Blenkin, G., Rose, J. and Yue, N. (1996) Government policies and early education: perspectives from practitioners, *European Early Childhood Education Research Journal*, 4(2): 5–21.

Bowlby, J. (1953) *Child Care and the Growth of Love*. Harmondsworth: Penguin.

Bradshaw, J. (1990) *Child Poverty and Deprivation in the UK*. London: National Children's Bureau.

Bredekamp, S. (1987) *Developmentally Appropriate Practice*. Washington DC: National Association for the Education of Young Children.

Brindle, D. (1994) Poverty highlighted by school meals survey, *The Guardian*, 31 January.

Bronfenbrenner, U. (1974) Developmental research, public policy and the ecology of childhood, *Child Development*, 45: 1–5.

Bronfenbrenner, U. (1975) Reality and research in the ecology of human development, *Proceedings of the American Philosophical Society*, 119: 439–69.

Bronfenbrenner, U. (1979) *The Ecology of Human Development*. Cambridge, Massachusetts: Harvard University Press.

Bruner, J. (1974) *The Relevance of Education*. Cambridge, Massachusetts: Harvard University Press.

Bruner, J. (1986) *Actual Minds Possible Worlds*. Cambridge, Massachusetts: Harvard University Press.

Bruner, J. (1990) *Acts of Meaning*. Cambridge, Massachusetts: Harvard University Press.

Bruner, J. and Haste, H. (1987) *Making Sense*. London: Methuen.

Burman, E. (1994) *Deconstructing Developmental Psychology*. London: Routledge.

Butler, A.J.P. (1996) Review of children and violence, *Child Abuse Review*, 5(4): 297–8.

Byrne, E. (1993) *Women and Science: The Snark Syndrome*. London: Falmer.

Calder, P. (1990) Educare can advantage the under threes, in *Babies and Toddlers: Carers and Educators*, pp. 21–30. London: National Children's Bureau.

Calder, P. (1995) New vocational qualifications in child care and education in the UK, *Children and Society*, 9(1): 36–54.

Calder, P. (1996a) Methodological reflections on using the early childhood environment rating scale as a measure to make cross-national evaluations of quality, *Early Child Development and Care*, 126: 27–37.

Calder, P. (1996b) Ideologies, policies and practices in nurseries in East Berlin before and after the fall of the wall, *International Journal of Early Years Education*, 4(3): 49–60.

Calder, P. (1996c) National vocational qualifications in child care and education: an advance?, *Early Child Development and Care*, 119: 39–50.

Calder, P. (1997) The development of early childhood studies degrees in Britain: future prospects. Poster presented at *7th European Early Childhood Education Research Association Conference, Munich, 3–6 September*.

Carnegie Corporation of New York (1994) *Starting Points: Meeting the Needs of our Youngest Children*. New York: Carnegie Corporation.

Central Advisory Council for Education (1967) *Children and their Primary Schools (Plowden Report)*. London: HMSO.

Chao, R.K. (1994) Beyond parental control and authoritarian parenting style: understanding Chinese parenting through the cultural notion of training, *Child Development*, 65: 1111–19.

Clift, P., Cleave, S. and Griffin, M. (1980) *The Aims, Role and Deployment of Staff in the Nursery*. Windsor: NFER.

Cochran, M. (ed.) (1993) *International Handbook of Child Care Policies and Programs*. Westport, Connnecticut and London: Greenwood Press.

Cohen, B. (1990) *Caring for Children: the 1990 Report*. London: FPSC/SCAFA.

Cole, M. (1996) *Cultural Psychology: A Once and Future Discipline*. Cambridge, Massachusetts, and London: Belknap Press of Harvard University Press.

Committee of Vice Chancellors and Principals (1993) *Strategy for Vocational and Higher Education*. London: CVCP.

Corsaro, W. and Emiliani, F. (1992) Childcare, early education and children's peer culture in Italy, in M. Lamb, K. Sternberg, C.P. Hwang and A. Broberg (eds) *Childcare in Context*. London: Lawrence Erlbaum.

Council of Europe (1996) *The Child as Citizen*. Strasbourg: Council of Europe.

Currer, C. (1991) Understanding the mother's point of view: the case of Pathan women in Britain, in S. Wyke and J. Hewison (eds) *Child Health Matters*. Buckingham: Open University Press.

Curtis, A. (1986) *A Curriculum for the Pre-school Child: Learning to Learn*. Windsor: NFER-NELSON.

Dahlberg, G. and Åsén, G. (1994) Evaluation and regulation: a question of empowerment, in P. Moss and A. Pence (eds) *Valuing Quality in Early Childhood Services*. London: Paul Chapman.

David, T. (1990) Under Five – Under-educated. Milton Keynes: Open University Press.

David, T. (1993) *Child Protection and Early Years Teachers' Coping with Child Abuse*. Buckingham: Open University Press.

David, T. (1996a) Their right to play, in C. Nutbrown (ed.) *Children's Rights and Early Education*. London: Paul Chapman.

David, T. (1996b) Researching early childhood: method matters, *International Journal of Early Childhood*, 1: 1–7.

Dearing, R. (1996) *Review of Qualifications for 16–19 Year Olds*. London: School Curriculum and Assessment Authority.

Dearing, R. (1997) *The National Committee of Inquiry into Higher Education Report 10 (Teacher Education and Training: a study)*. London: NCIHE.

Deloache, J.S. and Brown, A.L. (1987) The early emergence of planning skills in children, in J. Bruner and H. Haste (eds) *Making Sense*. London: Cassell.

Department for Education (1993) *The Initial Training of Primary School Teachers: New Criteria for Courses*, Circular 14/93.

Department for Education and Employment (1996a) *Nursery Education Scheme: The Next Steps*. London: DfEE.

Department for Education and Employment (1996b) Circular Letter 1/96. London: DfEE.

Department for Education and Employment (1997a) *Excellence in Schools*, Cm 3681. London: HMSO.

Department for Education and Employment (1997b) *Teaching: High Status, High Standards Requirements for Courses of Initial Teacher Training*, Circular 10/97. London: DfEE.

Department for Education and Employment (1997c) Circular Letter 1/97. London: DfEE.

Department for Education and Employment (1997d) *Nursery Education Vouchers and Early Education 1997/98*. London: DfEE.

Department for Education and Employment (1997e) *New Requirements for All Courses of Initial Teacher Training*. Circular 1/97. London: HMSO.

Department for Education and Employment (1997f) *Early Years Development Partnerships and Plans*. London: DfEE.

Department for Education and Science (1990) *Starting with Quality*. Report of the Committee of Inquiry into the Quality of the Educational Experience Offered to 3- and 4-year-olds, chaired by Mrs Angela Rumbold, CBE, MP. London: HMSO.

Department of Employment (1989) *Employment for the 1990s*. London HMSO.

Department of Health (1989) *An Introduction to the Children Act*. London: HMSO.

Department of Health (1991) *The Children Act 1989 Guidance and Regulations Vol. 2: Family Support, Daycare and Educational Provision for Young Children*. London: HMSO.

Department of Health, Social Services Inspectorate (1991) *Children in the Public Care: A Review of Residential Care*. London: HMSO.

Donaldson, M. (1978) *Children's Minds*. Glasgow: Fontana/Collins.

Donaldson, M. (1993) *Human Minds: An Exploration*. Harmondsworth: Penguin.

Drummond, M.J., Lally, M. and Pugh, G. (eds) (1989) *Working with Children. Developing a Curriculum for the Early Years*. Nottingham: Nottingham Educational Suppliers, Arnold and National Children's Bureau.

Duffy, B. and Griffin, S. (1994) *A Vision for Early Childhood Care and Education*. London: Early Childhood Education Forum.

Dunkin, M. and Precians, R. (1991) Orientation to Teaching of Award Winning Teachers (mimeo). Sydney: University of Sydney.

Early Childhood Education Forum (1995) Draft discussion document. London: Early Childhood Forum (October).

Early Childhood Education Forum (in press) *Quality in Diversity in Early Learning*. London: National Children's Bureau.

Edwards, A. and Knight, P. (1994) *Effective Early Years Education*. Buckingham: Open University Press.

Edwards, C., Gandini, L. and Forman, G. (eds) (1993) *The Hundred Languages of Children*. Norwood, N.J.: Ablex Publishing.

Eraut, M. (1994) *Developing Professional Knowledge and Competence*. London: Falmer.

European Commission Network on Childcare (1996a) *A Review of Services for Young Children in the European Union, 1990–1995*. Brussels: Commission of the European Communities.

European Commission Network on Childcare (1996b) *Quality Targets in Services for Young Children*. London: Thomas Coram Foundation/European Commission.

European Commission Network on Childcare (1996c) *Men as Workers in Childcare Services*. Brussels: European Commission.

Fawcett, M. (1997) Perspectives on an early childhood studies degree. *OMEP Update*, No. 86.

Field, T. (1991) Quality infant daycare and grade school behaviour and performance, *Child Development*, 62: 863–70.

Fiumara, G.C. (1990) *The Other Side of Language. A Philosophy of Listening*. London: Routledge.

Foucault, M. (1977) *Discipline and Punish*. London: Allen Lane.

Friese, P., Jorgensen, S.F. and Aero, L. (1995) *The Training of Social Educators in Denmark*, The Rectors Conference of National Institutes for Social Educators, International Committee.

Furlong, J. and Kane, I. (1996) *Recognising Quality in Initial Teacher Education*, occasional paper no. 6. London: University Council for the Education and Training of Teachers.

Gale, A. (1997) The reconstruction of British psychology. C.S. Myers Lecture. *The Psychologist*, 19(1): 11–15.

Gardner, H. (1993) *The Unschooled Mind*. London: Fontana.

Gergen, K. (1985) The social constructionist movement in modern psychology, *American Psychologist*, 40: 266–75.

Ghouri, N. (1997) Ministers pressed on early years, *Times Educational Supplement*, 24 October.

Gillan, C. (1996) Letter in *Work and Family: Ideas and Options for Childcare. A consultation paper*. London: DfEE.

Goleman, D. (1996) *Emotional Intelligence*. London: Bloomsbury.

Graue, M.E. and Walsh, D. (1995) Children in context: interpreting the here and now of children's lives, in J.A. Hatch (ed.) *Qualitative Research in Early Childhood Settings*. Westport, Connecticut: Praeger.

Griffin, S. and O'Hagan, M. (1996) National Vocational Qualifications/Scottish Vocational Qualifications (NVQs/SVQs), in G. Pugh (ed.) *Education and Training for Work in the Early Years*. London: National Children's Bureau.

Gura, P. (ed.) (1997) *Reflections on Early Education and Care, Inspired by Visits to Reggio Emilia, Italy*. London: BAECE.

Harding, S. (1991) *Whose Science, Whose Knowledge? Thinking from Women's Lives*. Buckingham: Open University Press.

Harre, R. (1983) *Personal Being: A Theory for Individual Psychology*. Oxford: Blackwell.

Harre, R. (1986) The steps to social constructionism, in M. Richards and P. Light (eds) *Children of Social Worlds*. Cambridge: Polity Press.

Hazareesingh, S., Simms, K. and Andeson, P. (1989) *Educating the Whole Child – A Holistic Approach to Education in the Early Years*. London: Building Blocks/Save the Children.

Heron, M. (1994) Race for a slice of the future, *Further Education*, 15 April.

Hevey, D. (1995) Still in a muddle about early years training?, *Co-ordinate*, 48: 8–11.

Hevey, D. and Curtis, A. (1996) Training to work in the early years, in G. Pugh (ed.) *Contemporary Issues in the Early Years*. 2nd edn. London: Paul Chapman.

Hevey, D. and Windle, K. (1990) Unpublished report of Working with Under Sevens Project, Occupational Mapping Survey.

Holtermann, S. (1995) *Investing in Young Children: A Reassessment of the Cost of an Education and Day Care Service*. London: National Children's Bureau.

Ingleby, D. (1986) Development in context, in M. Richards and P. Light (eds) *Children of Social Worlds*. Cambridge: Polity Press.

Jorde-Bloom, P. (1988) *Early Childhood Work Environment Rating Scale*. Champaign, Ill: University of Illinois.

Jowett, S. and Sylva, K.(1986) Does kind of pre-school matter?, *Educational Research*, 28(1): 21–31.

Katz, L.G. (1996) Child development knowledge and teacher preparation: confronting assumptions, *Early Childhood Research Quarterly*, 11: 135–46.

Kellmer-Pringle, M. (1980) *The Needs of Children*. 2nd edn. London: Hutchinson.

Kennedy, H. (1997) *Learning Works – Report to Further Education Funding Council*. Coventry: FEFC.

Kessen, W. (ed.) (1975) *Childhood in China*. New Haven, New Haven, Conn.: Yale University Press.

Kessen, W. (1979) The American child and other cultural inventions, *American Psychologist*, 34(10): 815–20.

Kessen, W. (1983) The child and other cultural inventions, in F.S. Kessel and A.W. Siegal (eds) *The Child and Other Cultural Inventions*, pp. 26–47. New York: Praeger.

Kontos, S., Howes, C., Shinn, M. and Galinsky, E. (1995) *Quality in Family Child Care and Relative Care*. New York: Teachers College Press.

Kumar, V. (1993) *Poverty and Inequality in the UK. The Effects on Children*. London: NCB.

Labour Party (1996) *Early Excellence – A Head Start for Every Child*. London: Labour Party.

Lambert, J.F. (1996) Des regles et du jeu. Paper presented at the *European Seminar of OMEP, UNESCO Paris, 24–27 October*.

Lera, M.J., Owen, C. and Moss, P. (1996) Quality of educational settings for four-year-old children in England, *European Early Childhood Education Research Journal*, 4(2): 21–33.

Lubeck, S. (1993) Die Suche nach einer neuen Zukunft für die Betreuung und Erziehung von Kindern – Eine Untersuchung politischer Entscheidungsmöglichkeiten im transnationalen Vergleich, in W. Tietze and H.-G. Rossbach (eds) *Erfahrungsfelder in der frühen Kindheit. Bestandsaufnahme, Perspektiven*. Freiburg i. Br.: Lambertus.

Lubeck, S. (1996) Deconstructing 'Child development knowledge' and 'teacher preparation', *Early Childhood Research Quarterly*, 11: 147–67.

Mahony, P. and Hextall, I. (1997) *The Policy Context and Impact of the Teacher Training Agency*. London: ESRC.

Makins, V. (1997) *Not Just a Nursery: Multi-agency Early Years Centres in Action*. London: National Children's Bureau.

Mezirow, J. (1981) A critical theory of adult learning and education, in *Adult Education*, 32(1): 3–24.

Miles, R. (1994) *The Children We Deserve*. London: Harper Collins.

Millett, A. (1995) *Securing Excellence in Teaching: Teacher Training Agency – First Annual Lecture*. London: Teacher Training Agency.

Morris, E. (1977) Ministers pressed on early years, in N. Ghouri *Times Educational Supplement*, 24 October.

Morss, J. (1990) *The Biologising of Childhood: Developmental Psychology and the Darwinian Myth*. Hove: Lawrence Erlbaum Associates.

Morss, J. (1996) *Growing Critical: Alternatives to Developmental Psychology*. London: Routledge.

Mortimore, P. and Mortimore, J. (1992) *The Innovative Use of Non-Teaching Staff in Primary and Secondary Schools Project*. Institute of Education, University of London.

Moss, P. (1996) Perspectives from Europe, in G. Pugh (ed.) *Contemporary Issues in the Early Years*, pp. 30–50. London: Paul Chapman.

Moss, P. (1997) Birth of a big idea, *Times Educational Supplement*, April.

Moss, P. and Penn, H. (ed.) (1994) *Valuing Quality in Early Childhood Services*. London: Paul Chapman.

Moss, P. and Penn, H.(1996) *Transforming Nursery Education*. London: Paul Chapman.

Moss, P. and Petrie, P. (1997) *Children's Services: Time for a New Approach. A discussion paper*. London: Thomas Coram Research Unit, Institute of Education, University of London.

Moss, P., Owen, C., Statham, J., Bull, J. and Cameron, C. (1995) *Survey of Day Care Providers in England and Wales*. London: Thomas Coram Research Unit.

Moyles, J. (1992) *Organization for Learning in the Primary Classroom: A Balanced Approach to Classroom Management*. Buckingham: Open University Press.

Moyles, J. and Suschitzky, W. (1994) The comparative roles of nursery teachers and nursery nurses, *Educational Research*, 36(3): 247–58.

Moyles, J. with Suschitzky, W. (1997a) *Jills of All Trades . . .? Classroom Assistants in KS1 Classes. A report for the Association of Teachers and Lecturers*. London: ATL and University of Leicester.

Moyles, J. with Suschitzky, W. (1997b) Jills of All Trades . . .? Classroom Assistants in KS1 Classes, University of Leicester in collaboration with the Association of Teachers and Lecturers. *Times Educational Supplement*, March 1996.

Moyles, J. with Suschitzky, W. (1997c) *The Buck Stops Here . . .! Nursery Teachers and Nursery Nurses Working Together*. A report on research funded by The Esmée Fairbairn Charitable Foundation. University of Leicester.

Moyles, J. with Suschitzky, W. (in preparation) *Too Busy to Play?* Buckingham: Open University Press.

NAEYC/NAECSSDE (1991) Guidelines for appropriate curriculum content and assessment in programs serving children ages 3 through 8, *Young Children*, 46(3): 21–38.

National Children's Bureau (1993) *The Future of Training in the Early Years. A Discussion Paper*. London: National Children's Bureau, Early Childhood Unit.

National Commission on Education (1993) *Learning to Succeed*. London: Heinemann.

Newson, J. and Newson, E. (1963) *Patterns of Infant Care*. Harmondsworth: Penguin.

Newson, J. and Newson, E. (1967) *Four Years Old in an Urban Community*. Harmondsworth: Penguin.

NNTARN (Nursery Nurse Tutors Anti-Racist Network (1987) *Selecting Students to Ensure Equality of Opportunity*. London: NNTARN.

Nottingham Andragogy Group (1983) *Towards a Developmental Theory of Andragogy*. Nottingham: Department of Adult Education, University of Nottingham.

Nunes, T. (1994) The relationship between childhood and society. *Van Leer Foundation Newsletter*, Spring, pp. 16–17.

Nutbrown, C. (ed.) (1996) *Children's Rights and Early Education*. London: Paul Chapman.

Nutbrown, C. and David, T. (1992) Key issues in early childhood education, *Early Years*, 12(2): 18–21.

Oberhuemer, P. and Ulich, M. (1997) *Working with Young Children in Europe: Provision and Staff Training*. London: Paul Chapman.

Office for National Statistics (1996) *Living in Britain: Results from the 1994 General Household Survey*. London: HMSO.

Office for Standards in Education (1995a) *Framework for Inspection of Children Under 5*. London: Ofsted.

Office for Standards in Education (1995b) *Framework for Inspection of Nursery and Reception Classes*. London: Ofsted.

Office for Standards in Education (1995c) *Guidance on the Inspection of Nursery and Primary Schools: The Ofsted Handbook*. London: HMSO.

Office for Standards in Education (1995d) *School Centred Initial Teacher Training 1993–1994, a report from the Office of Her Majesty's Inspector of Schools*. London: Ofsted.

Office for Standards in Education (1997a) *Framework for Assessment of Quality*. London: Ofsted/TTA.

Office for Standards in Education (1997b) *Report from Her Majesty's Inspector of Schools – 17/97 ITTSP. Cumbria Primary Teacher Training – Maryport Junior School*. London: Ofsted.

Office for Standards in Education (1997c) *Report from Her Majesty's Inspector of Schools – 41/97 TTS2. Mill House Consortium*. London: Ofsted.

Olmsted, P.P. and Weikart, D.P. (eds) (1989) *How Nations Serve Young Children. Profiles of Child Care in 14 Countries*. Ypsilanti, Michigan: HighScope.

O'Neill, J. (1994) *The Missing Child in Liberal Theory*. London: University of Toronto Press.

OPCS (1996) *Labour Force Survey*. London: OPCS Monitor.

Parker, I. (1989) *The Crisis in Modern Psychology and How to End It*. London: Routledge.

Pascal, C., Bertram, T. and Ramsden, F. (1994a) *Effective Early Learning: the Quality Evaluation and Development Process*. London: Amber.

Pascal, C., Bertram, T. and Ramsden, F. (1994b) *The Effective Early Learning Research Project: The Quality Evaluation and Development Process*. Worcester: Worcester College of Higher Education.

Pence, A. and McCallum, M. (1994) Developing cross-cultural partnerships: implications for child care quality research and practice, in P. Moss and A. Pence (eds) *Valuing Quality in Early Childhood Services*. London: Paul Chapman.

Penn, H. (1997) *Comparing Nurseries. Staff and Children in Italy, Spain and the UK*. London: Paul Chapman.

Penn, H. (in press) What age should teacher training cover?, in A. Hudson and D.M. Lambert (eds) *Exploring Futures in Initial Teacher Education: Changing Key for Changing Times*. London: Cassells.

Penn, H. and McQuail, S. (1997) *Childcare as a Gendered Occupation*. Research Report RR23. London: DfEE.

Piaget, J. (1954) *The Construction of Reality in the Child*. New York: Basic Books.

Polanyi, M. (1959) *The Study of Man*. Chicago: University of Chicago Press.

Postman, N. (1985) *The Disappearance of Childhood*. London: Comet/W.H. Allen.

Pugh, G. (1988) *Services for Under Fives: Developing a Co-ordinated Approach*. London: National Children's Bureau.

Pugh, G. (ed.) (1996a) *Contemporary Issues in the Early Years*. 2nd edn. London: Paul Chapman.

Pugh, G. (ed.) (1996b) *Education and Training for Work in the Early Years*. London: National Children's Bureau.

Pugh, G. and McQuail, S. (1996) *Effective Organisation of Early Childhood Services*. London: National Children's Bureau.

Qvortrup, J. (1990) A voice for children in statistical and social accounting, in A. James and A. Prout (eds) *Constructing and Reconstructing Childhood*. London: Falmer.

Raban, B. (1995) Early Childhood Years – Problem or Resource?, Inaugural Lecture, Melbourne University, Australia, 27 July.

Rees, M. (1995) Support in the early years classroom, *Early Years*, 16(1): 41–5.

Richman, N. and McGuire, J. (1988) Institutional characteristics of staff behaviour in day nurseries, *Children and Society*, 2: 139–51.

Riegel, K.F. (1979) *Foundations of Dialectical Psychology*. London: Academic Press.

Robson, C. (1993) *Real World Research: A Resource for Social Scientists and Practitioner-Researchers*. Oxford: Blackwell.

Rodd, J. (1994) *Leadership in Early Childhood: The Pathway to Professionalism*. Buckingham: Open University Press.

Rodger, R. *et al.* (1994) *The Identification of Factors Influencing the Quality of Provision for Children under Five*. The Manchester Metropolitan University/Salford LEA Partnership Research Project.

Rose, H. (1994) *Love, Power and Knowledge: Towards a Feminist Transformation of the Sciences*. Cambridge: Polity.

Saraceno, C. (1977) *Experiencia y Teoria de las Comunas Infantiles*. Barcelona: Fontanella.

School Curriculum and Assessment Authority (1996) *Nursery Education: Desirable Outcomes for Children's Learning on Entering Compulsory Education*. London: SCAA.

School Curriculum and Assessment Authority (1997) *The National Framework for Baseline Assessment*. London: SCAA.

Schweinhart, L.J., Barnes, H.V. and Weikart, D.P. (1993a) *Significant Benefits: The High-Scope Perry Pre-school Study through Age 27*. Ypsilanti, Michigan: HighScope.

Schweinhart, L.J., Weikart, D.P. and Toderan, R. (1993b) *High Quality Preschool Programs Found to Improve Adult Status*. Ypsilanti, Michigan: HighScope.

Shorrocks, D., Daniels, S., Frobisher, I., Nelson., Waterson, A. and Bell, J. (1992) *ENCA 1 Project: The Evaluation of National Curriculum Assessment at Key Stage*. Leeds: School of Education, University of Leeds.

Shotter, J. (1993) *Cultural Politics of Everyday Life: Social Constructionism, Rhetoric, and Knowing of the Third Kind*. Buckingham: Open University Press.

Smidt, S. (1993). Mums' army or professional body: what future for early years education? *Primary Teaching Studies*, Summer, pp. 23–9.

Smith, A.J., Harre, R. and Langenhove, L.V. (1995) *Rethinking Psychology*. London: Sage.

Stanton, A. (1989) *Invitation to Self-Management*. London: Dab Hand Press.

Steedman, C. (1988) The mother made conscious, in M. Woodhead and A. McGrath (eds) *Family, School and Society*. London: Hodder and Stoughton/Open University.

Stott, F. and Bowman, B. (1996) Child development knowledge: a slippery base for practice, *Early Childhood Research Quarterly*, 11: 169–83.

Sutherland, S. (1997) *Teacher Education and Training: A Study*, Report No. 10. London: NCIHE.

Sylva, K. (1992) Conversations in the nursery: how they contribute to aspirations and plans, *Language and Education*, 6(2–4): 141–8.

Sylva, K. (1994) The impact of early learning on children's later development, in C. Ball (ed.) *Start Right: The Importance of Early Learning*. London: RSA.

Sylva, K. and Wiltshire, J. (1993) The impact of early learning on children's later development, *European Early Childhood Education Research Journal*, 1(1): 17–40.

Sylwander, L. (1996) Why we need an ombudsman for children, in *The Child as Citizen*. Strasbourg: Council of Europe.

Teacher Training Agency (1995) *Advice to the Secretary of State on the Continuing Professional Development of Teachers*, October. London: Teacher Training Agency.

Teacher Training Agency (1997) Chief Executive's letter 12/8/97, *ITT Allocation for 1998/99 to 2000/2001*. London: Teacher Training Agency.

Therborn, G. (1996) Child politics, *Childhood*, 3(1): 29–44.

The Times (Editorial) (1995) Three kind mice, *The Times*, 12 September.

Trevarthen, C. (1992) An infant's motives for speaking and thinking in the culture, in A.H. Wold (ed.) *The Dialogical Alternative*, pp. 99–137. Oxford: Oxford University Press.

UNICEF (1996) *The State of the World's Children 1995*. New York: UNICEF.

United Nations (1989) *The Convention on the Rights of the Child*. New York: United Nations.

Universities Council for the Education of Teachers (1997) *The Role of Universities in the Education and Training of Teachers*, occasional paper no. 8. London: UCET.

Utting, D. (1995) *Family and Parenthood: Supporting Families, Preventing Breakdown*. York: Joseph Rowntree Foundation.

Webb, L. (1972) *Purpose and Practice in Nursery Education*. London: Blackwell.

Whitebook, M., Howes, C. and Phillips, D. (1990) *Who Cares? Child Care Teachers and the Quality of Care in America*, Executive summary of the National Child Care Staffing Study, Berkeley, Child Care Employee Project.

Wildeboer, B. (1997) Report of the Study into the Feasibility of a Level 4 National Vocational Qualification in Early Years Care and Education. Unpublished.

Wilkinson, R. G. (1994) *Unfair Shares*. London: Barnardos.

Wolf, A. (1989) Can competence and knowledge mix?, in J.W. Burke (ed.) *Competency Based Education and Training*. London: Falmer.

Woodhead, M. (1988) When psychology informs public policy. The case of early childhood intervention, *American Psychologist*, 43(6): 443–54.

Woodhead, M. (1990) Psychology and the cultural construction of children's need, in A. James and A. Prout (eds) *Constructing and Reconstructing Childhood*, pp. 141–61. London: Falmer.

Woodhead, M. (1996) In search of the rainbow. Pathways to quality in large-scale programmes for young disadvantaged children. *Early Childhood Development: Practice and Reflections, 10*. The Hague: Bernard van Leer Foundations.

Index

WORKING WITH THE UNDER-3s: RESPONDING TO CHILDREN'S NEEDS

Lesley Abbott and Helen Moylett (eds)

In order to do justice to the range of issues surrounding the care and education of the under-3s and to meet the many and varied needs of the adults who work with them, two books have been written under the title *Early Interactions*.

The books incorporate the views of a wide range of people with a wealth of experience in the early years field as both practitioners and trainers. They are intended as an accessible, informative and challenging resource for all those involved in the care and education of children under 3. Multiprofessional and interdisciplinary teamwork is essential in working with young children and their families and as the Rumbold Report (1990) emphasizes – 'no one person will possess all the knowledge and skills required for this important responsibility'. The books provide a range of perspectives and will appeal equally to professionals, parents and anyone who cares about young children. They are particularly valuable as a resource for use in training at all levels.

Working with the under-3s places a special responsibility on adults to both recognize, and respond appropriately to, their rapidly changing needs. A range of contributors share their experience and expertise in chapters which focus on adults working with children in a range of contexts. Early interactions take place in a variety of ways and contributors to the book explore opportunities which allow adults to respond to children's needs, particularly with reference to the development of the child's self concept. Different perspectives on developing children's language and literacy skills are offered, together with a focus on communication through creative and aesthetic experiences.

Contributions by parents, practitioners and trainers offer perspectives which will challenge and provoke readers to reflect on their own experiences and practice. The book is intended for all those training or working with the under-3s, including parents and other carers.

Contents

Contributors

Caroline Barratt-Pugh, Fiona Fogarty, Julia Gillen, Brenda Griffin, Ruth Holland, Brenda Kyle, Helen Moylett, Hilary Renowden.

176pp   0 335 19839 2 (Paperback)   0 335 19840 6 (Hardback)

WORKING WITH THE UNDER-3s: TRAINING AND PROFESSIONAL DEVELOPMENT

Lesley Abbott and Helen Moylett (eds)

In order to do justice to the range of issues surrounding the care and education of the under-3s and to meet the many and varied needs of the adults who work with them, two books have been written under the title *Early Interactions.* The books incorporate the views of a wide range of people with a wealth of experience in the early years field as both practitioners and trainers. They are intended as an accessible, informative and challenging resource for all those involved in the care and education of children under 3. Multiprofessional and interdisciplinary teamwork is essential in working with young children and their families and as the Rumbold Report (1990) emphasizes – 'no one person will possess all the knowledge and skills required for this important responsibility'. The books provide a range of perspectives and will appeal equally to professionals, parents and anyone who cares about young children. They are particularly valuable as a resource for use in training at all levels.

The training and support needs of early years workers is a key issue and provides a focus for debate in the present educational climate. Working with under-3s carries a particular responsibility. The contributors to this book represent a wide range of experience and involvement as practitioners and trainers which they share in interesting and accessible chapters. The book is intended for all those responsible for, or training to work with, children under 3 on a variety of courses. Topics covered include: new approaches to training, continuing professional development, equal opportunities, working with parents and carers, men working with under-3s, special educational needs, child protection, and the inspection process. Key issues are identified for consideration by all those working with young children.

Contents

Introduction – 'I know I can do it': training to work with the under-threes – 'Have experience: want to learn': creating a new pathway to professionalism with a little European money and a lot of hard work from our friends – 'I'm not working with the under-threes!': the need for continuing professional development within the early years team – 'Buildings as well as systems can appear as negative to males in early years settings': exploring the role and status of the male educarer working with the under-threes – 'We need to know': identifying and supporting very young children with special educational needs – 'I'm like a friend, someone to that to . . . but a professional friend': how educators develop positive relationships with parents and children – 'There are lots of activities for him to do and plenty of help and care from the educarers': supporting under-threes and their parents in a parent-toddler group – 'Who is listening?': protecting young children from abuse – 'Our very best show': registration and inspection implications for working with under-threes – Concluding thoughts: drawing the threads together – Index.

Contributors

Lesley Abbott, Shirley Barnes, Jean Coward, Terry Gould, Anne-Marie Graham, Jenny Lively, Chris Marsh, Karen McMahon, Sylvia Phillips, John Powell, Rosemary Rodger.

192pp   0 335 19837 6 (Paperback)   0 335 19838 4 (Hardback)